Routledge Revivals

The Dangerous Sex

First published in 1966, *The Dangerous Sex* shows how the irrational concept of the "dangerous sex" evolved and how it was – and is – used by man to maintain his dominance. The author examines sexual practices and beliefs, marriage customs and rituals, and social behaviour in every society and every age from pre-historic times to the present day. The result is a revealing picture of the deep-seated male hostility that generates the way of the sexes and has fed it throughout human history. It is also a blazing indictment of this ingrained psycho-social pattern, as it unconsciously destroys and disrupts huge areas of human happiness. In this enquiry into misogyny, H. R. Hays suggests that men must face their own compulsions before a true and balanced relation between the sexes is achieved. This book therefore throws a new light on the problems of feminism, the feminine mystique and the whole controversy concerning the place of women in society, and will be of interest to students of literature, gender studies, anthropology and psychology.

The Dangerous Sex
The Myth of Feminine Evil

H. R. Hays

Routledge
Taylor & Francis Group

First published in 1966
By Methuen & Co. Ltd

This edition first published in 2023 by Routledge
4 Park Square, Milton Park, Abingdon, Oxon, OX14 4RN

and by Routledge
605 Third Avenue, New York, NY 10017

Routledge is an imprint of the Taylor & Francis Group, an informa business

Publisher's Note
The publisher has gone to great lengths to ensure the quality of this reprint but points out that some imperfections in the original copies may be apparent.

Disclaimer
The publisher has made every effort to trace copyright holders and welcomes correspondence from those they have been unable to contact.

A Library of Congress record exists under LCCN: 64018006

ISBN: 978-1-032-49140-0 (hbk)
ISBN: 978-1-003-39238-5 (ebk)
ISBN: 978-1-032-49147-9 (pbk)

Book DOI 10.4324/9781003392385

The Dangerous Sex

THE MYTH OF FEMININE EVIL

by H. R. Hays

METHUEN & CO. LTD
11 New Fetter Lane, London E C 4

First published in Great Britain in 1966
© 1964 by H. R. Hays
Printed in Great Britain
for Methuen & Co Ltd
by Western Printing Services Ltd, Bristol

Thanks are due to the Indiana University Press for permission to quote from Rolfe Humphries' translations of Ovid's *Art of Love* and Juvenal's *Satires*. The author also wishes to express his gratitude to Dr Fredric Wertham and Dr Rose Rieger, who read the manuscript, for helpful comments and suggestions.

To my wife,
JULIETTE,
and my daughter,
PENELOPE,
the two members of the dangerous sex
I know the best

Contents

CHAPTER ONE

Male and Female Men

All authorities agree that men and women are different. In the words of the stage Annie Oakley, her little baby brother who had never read a book could distinguish easily between the sexes: 'All he had to do was look.' The nature of this difference in reality and myth has had a profound effect upon the course of human civilization. While there is no doubt that men, in general, are somewhat larger and endowed with heavier muscles than women, the basic divergence of course arises from different genitals and different sex processes. The two sexes would seem to be complementary and partners in reproduction. Yet, despite the gaiety of the sentiment 'Vive la différence', there never has been a time when women have been accepted easily and naturally as female men, in other words as equals and contributing members of society.

Until very recently, except for sporadic rebels of both sexes, the public and comforting position has been that women are naturally appendages of men, scarcely more than a tail wagged by the male ego. This state of affairs has been treated as a problem, modern women have rebelled against it, but surprisingly little effort has been made to understand it. An investigation of the attitude of men towards women involves scrutinizing the behaviour of the primitives, gathering evidence from history and myth and analysing the image of women created by writers significant in Western culture. The insights of depth psychology can also shed some light on the irrationality of a situation in which one half of the human race regards the other at best with condescension and suspicion, at worst with hatred and fear. A few test borings in the past will show that these words are none too strong to characterize man's attitude towards his mate.

Arab tradition provides us with some examples of the derogatory attitude. One group of Bedouins says that women were created from the sins of the satans, another that she was manufactured from the tail of a monkey. From the South Slavs we get other details; in this case God absentmindedly laid aside Adam's rib when He was performing the operation recorded in the Bible. A dog came along, snatched up the rib and ran off with it. God chased the thief but only succeeded in snatching off its tail. The best that could be done was to make a woman out of it. The Hebrews also make a contribution to the vilification of women with the daily prayer, 'I thank Thee, Lord, for not having created me a woman.'

Only a few people practised female infanticide, however; among them the Papuans of the Torres Straits. The Zulu who slaughter an ox as an offering when a boy is born are kinder and merely say, 'Why should we kill an ox for a girl? She is merely a weed.'

A Bulgarian folk rhyme expressing the sentiments of a man who has nine daughters is perhaps the ultimate in savagery.

> If the tenth, too, is a girlchild,
> I will cut both of your feet off,
> To the knees I'll cut your feet off,
> Both your arms up to the shoulders,
> Both your eyes, too, I will put out,
> Blind and crippled you will be then,
> Pretty little wife, young woman.

Along with the undervaluation of women goes the notion that they are formed for submission and obedience. Erasmus tells the story of a German nobleman who married an untutored, inexperienced girl so that he could form her to his liking. The poor ignorant seventeen-year-old whom he picked was then instructed in literature and music by her husband and was expected to learn by heart passages of the sermons she sat through in church. When the girl grew so weary of this didactic marriage that she did nothing but cry day and night and beat her head on the ground as though she wanted to die, her exasperated husband turned to his father-in-law for help. The latter suggested beating her into submission. The husband insisted the girl's father must reform her. The father took occasion to tell her that she was so homely and disagreeable that he had feared he would never get her married. He also informed her that if her husband were not so good-natured he would have treated her like a serving girl. Frightened and apparently convinced, the young girl fell down at her father's and then her husband's feet and promised she would be for ever mindful of her duty.

The unfortunate experience of the nobleman leads us to the examination of an eighteenth-century scandal which is not without sociological significance. Isaac Preston, captain of H.M.S. *Seaford*, was married in 1786. His wife, Jane, was described as 'a person of very modest carriage and of a very meek and affable, obliging, tractable, submissive, obedient temper and behaved to her said husband with the greatest tenderness, submission and duty'.

This in itself gives us a very clear picture of the virtues a woman was supposed to cultivate in this era. They did not avail the unfortunate Jane. 'On the 11th of January, only six days after their marriage ... he tore her cap from her head, and gave her a blow on the ear with his clinched fist and threw her with great violence out of the room.' From then on Jane was his daily punching bag. He also made her kneel for two hours in different parts of the room by his bedside before he would permit her to go to bed. When she became pregnant, he hit her in the belly with a book. Some of his endearments were biting her face, spitting in it, and boxing her ears. After some years of this treatment Jane, whose health had suffered considerably, escaped and Preston was brought to trial. A parade of witnesses testified to his behaviour. The verdict was a divorce for Jane while her husband was directed to pay ninety pounds per annum for her support.

The whole aura of obedience, submission and second-class citizenship which surrounds this sordid tale is highlighted by its exceptional sadistic nature. Yet, in the light of Hogarth's brutal types, we wonder how exceptional it was.

Skipping to the United States in 1845, an anniversary address by the Reverend Joel Hawes delivered at Mount Holyoke Seminary outlines the ideal woman. It is entitled *A Looking Glass for Ladies, or the Formation and Elegance of the Female Character*. Mount Holyoke of course exemplified the higher education for women. In this period in mid-century America, utopianism, feminism, reform, and all sorts of social experiments were already in the air. The clergyman, however, is serenely condescending. 'The husband is ruined who does not find his house a respectable, social, neat and happy home; and such a home he will never find if his wife is a slattern or is indolent and unskilled in domestic affairs.' When Hawes touches on education he has this to say: 'The virtuous woman is perhaps self-educated; at any rate, so educated as to know how to think, observe, compare, reason and converse and to perform with propriety and usefulness the duties of her station.'

Once this amiable creature has been taught to talk articulately enough to run a household, 'she needs piety to eradicate and correct the weaknesses and faults of her natural character, pride, vanity, envy, jealousy and the like. She needs piety as a stimulus to mental improvement, and to a proper use of her time, talents and means of doing and getting good.'

According to the Reverend Hawes the education afforded by Mount Holyoke did have wider application. The virtuous woman could make herself useful in missionary work and 'none can teach their own sex like pious, intelligent, well-educated women'.

About this same time Henry Fowler, editor of the *American Phrenological Journal*, published a little matrimonial guide. Fowler in his time enjoyed the sort of prestige that a leading psychoanalyst might today. Fowler is chiefly concerned with shielding women's minds from the facts of life. 'Young ladies must of course read every new novel, though nearly every one of them contains exceptional allusions, perhaps thinly covered with a gauze of fashionable refinement but on that very account the more objectionable. . . . Shame to every novel reading woman! They cannot have pure minds and unsullied feelings. Cupid and the beaux, and waking dreams of love, are fast consuming their health and morals!'

P. Moebius, a German scientist who had an explanation for everything, in a book *Concerning the Physiological Intellectual Feebleness of Women*, published in 1907, settled the matter. He had taken a look at the female brain and reported, 'Extraordinarily important parts of the brain necessary for spiritual life, the frontal convolutions and the temporal lobes, are less well developed in women and this difference is inborn.' Hampered by their inferior organs of thought, it was natural that 'hypocrisy, that is lying, is the natural and indispensable womanly weapon'. Then, too, 'That the sciences, in the strictest sense, have received no enrichment from women and never shall is therefore understandable.' It was all for the best, however, because: 'If we wish a woman to fulfil her task of motherhood fully, she cannot possess a masculine brain. If the feminine abilities were developed to the same degree as those of the male, her maternal organs would suffer and we should have before us a repulsive and useless hybrid.' This was the opinion of a psychologist of some reputation.

Otto Weininger, a German writer who considered himself a philosopher, alerted the world to the dangers of the feminist. His book, *Sex and Character*, first published in 1903, was republished in Germany every year up to 1920 and translated into half a dozen other languages as well. Filled with ominously pre-Nazi anti-Semitism, this treatise maintained that women were erotically voracious monsters. 'One can scarcely believe that women have ever been really different. And now the sensual element may well be stronger than before since an extraordinary large element in the feminist movement is only a transformation from motherhood to prostitution; it is far more whore-emancipation than woman-emancipation and certainly the chief result will be the predominance of the sluttish element in woman. What seems to be new is the attitude of men. Under the influence of Jewry they are close to accepting women's own evaluation of themselves and to assume the role assigned to them.' The role assigned to men, Weininger continued, was that of a dehumanized instrument of female lust. 'Woman wants man sexually because she only succeeds in existing through her sensuality.'

Only half a century ago the struggle for woman' suffrage was a burning issue. The sentiments of those who opposed giving women the vote are revealing. Edwin Bok, then a famous author, was interviewed in the New York *Times* in 1909. 'A woman, first of all and above all sees everything in the personal and concrete; it is her nature, it is constitutional,' Mr Bok said sadly but wisely. He went on: 'It is in no respect a charge against her, it is fundamental and inherent but that very elemental factor in her temperament would lead to a personal element in politics that would be disastrous to parties or policies.' He then made a flat statement, still more reveal-ing of the male attitude. 'A woman, by her very nature is a personifi-cation of nervous energy or sentiment. That nervous energy and emotion were given her for expression in her natural channels – that of motherhood.' Mr Bok viewed the situation with alarm. 'Suffra-gettes are working for a fancied equality, an equality that they can not see is impossible because of the inequality which nature itself has created, and which if it is made an equality, always brings about the injury of the weaker factor.'

If Bok's rhetoric seems a little confused, the legal mind of ex-Justice Henry Billings Brown, who spoke before the Ladies' Con-gressional Club of Washington the following year, cuts through to fundamentals. 'The best schools and colleges are open to such of them as desire a higher education until a new danger now threatens us of creating in them a distaste for manual labor, which has almost removed the native American girl from her natural vocation of housekeeping. Domestic service, which must be provided in every country, if social distinctions are to exist at all, is relegated to aliens and colored people. . . .' However, this reprehensible desire on the part of women to escape from their proper tasks as domestic servants is only one side of the problem. Brown keeps in mind those so easily sullied minds. 'My fear is that the right to vote will not elevate their character, but will rather minister to a growing desire of the sex to vindicate their rights by competing with men in what has hitherto been regarded as man's peculiar province. My fear is that success in this effort may do much to brush away that bloom of delicacy and refinement which from time immemorial has won the admiration and evoked the chivalry of the stronger sex, that in becoming politicians they will lose something of the instincts of motherhood.'

The historian Francis Parkman, in a pamphlet opposing woman's suffrage, explained, 'Everything else in their existence is subordinated to their indispensable functions of continuing and rearing the human race and during the best years of their life, this work, fully discharged, leaves little room for any other.'

Although these rationalizations now seem quaintly dated since time has proved their absurdity, they are nevertheless evidence of the smug assumption that woman's biological difference sets her apart, that she is essentially inferior, destined to be a willing slave, a domestic drudge, an incubator for the race. Although we can point to modern political and educational equality, to the general acceptance of women as skilled, unskilled and professional workers, and the greater freedom in general which they now enjoy, Simone de Beauvoir, in her exhaustive examination of the situation, is far from happy with women's present position. She still finds a lack of ease between the sexes, survivals of all the old discriminations – a sense of *otherness*, to use her phrase. In other words, as has been said before, women are not regarded as female men.

What is the reason for this otherness, this special treatment which on the one hand downgrades woman to man's appendage and, on the other, as Beauvoir shows, sometimes elevates her to an absurdly unreal and hypocritical ideal?

In the first place the testimony of history leaves no doubt that both the primitive and civilized world has been a man's world. In the past, male dominance has been unchallenged. The majority of ideas and symbols which have shaped culture have always been masculine; even when women were allowed to appear on the stage of society they have been as men have made them.

It is true that women are more biologically hampered than men. In very early cultures women were handicapped first by the long gestation period of the human infant. Since pregnancy occurred very often in the prime of their lives, it deprived them of the freedom to roam about and doubtless accounts for the male monopoly of hunting and fishing. Then, too, high infant mortality, the slow development of the child from infancy to puberty, a period of years during which the young of the species must be nursed at the breast and protected, continued to curtail the scope of feminine activities. Men were free to leave the nest, to roam the forest at will, to express their hostilities by spearing animals for food and carrying out delightful bloody raids against their neighbours. All of this provided them with material for myth and ceremony, for dance and drama. They had time to put feathers in their hair, rattles on their wrists and ankles, to paint their faces and shape their egos in any way that pleased them.

We should expect, then, that the contribution of primitive women would be limited to carrying on the species. In other words, their place was in the home because there was no help for it; they were simply inferior. Yet anthropological data shows that they were extremely productive in certain areas. While it is true that men manufactured weapons and tools to procure and cut meat, women probably invented nets and founded the fishing industry. Women have always been associated with basketry, weaving and pottery. There is good reason to believe that they invented these arts because the task of gathering and collecting was always in their hands. They could make short excursions near the camping place with the little one astride of the hip, followed by the children who were able to walk. (In fact, Pygmy women actually accompany their men on the hunt and act as beaters to help drive animals into the nets.) Above all, they collected the bark fibre and the pliant withes which they shaped into platters, pouches and storage receptacles. Indeed, their technique developed to such an extent they were able to make baskets which would hold water.

Various intricate methods of weaving, tying and stitching laid the basis for repetitive forms. By using strands of different colours contrast could be obtained. Women weavers also discovered earth and vegetable dyes with which to ornament their artifacts. Since each stitch takes up the same space, they were able to produce a series of uniform decorative forms. This, of course, indicates that early woman weavers could count to ten. Basketry designs included lines, triangles, squares, polygons of all sorts, meanders and cyclical curves which meant that the female artisan was obliged to keep in mind a quite intricate series of numbers. Although it has become a truism to say that women have shown no aptitude for mathematics, the evidence of pre-history indicates that women were practical geometricians from the earliest times and probably more advanced in the use of numbers than their mates.

The earliest solid receptacles were also made by women from soapstone or steatite, laboriously pecked out and ground into shape. From basketry came pottery, perhaps originating in the habit of lining a woven platter with a little clay in order to place hot coals upon it. Women's geometrical sense continued to be displayed in graceful bowls and jugs decorated with the repeat motifs worked out in basketry. Natural forms had already been copied in the weaving stitch. They also appeared in painted pottery decoration. In addition, in the Mississippi Valley, Middle America and elsewhere little figures of men or animals were attached to spouts, handles or legs. In connection with the pottery industry, therefore, women have a valid claim to have originated some types of representative painting and sculpture.

In various non-literate societies the ceramic tradition is still carried on by women who maintain a high level of technical proficiency. (It must be remembered that the artisan had to learn how to temper pottery with sand or crumbled shell to prevent it from cracking in the firing. The Pueblo Indian women still carry on a highly developed art which is centuries old. The writer has watched Shipibo women on the Ucayali River in the Peruvian jungle shaping clay pots by the coil method, smoothing and thinning them until when baked, they ring like porcelain. The designs subsequently painted upon them employ a contrasting thin and thick line with exquisite results.One of the standard sights when the tourist visits Oaxaca, in Mexico, is the woman potter shaping black bowls and tripod pots which are polished to a steely glitter and incised with simple designs. And this, too, is a ceramic tradition which can be traced back to the earliest period of Zapotec culture.

Interestingly enough, among the Veddas of Ceylon, a people who formerly lived on the lowest level of material culture without decorative arts or even bodily adornment, it was the women who, on the walls of rock shelters, drew a few crude pictures with their fingers after dipping them in liquid clay. The results are quite similar to certain rock drawings from the Spanish Stone Age. Perhaps the heritage of Paleolithic art was not entirely created by men!

There is a good deal of evidence, therefore, to prove that women in simple societies are not without creative energy. Later, it is true, with specialization and when these manufactures become a business, men take over. With the potter's wheel which allows for early mass production, the profit motive attracts the male artisan.

Civilization of course owes the textile industry to women. All over the world, a spindle with a little clay weight at the end dangled or still dangles from the woman's fingers as she ceaselessly manipulates the cotton or woollen thread. The oldest loom, still in use in Middle America, is attached at one end to the woman's belt and at the other to a tree or house post. The skill at counting and manipulating numbers is carried over from the more ancient and limited art of basketry into the charming patterns seen in the wraparound skirt of the contemporary Guatemalan Indian woman.

From textiles came the art of the couturier. But even before that, women were tailors, since dressing of animal skins and sewing was their province. A special half-moon-shaped flint knife, called by the Eskimo the *ulo*, was invented by the female leather worker for scraping and cutting. After skinning a seal, the Eskimo woman scrapes off the blubber with the ulo. The hide is then washed, rubbed in snow, dried and often chewed to make it pliable. For rawhide the skin is sweated to loosen the hair which must be laboriously scraped off. The ulo's descendant is still in evidence, used with a wooden chopping bowl, in the modern kitchen.

Indian women were the moccasin makers, decorating them with dyed porcupine quills; Eskimo women continue to create excellent fur boots, and elsewhere women manufacture various types of sandals, so still another important craft, that of the shoemaker, was originated by the female of the species.

There is no doubt that women invented bread. Since in the gathering phase it is they who collect roots and, above all, grass seeds, they first discovered the various uses of such vegetable food. The Panamint woman of California harvests sand grass seed, carrying in one hand a funnel-shaped basket and in the other a paddle made of wickerwork resembling a tennis racquet. With this she beats the grass panicles over the edge of the basket, causing the seeds to fall in. The Algonkian Indian woman paddles a canoe among the wild rice at the lake's edge and with a wand beats the grain on to a mat spread in the canoe. From these activities it is easy to trace the evolution of the milling and baking industry. It was undoubtedly women who hit upon the idea of domesticating grain and improving its seed-bearing ability, thereby causing one of the greatest revolutions in human culture. In societies in transition from hunting to village life women developed the stone muller and the flat mortar, or metate, on which they pulverized the grain. They, too, developed the clay storage bins which could be buried in the ground and are today recovered from sites in the Near East dating to 7000 B.C.

Women in transitional societies are still most closely associated with agriculture. The digging stick, a staff pointed at one end and sometimes hardened by charring in the fire, was the women's tool for grubbing up roots. When she domesticated plants the digging stick continued to be her chief agricultural tool; in some areas she still uses it today. All over Africa where she has graduated to the hoe, though the men help with the burning and some of the heavier clearing, the women do the planting and cultivation. On the whole, slash-and-burn agriculture is a feminine occupation. But when the plough makes this pursuit into an industry which produces a surplus, when slavery or peonage pays off, men step in and organize the work in the fields in the name of a god or priest-king who runs the business and technically owns the land.

Economic determinists solve the problem of women's peculiar position in the world by saying that capitalism is to blame. The classic Russian argument runs as follows: During the hunting and transitional cultures matriarchy was the rule, women were dominant, all was peace and democracy. Original sin somehow caused the males to revolt and set up an odious patriarchal system which has exploited everybody ever since.

Most Western anthropologists do not feel that a first phase of matriarchy can be proved. Furthermore this type of culture does not mean that women are dominant. About all it means is that inheritance is traced through the female line. Instead of a man's father being the authoritarian male in the family, his mother's brother assumes the job.

The Russian argument states that the weak are always exploited and since women are weaker than men, they are victims of the profit motive and automatically members of the working class. From this it should follow that women in Russia would be enjoying a modern utopia. Actually, after experimenting with liberal attitudes towards sex relations, the Soviet Union returned to the patriarchal family and a rather puritan attitude. This definitely shows that women are not merely exploited workers. To quote Beauvoir, 'It is impossible to regard woman simply as a productive force: she is for man a sexual partner, a reproducer, an erotic object – an Other through whom he seeks himself.'

One line of thought, pursued by depth psychology, arrives at the conclusion that the possession of a penis makes all the difference. Women have never overcome the original shock of discovering that men possess this useful and imposing instrument and consequently have been obliged to give up and play second fiddle. It has been pointed out, however, that Freud never questioned male superiority and always imperturbably reasoned from the male point of view. A female Freud might just as easily maintain that the male organ is an unsightly and inconvenient protuberance, while the vulva is surrounded with mystery and romance, being hidden, secret and enticing.

The externality of the penis, however, the fact that it can be grasped as though it were apart from the body and that it possesses a kind of semi-independent erective life of its own, might possibly be cited as a basis of man's tendency towards symbolization. The penis is easily equated with a weapon, a tree, etc.; man is able to project his maleness into other things, while the female is in the position of acceptance and the embryo grows within her body.

Weston La Barre suggests, 'A woman can give proof of her femaleness in a very simple and irrefutable way, by having a baby – but a male must always *prove* something, his manhood within the group. What reason, indeed, would press women to create great poetry, music and art – when they can do better than that and make real human beings!'

The argument that men really envy women because of their ability to produce a child and are therefore spurred on to cultural creativity is a new one, carried even further by Ashley Montagu, who writes, 'Men have been jealous of women's ability to give birth to children and they have been jealous of her ability to menstruate but men have not been content with turning these capacities into disabilities for they have surrounded the one with handicapping rituals and the other with taboos that in most cases amount to punishments.'

Ashley Montagu's argument that men are jealous of the ability to menstruate rests solely on the case of those Australians who practise subincision – the periodic slitting of the urethra in order to draw blood. The slit penis is sometimes given a name etymologically close to that of the vagina. In his study of subincision Ashley Montagu indicates that menstrual blood is felt to be a purge resulting in magical purification. From this he argues that the males desired to purge themselves in the same way and hence they repeated the ceremonial bloodletting to imitate the female period. This does not, however, prove that men in general are jealous of the ability to menstruate. Subincision is only practised in certain areas of Australia and the Pacific. The belief that menstrual blood is dangerous and always to be avoided by men is almost universal and it is much more likely that it indicates, as we shall show later, a contrary attitude.

Actually, it is doubtful if men in very early stages of culture, where children are not economically useful, feel them to be enviable acquisitions. We know that, among some animals, the male often has to be restrained from killing its young; stallions and buck rabbits are an example. The British anatomist, Sir Solly Zuckerman, in his studies of the social life of apes, describes episodes in which the young were killed by the male in sexual scrimmages. Géza Róheim writes, 'There is no paternal instinct and the unconscious hatred is very strong. The father sees the child as a rival for his wife's love and a representative of his own oedipal guilt.' This hostility towards the young is also expressed in aggressive puberty ceremonies. Theodore Reik cites the cases of peoples in New Guinea and British Columbia who sacrifice the firstborn and, indeed, the story of Abraham and Isaac is a theological rationalization of the same basic instinctive rivalry.

These suggestions, therefore, throw little light on the peculiar position of women. On the whole, capitalistic greed or jealousy are superficial moralistic explanations. Even the biological fact of the male organ does not explain everything. If there is such a thing as penis envy it could result from the fact that the organ is a symbol of male domination.

Assuming that male dominance was originally assured through greater strength and greater freedom of mobility, this is not an inevitable reason why (with the enrichment of material culture and the contemporary lightening of the tasks of the housewife) women should continue to be creatively or intellectually stifled and generally still be told by men, 'Anything you can do I can do better.'

To find the answer we must delve into social psychology, and scrutinize the observances, myths and practices with which men have surrounded women in early types of society, and the survivals of these phenomena which have persisted in cultural tradition. For we are gradually beginning to realize that human beings are still primitives disguised in the mask of modern technology.

CHAPTER TWO

Of Anxiety and Ambivalence

Into the dangerous world I leapt,
Helpless, naked, piping loud,
Like a fiend hid in a cloud.

And indeed Blake's newborn baby has a reason to pipe, for we all enter the world in a state of anxiety which never wholly disappears until we leave it. As far as we can imagine, a healthy foetus in a healthy mother approaches the condition of perfect tranquillity. It is completely concerned with itself, all its needs are gratified automatically. It is therefore a prey to no hopes or fears, having indeed no cause whatsoever to feel emotion. Its condition is close to that of the Buddhist Nirvana and perhaps accounts, in terms of unconscious nostalgia, for this particular philosophy. At birth, however, the young child undergoes a rude awakening – all of a sudden the snug haven and the automatic service is withdrawn, stimuli assault it from the outside world, it experiences a terrible sense of loss which it is obliged to dispel by coming to terms with the non-self. Its first compensation is generally contact with the warmth of the mother's body and the nipple.

One school of depth psychology (Otto Rank) has gone so far as to attribute all later anxieties to reawakened memories of this birth trauma. Subsequent experience, however, offers plenty of other disturbing sensations. As Freud has pointed out, the human infant differs considerably from most other young mammals which in a matter of minutes or hours are able to move about and are already small replicas of their parents. The time spent within the womb seems to be short in comparison with most animals since human babies emerge into the world less complete. He concludes, 'As a result the influences of the real external world have a greater importance for it so that the value of the object which alone can protect it against them and take the place of the former intrauterine state is enormously enhanced. The biological factor then establishes the earliest situation of danger and creates the need to be loved which will accompany the child through the rest of its life.'

Later, as basic animal needs are gratified within a social situation, compromises have to be made and the naked selfishness of appetite modified. The simplest external trigger of anxiety is a need for something which is not satisfied, causing distress. Growing up in the human situation, which involves learning and the postponement of immediate satisfactions and sometimes the complete inhibition of appetite, builds up a series of memories of this unhappy experience. Anxieties can then be triggered from the inside, they became complicated by emotion and imagination and, in extreme form, can be related to undefined causes or translated into symbolic forms when the ego does not wish to acknowledge their source.

Since all human beings must grapple with anxieties in various ways throughout life, it is true that man's emotional attitudes are conditioned by this fundamental anguish. Real or anticipated deprivation threatens him, fear of the condition of distress in general. The Freudian view that a sense of loss is felt on separation from the mother is substantiated by the behaviourists who have established that one of the infant's primal fears is that of loss of support. Apart from negative anxiety, there are also agents in the external world which can harm the growing infant and these, too, as we shall show, contribute to anxiety.

The mother, the first object to give security and protection, becomes the most important love object in the infant's life. From this it follows that if anything goes wrong in this relationship serious psychic scars will result. The father is the second most important and with him the young boy identifies because they have the same bodily structure. Then, according to Freud, the boy discovers, with the growing sexuality of this feeling for his mother, that his father is an obstacle in the way of access to his mother and he begins to feel hostile towards his male parent. This perhaps takes place in the first few years of life and is not really conscious. But love, through identification, is also present and thus we have a cause of ambivalent emotional conditioning, the beginning of the 'I hate and I love you conflict'. In other words, the same object or stimulus in the external world may arouse desire or hatred or the two feelings may be almost simultaneous.

The boy's situation, which concerns us here since we are investigating male attitudes, is complicated by the shocking discovery that girls do not possess a penis. From this arises the fear that he may be in danger of losing his own. This is the classic Freudian explanation, which may or may not be accepted, but we are about to demonstrate the fact that castration fears are deep and ingrained. The Freudian explanation goes on to suggest that the boy thus begins to fear his father who may castrate him for his unconscious designs on his mother. This involves an associative jump. It seems to be true, however, since circumcision rites in various parts of the world are clearly a castration assault upon maturing males, and show that men would like to rid themselves of their youthful sexual rivals.

Géza Róheim, the only Freudian-trained observer to make an intensive study of the sex life of a preliterate people, added another cause of anxiety which can result in ambivalence towards sex on the part of the male child. He felt that the child's witnessing of parental intercourse (the 'primal scene') plays a traumatic role. It is certainly true that in the living arrangements of primitive people, like the Australian aborigines who go completely naked, the facts of life must be revealed to children quite early in life. In most cases, and this includes the Australians, an effort is made to carry out sex activities in private and this is enough to surround the matter with some sense of prohibition.

The Australians weave myths about *erunchas*, demonic copulating monsters, which Róheim felt were projected images dramatizing the anxiety awakened on viewing the primal scene. The child is excited, probably has erections and at the same time is afraid that his own small organ will be inadequate in comparison with those of his elders. Since Australian copulation is a rough affair, there is a tendency to see it in terms of a fight (a concept also expressed by contemporary children), which is also frightening.

Róheim generalized in support of the view that men's sexual

disequilibrium is biological. He cited the principle of retardation. Even when mature, man retains the unspecialized foetal form – he has been called a 'foetal ape'. As he grows up his bodily development is very slow and allows for gradual psychic maturation in the family group. His sex cells, however, like those of his animal ancestors, mature early, at about the age of five. This creates a unique situation: his sex is making demands but he is unable to copulate at this early age. Hence there is a conflict between his impulses and performance. This conflict, Róheim feels, is stimulated by the primal scene. 'We have absorbed our pleasure-giving and powerful parents into our undeveloped egos during the long period of our infancy and so form the basis of our ambivalence. . . .' Sex becomes a matter of both desire and fear.

Whether this sketch of the oedipal situation is accepted as universal and basic or not, there is no doubt that sex plays an enormous role in magic, myth and religion throughout the world. The evidence from primitive groups shows that it affects the forms by which men cope with their anxieties. It is always ambivalently treated; everywhere it tends to be considered as both beneficial and harmful but, on the whole, men seem to be more intensely aware of its dangers.

All this is fairly clinical, it may be objected. It was Freud, however, who first noted striking similarities between the anxiety behaviour of his patients and the ritual behaviour of primitive groups. Patients are sick people, but psychologists generally agree that mental illnesses reflect, in exaggerated form, basic psychic and emotional tendencies in all of us. Both children and preliterates express basic drives without many of the censorships, repressions and rationalizations of which civilization is so proud. There is a point, therefore, where infant, neurotic and primitive forms of behaviour resemble each other and for this reason, if we seek to understand human institutions, we cannot disregard these fundamental unconscious and irrational data.

The idea of magic is a good example. Neurotic patients sometimes are convinced that they can kill at a distance by willpower. August Strindberg entertained this precise fantasy. Australian magicians believe they can kill by pointing a bone and reciting the right spell. Now let us turn to infant behaviour. Freud cited the case of a one-

and-a-half-year-old boy who was suspiciously well behaved when his mother was obliged to leave him for a few hours. He never cried or clung to her, instead he occupied himself with playing a game of 'gone', making his toys disappear and bringing them back. When this was finally puzzled out by the analyst, Freud realized that the game was a compensation for the boy's repressed anxiety at the loss of the beloved object, his mother. In the first place, by making things go and come back, he became active; he gained a sense of power. He was able to say, 'I can make things go, too; I am not afraid to lose my mother.' In one case he played gone with himself by ducking below a mirror and bringing back his own image. Thus, by controlling loss and return, he was not helpless in the face of the unknown powers of the universe.

The parallel between the child's game and the magic practice of preliterates is remarkable. The child needed to go only one step further and to claim by his mimetic magic he was bringing his mother back. And if, coincidentally, she returned, his case would have been proved. The Tlingit Indian who performs a dance in a goat mask during which the dancer is killed in pantomime by the hunter, or the horned Yakut Indian who perfectly mimics a deer while other dancers shoot him is doing this to control the game supply. In this case anxiety is concerned with getting enough food.

It is clear that play, dramatization and ritual are all ways of compensating for or supposedly avoiding deep anxieties. Just as the little boy was able to control 'gone' and feel superior to his loss, so the representation of tragedy on the stage makes it possible for human beings to contain and shape one of the most profound castastrophes of life – death.

Another example of magical behaviour which brings in the ambivalent conditioning of emotion we have just been discussing is the attitude towards the king in certain African groups. The infant, who both hates and loves his parents, endows them with exaggerated power. The African tribesmen known as the Shilluk believe that their ruler is responsible for rain and hence for the prosperity of his people. Yet this same people, who treat the king as a respected and all-powerful father, in the past maintained the custom that he should be killed by one of his sons when his sexual powers began to fail in order to prevent crop failure.

Ancestor worship is widespread among preliterates, particularly in Africa. Although the anxiety aroused by the death of a loved person probably crystallizes in maturity, the cult of the dead shows clearly the results of early ambivalent conditioning. On the one hand the dead are thought to cause disease when they are annoyed and on the other they are urged to confer benefits upon the living. When they are considered helpful, their role as continuing members of the tribe is stressed, they are still the protecting parents. When they are believed to be making trouble, a mechanism known to depth psychology as projection comes into play. Since the hostile side of the ambivalent feeling towards those we love is not acceptable, it can be disguised by reversing it. 'I do not hate my father; it is he who hates me and would like to castrate me,' or 'I do not hate women, they are hostile to me' is the way the unconscious formula works.

Freudian revisionists, such as Clara Thompson, Eric Fromm and Harry Stack Sullivan, have tended to stress the desire for approval or fear of disapproval of the parents as the most important source of neurotic anxiety. Whether the emphasis is placed on sex drives or on interpersonal relations, the individual is always involved with coming to terms with the non-self. His desire for release of tension through physical satisfaction and his need for social approval are included in the general anxiety situation. We are concerned here with establishing the fact that socially organized attitudes towards women arise from basic tensions experienced by the male sex and consequently it is necessary to sketch the general techniques by which the preliterate and nonlogical male handles his psychic problems.

We have been maintaining that human institutions grow from deep and primal anxieties and are shaped by irrational psychological mechanisms, which we can best observe in the child, the primitive and the neurotic. An objection often raised against the depth psychology preoccupation with the individual is best stated by Jean Cazeneuve, who points out that Róheim believed the conflicts in the child are the source of the anguish which leads to the rite. Writes

Cazeneuve, 'We do not see why each individual does not seek his own solution in the form of neurosis.' Cazeneuve, like most critics who accuse the psychoanalyst of lacking a social orientation, is simply ignoring what Freud has written concerning the artist and the leader. In the first place, although it is common to discuss social developments as though they arose in some vague collective way, the truth is that everything has a beginning. Primitive ritual is no doubt developed (as Paul Radin has pointed out) by the contributions of individual shamans – anonymous primal poets and prophets whose contributions are accepted wholly or partially by the group and crystallized in tribal tradition. In certain very simple societies, such as those of the Bushmen and Pygmies, the shaman is the only outstanding individual. There is no doubt that he is subject to the same infantile anxieties as his fellows but, unlike them, he is a speculative and imaginative type of man and at the same time possesses an outstanding personality. He creates images and elaborate projections for his anxieties or he displaces them, to use the Freudian term, by substituting one thing for another and devising the symbol. It is certainly the shaman who invents mimetic rites similar to those of the small boy who played 'gone'. The shaman is also an artist; in all probability the frescoes on the walls of the Altamira and Lascaux caves were created by the religious painter who, in this case, was motivated by anxiety over food.

Freud wrote that the artist's creations were the imaginary satisfaction of unconscious wishes 'but they differed from the narcissistic products of dreaming in that they were calculated to arouse sympathetic interest in other people and were able to evoke and to satisfy the same unconscious wishful impulses in them, too'. But even dreams are not idle if they arise from the unconscious of the shaman-leader. All of American Indian religion is concerned with dreams; dances carried on for increase reasons by men's societies were supposed to have originated in the dreams of some gifted individual.

But, it may be asked, are not these rituals conscious, calculated productions of the human mind? In late and elaborate form, when specialized priests arise, they definitely are. But the almost universal technique for curing patients, used by shaman-doctors, found in

Africa, Australia, Melanesia, Malaya and the Americas, consists of sucking at the sick man's body to remove the cause of the disease. Róheim points out that this certainly derives from concern with the mother's breast and the most basic of all satisfactions. In this, and in other cases, a magical technique is founded on an unconscious base.

The normally anxious person, therefore, is content to have his conflicts contained in forms devised by the shaman. The compensations of art, indeed, also play a cohesive role; by believing and doing the same things, the individual tribesman is not alone, he gains group individuality and embarks on the road to nationalism.

And indeed it is this process which answers the question, if we should push Cazeneuve's query still further, of how the shaman manages to extend his influence. Freud still has a reasonable answer. In the first place the gifted, imaginative individual with a vivid personality may, in many cases, be a prey to epilepsoid seizures during which hallucinations come to him. There is a tendency to identify with the leader as a father figure and members of the tribe further identify with each other in their attachment to their leader. An extreme pathological example is that of Hitler, who exhibited all the disequilibrium of the shaman, embodied the anxieties and frustrations of the Germans, captured their sympathies and channelled their conscious and unconscious wishes in his grandiose schemes and rituals.

The shaman who moulds the anxieties of the group can be hostile and destructive or benign, depending upon his temperament and the pressures of the group. Interestingly enough, many of the writers whose work we shall investigate later in this book were decidedly disturbed or neurotic individuals.

But what about the environment, granted that anxiety is the active force in shaping many human institutions? Obviously the word environment covers geography, the demands and expectations of the group, once they have been formulated, and the personal experience of the individual shaman. Environment as a force in the selection of important symbols is easily recognized in the Near East. Here the problem of rainfall caused tension and pastoralism arose very early. A fertility bull became associated with rain gods. Geography provides anxiety over food, geography and the variables of history combine to select the bull as the pastoral symbol, but male sexual anxiety elevates him to a symbol of potency. We shall never know, however, what early shaman, with doubts about his virility, experienced a feeling of power and reinforcement by praying to a bull or carving his image. Nor shall we know whether he or some successor decided that such prayers would increase the bull's enthusiasm for covering the cows and producing more cattle. His final promotion to rain god no doubt involves many more contributions.

In the case of the symbols associated with women, a similar dialectic has occurred. They have been set apart, sometimes deified and endowed with attributes of abundance, but more often transformed into figures of terror and menace. Above all, the testimony of history indicates that they themselves did not originate the myths that have surrounded them; they have been the victims of the ambivalent magic with which dawn cultures were riddled.

To sum up, therefore, we have suggested that male anxiety is a basic drive in the formation of social institutions. We have attempted to show how magical ideas, coloured by the compulsions and imagination of the shaman, probably gave rise to ritual and belief. We have also outlined the Freudian explanation of ambivalence, the continual feelings of attraction and repulsion which chequer the whole life like a pattern of light and shade.

We shall now take up another possible source of anxiety and ambivalence which leads directly to a kind of primitive philosophy, sometimes expressed, sometimes only implied, yet dramatized in magic and ritual universally, and extremely important in determining the status of women. This is the concept of mana.

CHAPTER THREE

The Double Mask of Mana

The Pomo Indians of California consider all strangers to be dangerous and prone to exercise destructive magic.

In the Fiji Islands any person who had touched the head of a chief
could not touch food with his hands until he had gone through a
process of purification.

To the Dahomeans, twins are sacred; to the Ashanti they are
dangerous and are killed.

Among the Eskimo when a man dies all skins must be taken out
of the house to avoid contamination.

In the Celebes Islands when chickens cackle at an unusual hour
or lay abnormally large or small eggs, it is a sign of evil; they must
be killed.

In Indonesia if a pig couples with a goat both must be killed.

The Ba-ila of the Zambezi River believe that if a mole pokes its
head out of its hole, someone is going to die. This same people
refused to eat bananas when they were first introduced into their
culture, saying they were magically dangerous.

Among the Navajo anyone who touches a dead body must remove
his clothes and wash thoroughly before mingling with the living.

Amboina Island women, when a child is born with a caul, preserve
it and if the child becomes ill, dip it in water and give this water to
the child to drink.

In Hawaii before the owner entered a new house, a priest performed certain ceremonies and slept in it in order to avoid magical
dangers.

A study of these customs and countless others like them has
shown that all arise from a reaction to the exceptional or unfamiliar.
We have here, therefore, an area of anxiety somewhat different from

those we have just been discussing. An Eskimo intellectual put it clearly when he said, 'Everything unusual frightens us . . . that is why we have our customs.' Although some reactions to the unusual certainly crystallize at a conscious level in response to the specific environment, they probably grow from deeper roots.

Freud mentions the anxiety of small children being left with strangers. He states that 'in the undisguised antipathies and aversions which people feel towards strangers with whom they have to do we may recognize the expression of self love – of narcissism. This self love works for the preservation of the individual and he behaves as though the occurrence of the divergence from his own particular lines of development involves a criticism of them and a demand for their alterations.' Freud also points out that every living organism has mechanisms for protecting itself from extreme stimuli which cause tensions. The anxieties we have already discussed, those arising from loss and from sexual conflicts, cause tensions, but to these must be added the exceptional and unfamiliar.

We might expect that the exceptional and the unfamiliar would always be avoided or steps taken to eliminate them. An ambivalent reaction can be traced instead. Twins, which are an unusual birth, often cause anxiety. In a large number of cases one or both may be killed but they can also be considered sacred and raised to the status of heroes or gods. Among the Bambara of Africa an albino, also an unusual birth, was sacrificed in times of national crisis and thus a beneficial use made of its power. Among the Nias of western Sumatra albino children are simply killed at birth. Throughout the rites and ceremonies which deal with the exceptional and the strange there run both the desire to guard against the dangers emanating from it and the belief that its power can be manipulated for human benefits.

All this can be related to the anxieties of the family situation. The sexually attractive mother and the competing, potentially dangerous father loom as all-powerful and both cause tensions in the helpless infant. In primitive myth, which probably arises from childhood compulsions, both can become magical entities. A sense of extra-ordinary power, helpful or hurtful, in the non-self must certainly belong to the earliest level of experience in human beings. Later experience will be viewed in these terms.

It is therefore reasonable to suppose that the ambivalent conditioning of infant life prepares the preliterate to assume the same attitude towards later disturbing experience, alien people, unusual weather conditions, strange animals, comets, eclipses, extreme cases of good or bad luck. Hatred and love are paired with avoidance and acceptance and upon these basic reactions he erects his elaborate structures of emotional and semi-articulate philosophy.

To approach this from another point of view, the infant at birth has to come to terms with the outside world through contact. Security, warmth and nourishment are derived from the touch of the mother's skin. Pain, however, arises from contact with outside agencies which are too hot or too cold, which can bruise, burn, cut or irritate its tender cuticle.

The young child, whose chief occupation is sucking, tends to explore the outside world with its mouth. We have all seen the distracted mother removing foreign objects such as leaves, dirt, matches or scraps of paper, anything that the crawler finds, from his mouth.

Ernest Crawley, who was concerned with this fact, wrote: 'Thus ideas of contact are primitive in every sense of the word. They seem to go back in origin and character to the highly developed sensitivity of all animal and organized life forms, at once a biological monitor and a safeguard for the whole organism in relation to its environment.'

Psychic contacts parallel physical ones. The child learns to contain its ambivalence towards its family and associates its parents with security, but the touch of the alien, both physical and mental, is dangerous. From this comes the idea of contagion, magical contagion either good or bad, transmitted by contact.

The fear of alien people or strangers is characteristic of all social groups including modern nations. The Tupi-Guarani of western Brazil regard all strangers as dangerous; in western Polynesia they are thought to bring disease. The white man, in particular, inspired such apprehension that the Basutos of South Africa refused to eat food offered them by Europeans. The American unreasoning fear of Russians (and vice versa) is a modern example.

On the other hand friendship, intimacy, and erotic union are all expressed through touching, from the handclasp, the arm around the shoulder, to the kiss. The Polynesians touch noses as a greeting; the Australians begin their sexual play by rubbing the breasts together, Melanesians by delousing each other's hair. Genital contact is, of course, the most intimate and intense physical expression of unity known to man. Healing by touch is another example of the benefits of contact. Scrofula, called the king's evil, was supposed to be cured by the touch of a reigning monarch. In this case we can see a survival of the belief in the sacred fertility king.

The feelings that surround contact, therefore, and the alien and unusual are the same as the earliest ambivalencies of the small child. Since all non-rational human behaviour is organized in this scheme of duality, of attraction and repulsion, of love and hatred, in primitive cultures it becomes a kind of semi-articulate philosophy called, from the Melanesian term, mana.[1] Mana is often thought of as a supernatural power, either good or bad, infusing everything, but, more intensely, the alien and the unusual. Magical practice which attempts to regulate it and handle the resulting contagion sets up the notion of taboo, or avoidance of its magical dangers.

When a taboo, established by custom and myth, is broken, human beings develop various ideas concerning the unfortunate results. Contemporary superstitions prove the tenacity of the psychological process. Builders omit the thirteenth floor; and when a person avoids walking under a ladder, fear of bad luck is the reason given. On the clinical level, a neurotic patient who feels obliged to wash his hands many times a day rationalizes his unconscious fear by saying he is ridding himself of germs and hence illness. Christopher Robin avoids stepping on cracks in the pavement lest the imaginary bears get him. Primitive peoples, conditioned by early experience to feel the menace of the alien power of the external world, consider any misfortune which occurs after the breaking of a taboo to be a punishment. Since the psychological process works both ways, when a misfortune occurs the magical experts try to discover what taboos have been broken.

We have briefly sketched, so far, some of the mechanisms by which basic anxieties are crystallized into a primitive philosophy of ambivalence. Admittedly both men and women are a prey to these

[1] See Note, p. 295.

anxieties. We must remember, however, that the male is dominant, he sets the pattern of the human being and the alien. His body and his biological processes are familiar and understandable and, by observation, he can see that other males are the same and therefore can be accepted into the category of the self versus the alien.

But women are different. Despite's a man's need for his mother's breast and his sexual attraction to her, she is not of his kind. Even though he entertains unconscious hostilities towards his father he can identify with him. Woman, therefore, is alien, peculiarly filled with mana and, as we shall endeavour to show, a number of different situations combine to make him feel that her bad mana is more important than her beneficial potentialities.

Thus the shaman who occupies himself with shaping man's anxieties into social forms, who deals with the alien, disturbing forces, has particularly concerned himself with women and, in order to protect his fellow men from contagion and terror, from sickness, mutilation and death, has contrived to surround her with sanctions and avoidances which scarcely admit her into the same tribe. Later the artist takes over the role of shaman and perpetuates the image of the dangerous sex. First, however, let us see how contacts between men and women in primitive culture are circumscribed and regulated.

CHAPTER FOUR

I Am Unclean . . . '

When menstruating, a Surinam Negro woman lives in solitude. If anyone approaches her, she must cry out, 'I am unclean.'

The notion that women's sexual processes are impure is world-wide and persistent; the magical fear of menstrual blood is particularly intense. In the first place, the fact that blood flows from the female genitals at regular intervals sets women off from the other sex and gives them the exceptional properties of mana in a world in which men set the norm. The taboos which surround the first menstruation are particularly severe. The phenomenon itself is frequently explained as a supernatural wound, the result of an attack by a bird, a snake or a lizard. The origin of the female genital as a result of castration or sadistic attack is also illustrated in myths concerning the creation of women. Since male fantasy is dominant in human institutions, a very early time is often referred to in which there were only men and no women. The Negritos of the Malay Peninsula maintain there was once an ancestral creator entity, the monitor lizard. Since his contemporaries were all men, the lizard caught one of them, cut off his genitals and made him into a woman who became the lizard's wife and the ancestor of the Negritos. When Christopher Columbus discovered the Indians inhabiting Haiti, whom he named Caribs, he left a friar among them as a missionary. Friar Pane recorded a story concerning the Indian ancestors who had no women yet felt they should have some. One day they observed certain creatures who were falling out of the trees or hiding in the branches. These alien beings had no sex organs whatsoever. The Carib ancestors bound them and tied woodpeckers to them in the proper place. The birds pecked out the desired sexual orifices. Not only do we have here the theme of women being created by castration appearing on opposite sides of the world but, significantly enough, the image of the vulva as a wound also occurs in the fantasies of male psychoanalytical patients.

New Guinea carvings show images of women with a crocodile attacking the vulva, a hornbill plunging its beak into the organ or a penis-like snake emerging from it. On the one hand there is the idea of castration and on the other an image of the female genital being created by a sadistic attack by the penis, symbolized by lizard, bird beak, or snake. The mysterious and dangerous nature of the wound is uppermost in primitive tradition.

Blood in all of its manifestations is a source of mana. In the case of menstrual blood the ancient ambivalence is in evidence with the harmful aspect predominating. The dangers of contact and contagion are so great that women are nearly always secluded or forced to reside apart during their monthly periods. Special huts are built for them by the Bakairi of Brazil, the Shuswap of British Columbia, the Gauri of northern India, the Veddas of Ceylon, and the Algonkian of the North American forest. From this it can be seen that the custom covers the globe.

Then, too, a sort of fumigating sometimes takes place. Siberian Samoyed women step over fires of burning reindeer skin. They must also refrain from cooking food for their men. Among the Nootka of the Canadian northwest coast, at her first period a girl is given her private eating utensils and must eat alone for eight months. The Chippewa girl also eats alone, cannot cross a public road or talk to any man or boy. Eskimo girls at their first period are taboo for forty days. They must sit crouching in a corner, their faces to the wall, draw their hoods over their heads, let their hair hang over their faces and only leave the house when everyone else is asleep. Hermann Ploss describes a still more curious segregation practised by the Australians of Queensland. The girl is taken to a shady place. Her mother draws a circle on the ground and digs a deep hole into which the girl must step. 'The sandy soil is then filled in, leaving her buried up to the waist. A woven hedge of branches or twigs is set around her with an opening toward which she turns her face. Her mother kindles a fire at the opening, the girl remains in her nest of earth in a squatting posture with folded arms and hands resting downward on the sand heap that covers her lower limbs.'

We are not told how long she must remain in the condition of the heroine of Beckett's play, *Happy Days*, but it is evident that the soil is supposed to purify or nullify her dangerous condition.

Among the Dogon of East Africa the menstrual taboo is so strong that a woman in this condition brings misfortune to everything she touches. Not only is she segregated in an isolated hut and provided with special eating utensils, but if she is seen passing through the village a general purification must take place. The Wogeo of South Australia believe that if a man has contact with a menstruating woman he will die from a wasting disease against which there is no remedy whatsoever.

The Hindus observe an endless number of prohibitions during the first three days of a woman's period. She must not weep, mount a horse, an ox or an elephant, be carried in a palanquin or drive in a vehicle.

In Hebrew tradition the menstruating woman is forbidden to work in a kitchen, sit at meals with other people, or drink from a glass used by others. Any contact with her husband is a sin and the penalty for intercourse during her period is death for both. Indeed the misfortunes which men suffer when they break the menstrual taboo vary but they are always severe. A Uganda Bantu woman by touching her husband's effects makes him sick; if she lays a hand on his weapons, he will be killed in the next fight. The natives of Malacca believe that coitus, or even contact, will cause the man to lose his virility.

The prohibitions which we have just been discussing occur in ancient or primitive cultures. Menstrual anxiety, however, is so deeply ingrained in the male psyche that it lingers in folk tradition. The peasants of eastern Europe believe that a woman must not bake bread, make pickles, churn butter or spin thread during her period or all will go wrong. Here, of course, is a survival of the idea that food is particularly susceptible to the deadly contagion. In Silesian folklore women during their periods are forbidden to plant seedlings or work in the garden. The Roman author Pliny tells us that contact of menstruous women with new wine or ripe fruit will sour both. The same author provides us with examples of ambivalence: 'Hailstorms, whirlwinds and lightnings even will be scared away by a woman uncovering her body while her courses are upon her. . . . Also if a woman strips herself naked while she is menstruating and walks around a field of wheat, the caterpillars, worms, beetles and other vermin will fall off the ears of corn [wheat].' Algonkian women walk around a cornfield for the same reason. Menstrual blood is also thought to cure leprosy and is actually by European peasants sometimes put into a man's coffee as a love charm. In Russian folklore it is said to cure warts and birthmarks. These instances are enough to show that the basic principle of ambivalent mana is involved. The overwhelming amount of evidence proves, however, that men do not envy the female ability to menstruate but fear it.

An example cited by Havelock Ellis shows that even in the late nineteenth century educated men were not free of this superstition. In 1891 a British doctor, William Goodell, wrote that he had to shake off the tradition that women must not be operated upon during their periods. 'Our forefathers from time immemorial have thought and taught that the presence of a menstruating woman would pollute solemn religious rites, would sour milk, spoil the fermentation in wine vats, and much other mischief in a general way.' Ellis also cites several instances of violinists who were convinced that the strings of their instruments continually broke while their wives were indisposed.

Even Hermann Ploss and Max Bartels in their gynaecological and anthropological work *Woman*, first published in Germany in 1905, wrote: 'But it seems very doubtful whether these superstitions and traditions will ever be eradicated. They are far too deeply and far too widely ramified in the mind and emotions of humanity.'

It will be seen that all the basic predispositions to anxiety are involved. Women by their recurring supernatural wound are set apart as aliens from the male norm. Sensitivity to contact and contagion is aroused and the symbol of the whole complex is blood, the powerful magic liquid on which life depends.

But menstruation is not the only female process which is surrounded with precautions. Pregnancy and childbirth, although the focus of various ideas, again arouse anxiety connected with blood, impurity and contagion. In addition, the production of a live being from a woman's body undoubtedly endows her with the supernatural properties of mana. In most cases the woman must be segregated or else she must give birth alone in the forest as among the Negritos, some east coast African Negroes, the Kiwai Papuans and the Guaná of Paraguay. The Hottentots of South Africa, the Tahitians, the Todas of India and the Gilyaks of the island of Sakhalin are among those who build a special hut or tent.

The misfortunes brought about by pregnancy and childbirth parallel those of menstruation. Among the Indians of Costa Rica, a woman pregnant for the first time infects the whole neighbourhood; she is blamed for any deaths which may occur and her husband is obliged to pay damages. Cape Town Bantu males believe that looking upon a lying-in woman will result in their being killed in battle. Some Brazilian Indians are sure that if the woman is not out of the house during childbirth weapons will lose their power. The Sulka of New Britain feel that in addition men will become cowardly and taro shoots will not sprout. A purification ceremony consists of chewing ginger, spitting it on twigs which are held in the smoke of a fire, and repeating certain charms. The twigs are then placed on the taro shoots, on weapons, and over doors and on roofs.

Those who aid the parturient woman are also sure to be infected by the contagion. Garcilaso de la Vega, the chronicler of the ancient Incas, wrote that no one must help a woman in childbirth, and any who did would be regarded as witches. Among the Hebrews the midwife was regarded as unclean. The whole concept of 'lying in' – only recently dispelled by new medical theories requiring the new mother to be up and about as soon as possible – which was rationalized as necessary for the woman to regain her strength, originated in magical precautions, as is clearly shown by the extreme length of time during which primitive women were sequestered and by the ceremonies carried out to purify them. To cite a few examples: The time varied from forty days, among the Swahili of Africa, to two months among the Eskimo or two to three months in Tahiti. Significantly enough, the period was longer after the birth of a girl in India, among the Hebrews, among many New Guinea tribes, the Masai of West Africa, and the Cree Indians of North America.

An example of purification ceremonies is the bathing of Hebrew women in special bath-houses in which both menstruating and parturient women were cleansed. After her time of sequestration was over, the Hebrew woman was required to send a lamb and a dove to the priest as sacrifices. The Pueblo Indians treat the purification more lyrically. Five days after the child is born, its mother is ceremonially washed. She then walks in the retinue of a priest to view the sunrise, throwing up cornflowers and blowing them about in the air.

In accordance with the feeling that the exceptional is embued with mana, miscarriage, being more abnormal than ordinary birth, is regarded with particular apprehension. The African Bantu consider it a cause of drought. They also believe that if a woman succeeds in aborting herself and at once has sexual relations with a man his death will follow.

The samplings just given are selected from a wealth of evidence which demonstrates that the male attitude towards female sexual functions is basically apprehensive; women, in short, are dangerous. Taboos and fears of contagion, however, are not limited to the physical crises in their lives. When we investigate the ideas of contact still further, a host of activities requires avoidance of women in general.

Since nutrition is one of the basic needs of human beings, and food is brought into contact with the body, it is not surprising that food and eating are universally involved with magical precautions. Women being intrinsically dangerous, their relation to food is a psychological problem. We have already cited food and eating taboos in relation to menstruation. Among preliterates and in ancient civilizations it is the rule rather than the exception that women do not eat with their husbands. Although in later periods the idea that the dominant male must be served first also enters the picture, the germ of the custom is certainly the notion that female impurity will contaminate a man's food and do him harm. Throughout Africa men and women eat separately, and the same is true of many South

American tribes. In Melanesia and Polynesia the same segregation is observed. The Todas, those hill people of India who have already been cited, also observe the taboo, as do the sophisticated Hindus. If the wife of one of the Hindus were to touch his food it would be rendered unfit for his use. The same precaution was widespread in North America. The early traveller and artist George Catlin said he never saw Indians and squaws eating together. Henry Rowe Schoolcraft, the first American anthropologist, when he was an Indian agent among the Chippewa, married a half-Indian girl. Although his wife had been educated in England and helped him collect Algonkian folklore and her dark-skinned mother prevented a border incident by mediating between her people and the whites, the mother's conservatism was so intense that she could never be persuaded to eat with her son-in-law.

The two exclusive male activities of hunting and fighting are also very often associated with avoidance of women. Nothing is closer to man's maleness than his weapons and his hunting gear. In Tahiti, women are prohibited from touching weapons and fishing apparatus. In Queensland the natives throw away their fishing lines if women step over them, and elsewhere a woman is forbidden to step over objects, because in so doing the woman's sex passes over them and they are thus exposed to the seat of contagion. (When a Maori warrior wishes to absorb the phallic magic of a powerful chief, he crawls between his legs.) A Dakota Indian's weapons must not be touched by a woman and women of the Siberian hunting tribes must abide by the same taboo. If a woman touches a Zulu's assegai, he cannot use it again.

Cattle among the southern Bantu are an important form of male ego expression and in this case they are taboo to women. If women touch them the beasts will fall ill. Fighting cocks among the Malay are treated in the same way. This taboo, however, among the Bantu does not apply to girls who have not yet reached puberty or to old women who have passed the menopause, proving conclusively that it is the female sexual mana which is thought to do the damage.

The necessity of abstaining from intercourse with women before undertaking the chase and warfare has sometimes been explained as a fear of the debilitating effect of what is considered the weaker sex.

Indeed it is often so rationalized by the primitives themselves. That this is a late addition is indicated by the fact that fasting often accompanies the ritual surrounding hunting and war and fasting can scarcely be construed as a method of conserving strength.

Sexual abstinence before war and hunting is practised all over Polynesia and in many parts of Melanesia. The head-hunters of Assam, in India, are particularly strict in observing this taboo. In one case the wife of a headman spoke to her husband, unaware that he was returning with a group of warriors who had taken trophy heads. When she learned what she had done she was so disturbed that she grew sick and died. In British Columbia and other areas of North America which were inhabited by the hunting tribes, the taboo against contact with women before hunting or fighting was carefully observed. The Huichol of Mexico did so, and explained that a deer would never enter the snare of a man who was sleeping with his wife. It would simply look at the trap, snort 'pooh, pooh' and go away. Throughout Africa continence and avoidance were observed before war and hunting. Women were forbidden to approach the Zulu army except (as in the case of cattle) for old women past the menopause, because such women 'have become men'.

The hunting taboo can be exaggerated to the extent that the Bangalas of equatorial Africa remain continent while they are making nets to capture wild pigs and the Melanesian of the Torres Straits refrain from intercourse during the mating season of turtles (an important food), in a curious defiance of the principles of mimetic magic.

Most extreme of all is the taboo which functions on the principle that since the name is a part of the individual, its use will affect his well-being. The Bantu women of Nyasaland do not speak their husband's names or any words that may be synonymous. A Warra-munga woman of Australia may not mention the ordinary name of a man, which she knows, and in addition he has a secret name which she does not even know. Similarly the Hindus, whom we have continually cited as taboo ridden, do not allow a woman to mention her husband's name. She must speak of him as the 'man of the house' or 'father of the household' and if she dreams of his name this will result in his untimely death.

The tiny Bushmen, who are one of the oldest peoples and who support life by the simplest of hunting and gathering techniques, exemplify nearly all of the avoidances we have been discussing. Men and women sit on different sides of their crude shelters of woven twigs or grasses – if a man occupies a woman's place he will become impotent. When a man sets out to shoot an eland or a giraffe, he must avoid intercourse or the poison on his arrows will lose its power. A Bushman woman gives birth secretly in the bush. If a man inadvertently steps over the spot he will lose his ability to hunt.

A Bushman myth emphasizes the alienation of the two sexes almost in terms of their being different tribes. In the early times men and women lived apart, the former hunting animals exclusively, the latter pursuing a gathering existence. Five of the men, who were out hunting, being careless creatures, let their fire go out. The women, who were careful and orderly, always kept their fire going. The men, having killed a springbok, became desperate for means to cook it, so one of their number set out to get fire, crossed the river, and met one of the women gathering seeds. When he asked her for some fire, she invited him to the feminine camp. While he was there she said, 'You are very hungry. Just wait until I pound up these seeds and I will boil them and give you some.' She made him some porridge. After he had eaten it, he said, 'Well, it's nice food so I shall just stay with you.' The men who were left waited and wondered. They still had the springbok and they still had no fire. The second man set out, only to be tempted by female cooking, and to take up residence in the camp of the women. The same thing happened to the third man. The two men left were very frightened. They suspected something terrible had happened to their comrades. They cast the divining bones but the omens were favourable. The fourth man set out timidly, only to end by joining his comrades. The last man became very frightened indeed and besides by now the springbok had rotted. He took his bow and arrows and ran away.

On the other side of the world, among the Pueblo and Zuñi Indians, myths which tell of the emergence of their forefathers from the ground also divide the sexes into two camps, although in this case the women are portrayed as less efficient than the men in their attempts to reach the upper world. In these traditional stories such matters as sex and marriage are completely ignored, the sexes are viewed as groups living apart, a theme which may be a reflection of the periodic segregation of women.

The earliest types of religion at any rate codify male anxiety by proclaiming that women shall remain inactive for a considerable portion of their lives. The same religious sanctions prohibit them from participating in many human activities, partly excluding them from the human condition. And all the evidence points to the fact that this situation began with the simplest types of group association, in all probability as far back as the Paleolithic.

Despite these barriers of alienation and fear, the sex drive after all does ensure reproduction. The act of procreation, however, arouses still another type of ambivalence which affects the status of women and substantiates the view that the conditions of man's development as a social being prevent him from ever taking eros for granted.

CHAPTER FIVE

The Perils of Love

It may seem a far cry from the primitives we have just been discussing to the leading American writer of the nineteenth century,
Herman Melville, but the brilliant author of *Moby Dick* produced
two stories which are singularly illuminating from the point of view
of male attitudes towards sex.

Since Melville wrote in a period in which sexual anxieties were
sternly repressed, and was at the same time endowed with a rich
symbolical imagination and a passionate nature, his unconscious
spoke loudly in lyrical fables. Moreover, as we have already suggested, the artist must be ranked among the latter-day shamans.

The first of these significant stories, entitled 'I and My Chimney',
begins with a description: 'Within thirty feet of the turf-sided road,
my chimney – a huge, corpulent old Harry VIII of a chimney – rises
full in front of me and all my possessions.' Although the comparison
with Henry VIII is ostensibly one of size, the other chief associations
with the famous monarch are erotic. Later the description of the
chimney is more explicit. 'When in the rear room, set apart for that
object, I stand to receive my guests (who, by the way, call more, I
suspect, to see my chimney than me), I then stand, not so much
before, as, strictly speaking, behind my chimney, which is, indeed,
the true host.' As the story goes on, the unconscious phallic symbol
of the chimney becomes more and more apparent. The writer is
identified with it, it is the core of his house. Furthermore, 'What
care I, if, unaware that my chimney, as a free citizen of this land,
stands upon an independent basis of its own.' In other words it has
its own erective life. Again and again its great vertical size is emphasized. It is identified with the ego of the writer: ' "Sir, I look upon

49

this chimney less as a pile of masonry than as a personage. It is the king of the house." '

The whole plot of the story revolves around the wife's attempt to destroy the chimney!

At first she plans to knock a hole through it to make an entrance hall. The narrator objects. ' "But wife," said I, "the chimney – consider the chimney; if you demolish the foundation, what is to support the superstructure?" ' – which translated would mean that a man is nothing without his virility. All through this curious story, the wife's intense vitality is stressed and indeed her desire to dominate the narrator is openly described. 'She is desirous that, domestically, I should abdicate; that, renouncing further rule, like the venerable Charles V, I should retire into some sort of monastery. But indeed, the chimney excepted, I have little authority to lay down. By my wife's ingenious application of the principle that certain things belong of right to female jurisdiction, I find myself, through my easy compliances, insensibly stripped by degrees of one masculine prerogative after another.'

The story has no other plot than the defence of the chimney against the wife's attacks. She is said to regard it 'as the bully of the house'. When she plans to remove it entirely, its owner objects. 'No, no, wife, I can't abolish my back-bone.' An architect is brought in who tells him, 'Your chimney, sir; it can without rashness be removed.' To all such intrigues and plots the master of the chimney responds with delaying tactics and passive resistance. 'But when I consider her enmity against my chimney, and the steadiness with which at the last she is wont to carry out her schemes, if by hook or crook she can, especially after having once been baffled, why, I scarcely knew at what step of hers to be surprised.' His daughters join the wife in the plot against his symbolic virility but the story has no resolution and no other point than the patent sex opposition. In the end he is still on the defensive. 'I am simply standing guard over my mossy old chimney; for it is resolved between me and my chimney, that I and my chimney will never surrender.' The adjective "mossy" even suggests pubic hair.

We wonder what Melville's nineteenth-century readers made of such a frankly dramatized fear of castration.

Coupled with this tale is another, a two-part sketch the first of which is entitled 'The Paradise of Bachelors' and merely describes the relaxed atmosphere of male comradeship in a London club. The second sketch is significantly entitled 'The Tartarus of Maids' and is basically a documentary account of a visit to a New England paper mill operated by women workers. Melville's extravagances of description manage to endow the piece with truly amazing overtones. In the first place, the narrator is called the *seedsman*. He drives into 'a *dusky pass*, which, from the violent Gulf Stream of air unceasingly driving between its *cloven walls* of haggard rock, as well as from the tradition of a crazy spinster's hut having long ago stood somewhere hereabouts, is called the Mad Maid's Bellows-pipe'. The tale goes on to speak of a *sudden contraction* called the Black Notch. If the *shaggy-wooded mountains* surrounding the *purple hopper-shaped hollow* were not enough, we are told a stream flows through it, brick-coloured and called Blood River. Along this river are *grey-haired pines*. It is certainly no far-fetched interpretation to see in this female hell, as the title could be translated, a symbolization of a violent anxiety concerning the woman's genital. The seedsman, clearly the penis, which passes into this icy inferno, does so in winter, the episode being surrounded with apprehension and fear. The horse is evidently absorbed into the phallic symbolism of the seedsman, 'his nostrils at each breath sending forth two horn-shaped shoots of heated respiration'. But the phallic energy is not maintained, for suddenly 'right across the track – not ten minutes fallen – an old distorted hemlock lay, darkly undulatory as an anaconda'. The sexual encounter so strangely dramatized by the trip into the pass is surrounded with various anxieties. The emphasis on coldness seems to indicate the frigidity of the female partner, and the fallen hemlock is, of course, the failure of an erection. On the other hand a different kind of fear is also present, a fear of damage to the male organ because of obstacles in the pass. 'Black, my horse, as if exasperated by the cutting wind, slung out with his strong hind legs, tore the light pung straight up-hill, and sweeping grazingly through the narrow notch, sped downward madly past the ruined saw-mill. . . . With might and main, quitting my seat and robes, and standing backward, with one foot braced against the dash-board, I rasped and churned the bit, and stopped him just in time to avoid *collision, at a turn, with the bleak nozzle of rock, couchant like a lion in the way.*'

Melville returns to the image later in a way that shows he was compulsively and apprehensively concerned with a dangerous passage through a narrow aperture. 'I by degrees wound into the Mad Maid's Bellows-pipe, and saw the grim Black Notch beyond, then something latent, as well as something obvious in time and scene, strangely brought back to my mind my first sight of the grimy Temple Bar. And when Black, my horse, went darting through the Notch, perilously grazing its rocky wall, I remembered being in a runaway London omnibus, which in much the same sort of style, though by no means at an equal rate, dashed through the ancient arch of Wren.'

That a bizarre mixture of rampant unconscious symbolism and a certain awareness is present emerges in the careful apposition of the two sketches. Among the male group of bachelors, all is peace and tranquillity while the female world of the mill-workers is grim, consumptive, and squalid. And here another outrageous bit of symbolism occurs. In the room in which rags were cut up to be made into paper, 'like so many mares haltered to a rack, stood rows of girls. Before each was vertically thrust up a long, glittering scythe, immovably fixed at bottom to the manger-edge. The curve of the scythe, and its having no snath to it, made it look exactly like a sword.' The rags were ripped up on these blades but to Melville they held further symbolism. 'And each erected sword is so borne, edge-outward, before each girl. If my reading fails me not, just so, of old, condemned state-prisoners went from the hall of judgment to their doom: an officer before, bearing a sword, its edge turned outward, in significance of their fatal sentence.' Though Melville is consciously attacking the evils of the factory system, his unconscious is once more erecting proud phallic symbols which are treated as antagonistic to the female principle. They do not long maintain their independence. 'That moment two of the girls, dropping their rags, plied each a whet-stone up and down the sword-blade. My unaccustomed blood curdled at the sharp shriek of the tormented steel.' Amazingly enough, the guide who has led the seedsman into the rag room is named Cupid!

It may be objected that this peep into a Victorian writer's unconscious, with its violent castration fantasies, merely proves that Melville, though a genius, was a highly exceptional neurotic; and indeed many of his critics have detected evidence of passive or sublimated homosexuality in his psyche.

Let us listen to the testimony of an analyst on this subject. Karen Horney writes: 'Now this dread of the vagina appears not only in homosexuals and perverts but also in the dreams of every male analysand. A boat is sailing in a narrow channel and is suddenly sucked into a whirlpool, there is a cellar with uncanny bloodstained plants and animals or one is climbing inside a chimney and is in danger of falling and being killed.' Horney goes farther to explain that the dread of the female genital is extended to dread of women in general. 'Everywhere the man strives to rid himself of his dread of women by objectifying it. "It is not," he says, "that I dread her; it is that she herself is malignant, capable of any crime, a beast of prey, a vampire, a witch, insatiable in her desires. She is the very personification of what is sinister." '

We shall have occasion to document this objectification later on. The matter of fear of the female genital and of the act of intercourse with the opposite sex, however, now takes us back to primitive mythology. The Wichita Indians of North America have created a cycle of myths about a folk hero named Son of a Dog. One day the hero encountered two women, one of whom invited him home, hospitably urging him to marry her daughters. As it happened, she was a witch named Little Spider Woman. Her companion, also a witch, whose name was Buzzard Woman, took the young man aside and privately warned him that the two daughters had teeth in their vaginas which would cut off his penis. 'When you lie with them you must not have intercourse even though they try to persuade you. You will hear the gritting of the teeth in their vaginas. You must not sleep at night either because the old woman will come to see what you are doing. If you do not have intercourse with the girls, she will ask them why you don't. Therefore watch, for if you sleep you will be destroyed.' Nothing daunted, the hero resolved to follow her advice. He also took another tip from Buzzard Woman and pushed a log of wood ahead of him when he went into Little Spider Woman's hut. It was a wise precaution and saved him from being brained by a war club in the hands of the old witch. The daughters proved enticing as he slept, or rather pretended to sleep, between them. They attempted to titillate him but he controlled his ardour. Meanwhile the old witch pretended to snore but later got out of bed and again tried to kill him. The hero nimbly evaded her. The next day Son of a Dog secretly met with Buzzard Woman, who gave him two long whetstones. He was advised to pick the girl he found most attractive and to render her harmless by grinding off the vaginal teeth with one whetstone. The other girl he was to kill by thrusting the second whetstone up her vagina instead of his penis. Buzzard Woman also gave him a charm to put the evil witch to sleep. The following night Son of a Dog killed one girl by shoving a whetstone so far up her vagina that it could not be removed. He ground off the teeth in the other girl's genital, thus making her fit for male use. He then fled with the girl hotly pursued by Little Spider Woman. The good witch intervened, however, carried her evil rival up into the air and dropped her so that she died and the eloping couple were able to escape.

It is quite clear that Melville's rocky protuberances which threaten to dash the seedsman to pieces in the Black Notch are exactly parallel to the teeth in the vagina of the girls in the Wichita tale. Here we have American Indians exhibiting the same castration anxiety as the nineteenth-century novelist. Another form of the story, found among the Angmagsalik Eskimo, describes a dangerous woman who carries a live dog's head between her legs which bites off male organs. The Pomo Indians of California have a version which goes as follows: Wood Rat was courting the daughters of Morning Star. One of them said, 'Well, Wood Rat, if you like me all right, I will marry you but you must know that my father has placed thorns all about my vagina.' Rat then took a stone, broke off all the thorns, and married the girl.

Actually twenty-two versions of this myth have been found in North America alone. It occurs in the mythology of the Siberian tribes and in India and New Guinea.

Another version of the theme appears in the mythology of the Toba Indians of the Gran Chaco of South America. The chief characters in this story are Big Fox, a bawdy trickster, and Hawk. Both went hunting with a group of other beings who were a blend of animal and man. At this time men had no women. Hawk had the good fortune to encounter some women climbing down from the sky on ropes. Hawk cleverly cut the ropes, causing the women to fall down to earth. There were enough to provide all the men with mates. Hawk, however, had noticed that the women were provided with toothed vaginas and advised caution. Fox being sexually greedy could not wait and as soon as he started to make love to his woman she cut off his penis and testicles with her vagina. Fox died of his wound. A little later rain fell upon him which brought him to life. He made a new penis of wood and testicles from two black fruit. Then he went back and copulated with his wife. She tried her best to bite off his penis but only succeeded in denting it. The next day Hawk picked up a stone and broke off all the teeth in the women's vaginas except one which became the clitoris. He said, 'Now wait. Tomorrow your wives will be well again and you may copulate with them.'

Allied to these symbolic stories is the belief of the Arunta of Australia that a woman can 'sing' a finger, that is, charm it, and insert it into her vulva. The genitals of a man who has intercourse with her immediately afterwards will become diseased, and in all probability he will lose them entirely.

Still other images dramatizing the dread of women occur in the mythologies of both the Hindus and the Hebrews, cultures which we have already cited as particularly saturated with menstruation and birth taboos. The Hindu goddess Kali, the black mother, is depicted with four arms, two of which hold the decapitated heads of giants, one of the others a drawn sword. Around her neck is a necklace of men's heads or of skulls. She dances for joy on the body of her dead husband, Siva. The myth states that, drunk with the blood of the giants she had killed, in a blind exaltation she also killed her husband. Head taking, in Freud's view, is a symbol of castration. Kali has not only emasculated giants but has killed her husband, and the necklace of heads still further symbolizes her destructive power. The story of Judith is another example of an emasculating woman, this time shaped by theology into a heroic legend. Finally the story of Samson and Delilah softens the theme but nevertheless preserves its fundamental outlines. The cutting of hair is, of course, the symbol of castration, since the loss of strength is the same thing as a failure of masculine power.

How then can we explain this ingrained fear of the castrating women? In the first place the old theme of ambivalence is still present. Kali, the black mother, has a beneficent double, her sexuality is both good and bad, but on the whole the bad female mana predominates in most early cultures. C. F. Daly in discussing the image of Kali feels that 'fear of destruction which originates in the woman's periodicity accounts for the reaction which eventually drives men into the homosexual group'. Menstruation, as we have shown, is an important cause of magical anxiety but does not seem to account satisfactorily for the fear we are describing.

Actually, beginning with Freud, psychoanalysts have noted that a dread of women frequently appears in neurotic situations and especially, of course, in the case of homosexuality. This dread seems to be tied up with what in classical Freudian terms is called the 'phallic phase'. The very young infant's sexuality is believed to be distributed over oral, anal and cutaneous regions. Generally, while at the phallic phase, which occurs at four or five, sexuality crystallizes about the penis, the male begins to identify with his penis, prizes it highly and thus his anxiety about castration is intensified. Because of his identification with the organ, anything lost from his body becomes a symbolical castration.

In extreme homosexuality, the castration fear is never overcome and the dread of the female genital is intense. As a result the male turns to his own kind. The psychoanalyst Otto Fenichel suggests: 'It may be that the boy has a more primary reason to fear the female genital than castration (oral anxieties of a vagina dentata as a retaliatory fear for oral sadistic impulses).' In other words the sucking infant, which had an unconscious cannibalistic desire to consume the mother, projects an instinctive memory of its own sadism into the female vagina and transforms it into a biting mouth. That deep cannibalistic drives do exist is substantiated by primitive customs in which a part of the defeated enemy is eaten ostensibly to obtain his qualities. The explanation seems over-elaborate, however. Sartre, in his existential psychoanalysis, arrives at a simplistic type of explanation. 'The obscenity of the feminine sex is that of everything which "gapes open". It is a *summons to being* as all holes are. In herself woman appeals to a strange flesh which is to transform her into a fullness of being by penetration and dissolution. . . . Beyond any doubt her sex is a mouth and a voracious mouth which devours the penis – a fact which can easily lead to the idea of castration. The amorous act is the castration of the man; but this is above all because sex is a hole. We have to deal with a *presexual* contribution which will become one of the components of sexuality as a complex human attitude.'

Once more the hypothesis developed by Róheim from field experience is interesting and provocative. His explanation involves a theory of magic. He points out that parts of the body or products of the body predominate in magical spells used to affect their former owner. Hair or nail clippings, excrement, urine, semen, the navel cord, the foreskin, all such products are treated with care; they can be used in the usual ambivalent way for harm or help.

This, says Róheim, goes back to the phallic phase (which as we shall see later seems to persist in primitive cultures) when the whole body is identified with the penis. 'For the savage everything separated from the body brings danger. . . . The original anxiety is that something becomes separated from the body at coitus.' Freud expressed a similar idea. 'The effect of coitus in discharging tensions and inducing flaccidity may be a prototype of what these fears represent.' Róheim goes on to elaborate. 'The contrast between life and death in cohabitation seems to be between the male member standing erect (life) and its subsequent death after ejaculation.' He cites the Maori who used to work up a battle frenzy which resulted in their entering the struggle with an erection. The sexual spasm and death were equated. 'That which destroys man is the vulva,' an old Maori said. A Central Australian said, 'The vagina is very hot, it is fire and each time the penis goes in it dies.' In the myth of Maui, the Polynesian trickster, the death of the hero takes place when he creeps into the vagina of his ancestress, Hina; in other words he identifies with his penis and dies in symbolic coitus. Róheim concludes from this, 'Actually it is the seminal fluid which leaves the body but there is an unconscious tendency to dread the total cutting off of the penis, i.e. castration, as the inevitable consequence of coitus.'

It is obvious that such ideas take us further on in the life of the individual and involve traumas which arise at puberty and with actual connection with the other sex. It appears that a whole network of anxieties surrounds the maturing individual. We have already enumerated sense of loss, early castration fear, fear of the exceptional and unusual, and finally pubertal fears, some or all of which can form a basis for the elaborate structures of ritual which are erected around sexual relations. As Karen Horney points out, the boy just entering puberty is filled with apprehension towards women and 'only mature sexuality drives him over the border of anxiety'. Any normal male, looking back over his own development, will probably remember that, despite a burning sexual curiosity which was intensified at puberty, despite the interest in pornography and the intense desire to know what the female organ looked like, there was an unacknowledged sense of misgiving. The immature boy is not sure what he can do or should do with the longed-for female or what she will do to him.

Clearly rites connected with female virginity relate to this basic fear, rites which are culturally transmitted and pass on the group formulation of the dread of women. In many cases the husband himself does not deflower his bride. Sometimes an old woman or an old man of the tribe does it manually; again, ritual intercourse by a priest does the job. While, as Ernest Crawley points out in *The Mystic Rose*, this may be a magical precaution in order to avoid the exceptional mana of the first time, a kind of ceremony of transition by which a woman's dangerous organ is neutralized by a magically armed person, it is also probable that it assuages the young man's dread and, indeed, the process of defloration can be painful and frustrating.

Róheim's theory equating loss of semen, dread of castration and image of death is further elaborated. For him the early concept of the soul, or vital principle, also has a sexual base. 'Just as coitus is in a certain sense of castration, death appears as the final coitus or castration of life.' (Indeed throughout Western literature the image of death as a lover recurs constantly.) The soul, for Róheim, is a king of sexualized double image of the ego and since the ego is, in the phallic phase, identified with the penis and its product, fear of damage or death to the soul through magic is a castration fear. He points out that among the Hindus, 'The climax of the Yogi's art is not to let the "drop", the semen, leave him and to compel it to return to him from the female organ if it is on its way; by doing this he vanquishes death, for the drop he retains means life and the drop that falls from him is death.'

Róheim's explanation does seem to illuminate a great deal of magical practice and suggests one basis for fear of the sexual act with women. In primitive mythology, however, there is still another image which appears in relation to the dread of woman's sexuality, and that is the snake. We have already seen that the snake is a phallic symbol and is sometimes blamed for originating menstruation by biting the vagina. The snake, however, also participates in a different context among the Caribs of the Orinoco forest. In this tale the father of the hero twins (characters who appear all over the world) seeks a wife who is provided for him by Alligator. Alligator, however, has no real daughter; he has carved one from a plum tree, but it turns out that she has a snake in her vagina. The father eventually removes the snake, making her fit for her husband's use. The significance of this story arises from the fact that in psychoanalytical cases, homosexuals are often found to cherish fantasies of a phallic woman. Karen Horney equates this fear of a snake or penis in the vagina as a fear of the father. The phallic snake which may bite and castrate seems to be a double image in which the toothed vagina is blended with the father's penis that stands in the way of the son's sexual impulses. Robert Gessaim mentions a homosexual patient whose fantasy centred about a woman with a dangerous dog which would bite him. A physician, recording the hallucinations of alcoholic patients, quoted one man, a heterosexual, as saying, 'They said they would have a police dog tear out my organs . . . a woman will bite off the organs. . . .' The similarity between primitive myth and contemporary neurotic fantasy certainly indicates how deep-seated this type of male anxiety is.

*

If in addition to the menace of the recurring wound, the cleft between a woman's thighs is felt to be a castrating scissors, we begin to perceive, more and more, how intensely alien the second sex is thought to be, how all the noxious mana of the exceptional is bound to cluster around half the human race. As a result, not only contact with women but the heterosexual act of intercourse itself begins to be endowed with dangers. For instance, a native of New Britain who has just engaged in the act must not go near a wounded man or the man will die. Similarly the African Masai believe that a couple engaged in making honey wine must be continent for two days before and during the six days of the brewing or the wine will be undrinkable and the bees will fly away.

Prohibitions decreeing that a newly married pair must not consummate their relationship for a specified time are also connected with the dangers of sex, of virginity, and of the first participation in an exceptional situation. The Canelos of Ecuador say that if a husband and wife sleep together on the first night the husband will die. The Thompson Indians of Canada insist an abstinence for four nights. Among the Aztecs rituals went on for four days before the newly married pair were allowed to begin their sex life.

The Wogeo of South Australia are a good example of this generalized fear of sex. Herbert Ian Hogbin writes, 'Perhaps the most fundamental religious conception relates to the difference between the sexes. Each sex is perfectly all right in its own way but contact is fraught with danger for both. The chief source of peril is sexual intercourse when contact is at its maximum. The juices of the male then enter the female and vice versa. Women are automatically cleansed by the process of menstruation but men, in order to guard against disease, have periodically to incise the penis and allow a quantity of blood to flow.'

Margaret Mead's Mountain Arapesh of New Guinea are a good example of a group which combines all the fears and sanctions we have been discussing. A gentle peaceable people, they fear all extreme expressions of sex, and female sexuality in particular. Coastal Arapesh women are supposed to be highly passionate. If a mountain man is foolish enough to marry one he must be on his guard. If his yams don't prosper and he fails to find game, 'let him abstain from relationship with this dangerous oversexed woman still many more moons, lest the part of his potency, his own physical strength, the ability to feed others which he most cherishes, should be permanently injured'. The flying fox bat is a symbol of the oversexed woman. In one legend a man traps these animals. In revenge they organize the birds who cut off the man's penis and drop it among the women, who bury it sorrowfully. The Arapesh male 'fears the female demon, in legends, the *unuk*, which is also the name for the morning star, who is predatory and lustful, with two teeth in her mouth and two in her vulva and disguises herself as his wife to lure a man into intercourse which will end in death'. The snake image also appears in the form of a phallic demon, the *marsalai*. This entity produces pregnancy in a woman, entering her vulva in the form of a snake and causing her to give birth to snakes. (We may probably see in this the phallic woman image blended with an articulate fear of the father's penis.) In one legend a woman marries the marsalai, bears young snakes which she nurses with loathing, and decides to do something about it. She cuts off the heads of both husband and children and boils them until they are soft and ruined.

Interestingly enough, menstrual blood which is thought to be extremely dangerous can be used to fight fire with fire. If a man sees the marsalai he will die unless he is treated with menstrual blood to counteract the evil mana. The dangers of the first experience of sex give rise to a belief parallel to that of the Wogeo of Australia. According to Hogbin, 'Bringing together the male and female in the sex act is always dangerous; after first intercourse both bride and bridegroom have to perform a ceremonial to exorcize the dangerous heat of sex contact from their bodies. If they do not perform these ritual acts, the woman will not have children and the man will not grow yams or find game.' The purification consists of the man letting blood from his penis while the woman urinates against a tree.

The same idea concerning the dangers of sex turns up in Africa among the Bambara, who have developed an elaborate mythology including an evil first female who symbolizes the impure earth and night sorcery. The Bambara practise circumcision and also excision of the clitoris. Both operations must be performed to allow the *wanzo*, the dangerous sexual principle which comes from the female spirit, to drip out with the blood lost by the operation.

On a folklore level the Finns also entertain beliefs very similar to those of the Mountain Arapesh. After sexual intercourse there develops an emanation termed *pĕ'z* of extreme harmfulness and highly contagious. Hermann P. Ploss wrote: 'All men are considered infected by pĕ'z after coitus until they perform special ceremonies of purification. . . . Woman is regarded as the source and focus of pĕ'z; human beings and animals suffer in various ways according to their respective natures if they have contact with a woman. Even if a woman steps over them, the infection may be transmitted. A child to whom this happens falls sick, a dog loses his scent and power of tracking game, also his vision of the spirits and wood demons and can no longer protect his master from their attacks. A man loses his strength, falls ill, loses his skill in the chase and becomes a weakling in every way.'

At this point it might be asked: If women are so dangerous, why do men have anything to do with them at all? Homosexuals, of course, do avoid them. Fortunately for the continuance of the race, next to hunger, the sex urge is the strongest instinctive drive. But men do, quite clearly, avoid women with ritual justification and express their dread or hostility in social forms. This leads us into an account of such forms in relation to the cultural heritage.

CHAPTER SIX

Men Without Women

East of Lake Tanganyika, in Bantu villages, the most important structure is the Iwanza or men's house. Hutton Webster describes it as
'a long room, twelve by eighteen feet, with one door, a low flat roof,
well blackened with smoke, and no chimney. Along its length there
ran a high inclined bench, on which cow-skins were spread for men
to take their siesta. Some huge drums were hung in a corner, and
logs smouldered on the ground.' Leaving their mothers, the boys
went into this institution at the age of about eight. From then on
during their young manhood they slept and ate there. Dances took
place in front of it by day or by night. It was a centre of gossip and
male recreation and a guest hall for visiting male groups.

Both Hutton Webster and Heinrich Shurtz, who wrote the
classic studies on men's societies, stressed the magical sex antagonism involved. Wrote Webster, 'Out of these beliefs have arisen many
curious and interesting taboos designed to prevent the real or
imagined dangers incident to the contact of the sexes. Sexual
separation is further secured and perpetuated by the institution
known as the men's house of which examples are to be found among
peoples throughout the world.'

Schurtz, who was innocent of any knowledge of psychoanalytical
theory, explained the institution on the basis that women were
possessive and hampering to men. In men an innate gregariousness
and a desire for brotherhood with their peers drove them to escape
into associations freeing them from the anti-social, isolated little
world of marriage.

Men's houses are found all through Melanesia. There, as well as
being clubhouses, they become centres of ancestor cults where bones
and decorated skulls are kept. In Polynesia they were dominated by

the aristocratic class. In Malaysia where the warrior element predominates, the Land Dyaks, for instance, use them as storehouses
for trophy heads. In the Solomon Islands canoes are kept in them.
In Africa sometimes initiation ceremonies such as circumcision takes
place in them.

The Tchambuli men's houses of New Guinea, described by
Margaret Mead, are built on the shore of a lake. One for each clan,
fifteen in all, they are perched on high stilts like long-legged birds.
The floors are of packed clay with raised platforms on each side.
They are thirty feet long with slender high steeples at each end, the
ridge-pole dipping in the centre like a crescent moon. On the
thatched leaf-patterned gable ends, there is a huge face carved in
low relief and painted red and white. When a new house is built the
steeples are made of wicker; wicker birds are set on the steeple tips.
Later the steeples are thatched over and wicker birds are replaced
with a wooden bird whose wings spring from the hollow body of a
man. Dwelling houses which shelter several families are called houses
of women in opposition to the male clubs.

Between the ages of eight and twelve a boy is scarified, patterns
are cut in his back by a maternal 'uncle'. After a long seclusion and
various rituals he is given presents and supposed to spend much of
his time in the men's house. Here he learns to play the flute, carve,
plait masks, and takes part in elaborate dramatic masked ceremonies.
Symbolic headhunting was a part of Tchambuli life and each boy
was expected to kill a war captive in his childhood, his spear hand
held by his father while the blood was splashed on upright (and
probably phallic) stones outside the ceremonial house. When Mead
studied this group, true male dominance and sex antagonism was
weakening although the outward forms persisted.

The antagonism between men and women, however, is expressed
in extreme form in the men's societies and initiation activities
among the Iatmül of New Guinea. Here the ceremonial house may
be 120 feet long with towering gables at the ends. Inside, the long
vista through the series of supporting beams suggests the darkened
interior of a church. The institution is not without religious significance since there are strong taboos against scratching the earth
floor or damaging the woodwork. A man must not walk through the

building and out the rear entrance but must always exit through a side door. As well as being a meeting place and a centre of social life it is a place of ritual activity, being imbued with the 'heat' of violence and killing. Long sessions of boastful debate and buffoonery go on in which rivalries are expressed in terms of elaborate and often fraudulent totemic heraldry. Sometimes the representative of one group threatens to rape members of the opposition and does an erotic pantomime. The ceremonial house is taboo to women because here the men make their masks and ceremonial equipment and carry out parts of their male ceremonies which involve musical instruments. Some of these activities take place within while the women outside can hear 'the mysterious and beautiful sounds made by the various secret instruments, flutes, gongs, bullroarers. . . .' At times the group sallies forth and performs on the dancing ground outside, while the women form an audience.

There is a clear connection between male sexuality, initiation of the boys and trophy headhunting. In the first place, as among the Tchambuli, the young boy is made to spear a bound captive while his clan uncle helps him lift the spear. In the initiation ceremony the boys are brutally scarified on the back. When they scream, slit gongs are beaten to drown the sound. They are drenched with icy water and a crocodile bone is thrust into the mouth ostensibly to find out if they have eaten taboo foods but in actuality it is merely used to wound their mouths. Significantly, during initiation the boys are called the 'wives of the initiators whose penises they are made to handle'. As Gregory Bateson sums it up, the end of all the initiation 'is the adoption by the novice of the masculine ethos but it seems the first step in inducing this process is to compel the novices to behave as women'. In this connection Lionel Ovesey's comment on a certain type of modern homosexual is pertinent. 'What about the "masculine" male who is homosexually attracted to his more "feminine" counterpart? Here also, the sexual component is primary but, of the other two, the power component takes precedence over the dependency component. . . . His object choice is a man but one as much like a woman as possible. If, in addition, the power component is strong, he attempts to redeem his masculine failure through a compensatory domination of his weaker partner. He seeks to have men submit to his penis orally and anally, but generally refuses to accept the reverse role. He denies his own dependency at the expense of the weaker man. In this he not only satisfies himself sexually but enhances his deflated masculinity by making a woman out of his partner.' It would seem then that the sexual brutalizing of the young boy and the effort to turn him into a woman both enhances the older warrior's desire of power, gratifies his sense of hostility towards the maturing male competitor, and eventually, when he takes him into the male group, strengthens the male solidarity in its symbolic attempt to do without women.

Headhunting among this people was originally a status affair; the man who had killed was allowed to wear a special flying-fox skin pubic apron. On returning from the raid, the warriors placed the heads on phallic standing stones outside the ceremonial house. The word for intercourse was 'to set up a standing stone'. To quote Bateson, 'We can clearly see the general position of headhunting as the main source of pride of the village while associated with this pride is property, fertility and the male sexual act.' For fertility we should read 'potency' and the sexual act is homosexual.

The type of culture we have just been describing is representative of a whole complex which involves the separation of men from women, ambivalent sadistic sexual assaults upon boys in initiation and a sadistic warrior ethos which is often expressed in trophy head taking. In general it appears to be related to the 'phallic phase' as described by depth analysis. This, as we have pointed out, is a stage in the development of the young male in which he identifies with his organ and because of unconscious castration fears rejects the female. In the words of Ernest Jones, 'In this connection we may remember that to the neurotic phallic boy, the idea of the female being castrated involves not a simple cutting off but an opening being made into a hole, the well known "wound" theory of the vulva.' We have already cited the wound theory as it appears in primitive mythology. Modern case histories of children indicate that the phallic phase involves comparison of male organs, urination competitions, etc., a narcissism which is easily transformed into homosexual practice. Along with this goes the notion of the phallus as a weapon in connection with sadistic impulses.

Evidence of the dread of women connected with primitive culture comes from two areas in the Pacific. Bronislaw Malinowski relates a story told him by the Trobriand Islanders. His informants insisted that the women of another tribe were hostile and dangerous to men. If a stranger were to pass by while these women were working in a yam patch they would seize him, abuse him sexually, and rape him. Malinowski was never able to find a first-hand witness of this act but everyone told him the story secondhand. Buell Quain reports almost the same tale from the Fiji Islands and again it is a stranger who is seized and raped. Since there is never any direct evidence for this female behaviour, there is every indication that it is a male fantasy created by the dread of women. This same theme has turned up in the United States in the form of a fictional episode in which a young serviceman is picked up by a couple of women in a car, taken to a motel, brutalized and raped. By projecting this fear in the form of hostility we get the Victorian anthropologist's picture of the 'primal horde' in which male brutes slaver up and down raping every female on sight. Surprisingly enough, the primal horde idea has been repeated in recent times by Theodor Reik. Even the male analyst, it seems, has little perspective on the fantasies of his own sex. Of course the gang rape of one unfortunate female in wartime or by juvenile delinquents is just another expression of group phallicism and fear of women projected in hostility.

It may be objected that 'homosexual group' is too strong a characterization for men's organizations. A good deal of romanticism has been woven about male comradeship in warfare and the wholesome manliness inculcated by the brutalities of hazing, the modern equivalent of initiation. Ethnological facts, however, are rather striking. If, in most cases, the group is only symbolically or passively homosexual, there is enough evidence of overt behaviour in some cultures to underline the homosexual component in this type of rejection of women.

Buell Quain states that the Fiji Islanders practised competitive group masturbation. Géza Róheim has more specific evidence. Ritual masturbation takes place among the Central Australians with comparison of erections. 'Yours is as big as a murmuntu [mythical dragon],' one man says. The other replies modestly, 'Mine is small but yours is as big as a gum tree.' The connection with war is exemplified by another homosexual ritual. Before setting out on a blood-avenging expedition, the Pitjentara excite themselves by masturbating one another. Among another group, the Nambutji, after initiation the boy's future father-in-law has intercourse with him and he is called a boy wife.

Róheim writes, 'The phallic phase of development with stress laid on the male genital and the exclusion of women is the basis of society. The group ideal is the old man, the keeper of the tjurunga (phallus).' He also states, 'The child discovers the vagina and interprets it as lacking a penis. It is from this interpretation that the close association between the castration complex and the phallic organization arises.' The bullroarer which is swung at initiation ceremonies is explicitly described as the penis of an ancestor, Malpunga.

In various cultures in Melanesia and also in South America bullroarers, flutes or trumpets, taboo to women, are used in ceremonies in which they represent male ancestors, quite clearly as phallic symbols.

When we turn to the island of Malekula of the New Hebrides we find a culture which is thoroughly and overtly homosexual. Here two forms of deformation of the male organ are practised. In one the foreskin is merely slit, in another it is cut all around and removed. Afterwards the phallus is wrapped in layers of palm leaves until it becomes outsized and the end is tucked under a bark-cloth belt leaving the testicles hanging free. (Elsewhere, in New Guinea, penis wrappers are manufactured which sometimes attain the length of a couple of feet.) John Layard, describing this treatment of the male organ, believes it is a seat of power and must be protected after the cutting which symbolizes a rebirth of spiritual life. Clearly the fundamental derive is that of the phallic phase, a homosexual glorification of the organ.

This is also evident from the custom of taking boy lovers. In the case of one group the older man is the guardian who officiates at initiation, in another, Layard reports, 'Up to the time when a boy assumes the bark belt, the badge of the adult male, he should not take a boy lover, but himself plays the role to some older man. It is only after he has donned the bark belt that he enjoys this privilege. It is clear then that for some time before a boy is circum-incised he belongs to one of the older men.' The boy accompanies his husband everywhere and indeed it is said that some Malekulan groups actually prefer sodomy to heterosexual love.

Another Malekulan group which does not practise actual sodomy perpetrates a series of 'hoaxes' upon the boys during initiation. One of these consists of the older men wrapping their phalluses with leaves until they are enormous. They lie in a row, their enlarged male organs making a continuity across their bodies. The boys are made to handle the false penises. Also at the end of the initiation period, 'An initiate climbs up inside the men's house to the apex of the roof, calling out to those who have died a violent death to come and have sexual intercourse with the new initiates.'

Describing this situation in terms of the natives' own rationalization, Layard writes, 'It would seem that both circum-incision and organized homosexuality are an expression of the extreme holiness of men over against women.'

The hoax involving the enlarged penises is believed to be a symbolism of the transmission of this holiness and potency through the male ancestral line. The Malekulan culture also involves the usual segregation in the men's house. Women are not permitted to eat with men and only men are allowed to sacrifice male pigs. Men cannot eat the flesh of sows because they are female. In addition women are not supposed to possess souls. The Malekulans were fierce fighters and, in the past, cannibals, a trait which often is combined with the phallic complex.

Among the Karaki tribes of south-west New Guinea, although circumcision is not practised, the bullroarer is acknowledged as a phallic symbol. An ancestor-creator supernatural being made his wife pregnant with the primal bullroarer. The Karaki practised head-hunting and when a raider struck his victim dead he was supposed to cry, 'The primal bullroarer is copulating with you!' Ritual cannibalism went with the headhunting, a bit of the cheek being eaten. These same Karaki carry out an initiation ceremony in which the boys are paraded through the village, beaten and handed over to the initiators who practise sodomy with them. For about a year each boy is at the service of a member of the opposite moiety of the tribe from his own.

The trait of headhunting which is associated with the male rejection of, or partial segregation from, women has a rather wide distribution. Psychologically it appears to be a symbolic substitute for castration and is allied to the ambivalent sexual attack upon the young men in circumcision and initiation. In actual war other males are castrated to obtain their potency; in this act the hostile power-seeking, homosexual eroticism is uppermost. Among the Galla and other tribes of Ethiopia a man is not fully initiated and able to marry until he has brought home the severed genitals of another male, a bit of evidence which strongly substantiates the castration interpretation of headhunting for, almost universally among the Malay, a man must bring home a head before he can marry.

According to Tony Saulnier's account of the Papuan expedition in which he participated, the same pattern occurs today among the Asmats and related tribes. Headhunting is practised by the Papuan tribes in the south marshlands, from the Eilanden to the Fly River in Australian New Guinea. Until a few years ago the men and women lived in separate huts – 'the women in small cabins perched very high up in the trees, the men grouped in large low rectangular huts. Men and women never visited each other; they met only in the bush.' This complete segregation of the sexes suggests that they did not even eat together. The Asmats also build large men's houses in which much of their ceremonial takes place. Headhunting is a central activity in the culture. A man cannot marry until he takes a head. When his son is born he must take another, for the child will not be strong or even will not live if the father does not bolster his family potency in this way. 'Some tribes apply this law with a certain amount of tolerance. Their members can have children without cutting off heads so long as they cut off at least one before initiation.' Asmat rationalization is that power is gained from the slain warriors by means of the head. 'Every man wanted to get hold of his enemies' strength, which is why he cut off his head and kept it.'

Sexuality is very important to these Papuans; the transfer of power takes place through the sex organs. In the initiation ceremony for the boys the severed head is placed between their legs so that their genitals may touch it. A design of superimposed men, with heads between their legs, appears on shields. Phallicism is also expressed in the wooden ancestor figures carved from a whole tree trunk. One root is left attached to the trunk in the shape of a perforated winglike projection which appears on the chest of the finished figure. It symbolizes the ancestor's virility; in the Asmat language the same word means 'totem wing' and 'virility'. In this culture, therefore, the sadistic power-seeking impulse is satisfied by symbolic castration of an enemy whose head is used to transmit sexual energy to the victor, his children, and to boys at initiation. Saulnier tells us nothing concerning homosexuality in the male group but the rigid segregation of the sexes in the past shows that the rejection of women is a part of the Papuan phallic complex.

Headhunting, phallicism and the sadomasochism of war were united among the Teutonic tribes of Europe. A whole series of rock carvings from Sweden dating from the second millennium B.C. shows male figures with their organs nearly always in a state of erection. Episodes in which two combatants attack each other with axes shows both fighters as ithyphallic. The later historic Teutons were known to take heads and to go into battle in a kind of sexual frenzy paralleling that of the Maori. The same is true of the Celts. The carvings of Camonica Valley in the Italian Alps which record a late Stone Age to Iron Age highly masculine culture also include many ithyphallic male figures and battle scenes in which both fighters exhibit erections.

The castration idea also turns up among the nineteenth-century Serbs whose culture remained fairly primitive. A ballad celebrating the Christian champion, Lukas, relates that this hero was in the habit of cutting off the life (penis) of all of his defeated enemies because he believed that by carrying about these trophies, 'the life of the conquered, which mean their power and might, would be transferred to him'.

To sum up, evidence from early cultures indicates that the phallic phase, combining a homosexual glorification of the penis, an underlying magical rejection of women, and strong sadomasochistic impulses, crystallizes in men's associations which concern themselves with initiation and warfare.

A more developed and idealized phase lingers in Greek civilization in which the men's house can be discerned behind the symposium, and the boy-lover of the philosopher and poet reflects the sodomy of primitive initiation. Greek inscriptions from the seventh century B.C. shows that the bond between the hero and his boy lover had a religious character and was sanctified by certain initiation ceremonies. In this connection the testimony of an early missionary, Thomas Williams, to the Fiji Islands is interesting. 'Instances of persons devoting themselves specially to deeds of arms are not uncommon. The manner in which they do this is singular and wears the appearance of a marriage contract; the men entering into it are spoken of as man and wife, to indicate the closeness of their military (!) union. By a mutual bond the two men pledged themselves to oneness of purpose and effort, to stand by each other in every danger, defending each other to the death and, if needful, to die together.' Although the homosexual relationship is not specifically mentioned, everything points to it, especially as the union had to be formally dissolved before either party could marry. The Fijian culture was strongly phallic – phallic stones were used in religious rites, there were men's houses and the youth was moulded into a harsh sadistic norm. The Reverend Williams insists that young boys were encouraged to strike their mothers to show their determination and rejection of the female sex.

To return to the Greeks, we are told by Theognis that the hero Diocles fought beside his lover in battle and in the moment of danger protected him with his shield, saved him, and himself fell. To quote Plutarch, 'In the Thessalian war against Eretria, among the Chalcidians there was a knight called Cleomachus of Pharsalus, a man with the soul of a hero. He insisted on being the first to charge the enemy warriors and first asked his lover, who was present, if he would be witness to the fight. The young man agreed, kissed and embraced him and adjusted his helmet. Then Cleomachus, filled with joyous bravery, took the best of the Thessalians with him and the opposing warriors were thrown into confusion and fled.'

In Thebes a sacred regiment of 300 practised sodomy and in Crete and Sparta it was a regular feature of the training of young warriors by their elders.

The phallic phase when prolonged in the life of the individual is considered by psychoanalysts to be an infantile survival. It is hard to see phallic social forms, which have lingered so persistently in history, as anything but infantile cultural elements which continue to have a harmful effect on relationships between the sexes. These regressive impulses are still capitalized upon in the actual conduct of warfare. Magnus Hirschfeld comments, 'There is little difference between the preparation for war in drill and actual participation in war itself for arousing erotic excitations of brutality and cruelty and also releasing homosexual components . . . the ideal type of soldier, the good subordinate officer is a sadist to those below him and a masochist to his superior.' To cite one recent historical example, the relationship between homosexuality and sadism in an organized men's group is clear enough among certain groups of Nazi storm troopers.

The examples of male associations antagonistic to women have so far been cited from the Old World and Oceania. An interesting parallel phenomenon occurs in South America. A group of people formerly inhabited Tierra del Fuego, the Ona and the Yahgan, who shared a common mythology and a common type of initiation. The Fuegians were hunters and gatherers possessing one of the simplest types of material cultures. Like their Oceanic counterparts, they were accustomed to build men's houses for initiation purposes in which secret rites went on for two years. The boys were made to sit in cramped positions and sharp splinters were driven into their flesh. They were also terrorized by the older men, who painted themselves and wore masks representing various nature spirits. In short, the familiar sadistic assaults took place. Once initiated, the boys then learned the identity of the maskers and became members of the secret society. The masked figures, nude and spotted with red and white paint, and wearing tall conical headdresses which hid their faces, also sallied forth at stated intervals to frighten the women.

The rationalizing myth involves a curious theme of reversal. In the Yahgan form, in the ancient time, women were completely dominant. They sat in the prows of the canoes and relegated the men to the stern. Women gave orders forcing the men to tend the fire, prepare the hides, and rear the children. The women built the ceremonial house and carried out the rites which went with it at each place where they halted, for they were a wandering group. They told the men they were looking for a powerful female spirit, Tanowa, whom they wished to induce to enter the ceremonial house. They finally arrived at a place named the Mouth of the Underworld. Here they masked and painted themselves and came out with loud cries, proclaiming themselves different spirits, and so terrifying the men that the poor males fled to their huts in terror. They were told that Tanowa had been found and that she had come out of the Mouth of the Underworld. One day, however, a successful hunter, Lem (who also happened to be the sun), surprised some women who had taken off their masks and were washing off the paint. The game was up and the result was a battle in which the women were defeated and turned into various types of animals and birds. Since that time the men took over the rites and terrified the women. There is no evidence that this was ever a historic cultural event or that women were ever dominant in early cultures. It seems likely therefore that the whole myth is, in psychoanalytical terms, a projection of male hostility and anxiety. Highly significant is the Mouth of the Underworld from which the terrible feminine spirit was supposed to emerge. This is clearly symbolic of the female genital organ around which the whole fantasy of the hostile dominant women is woven.

The Ona form of the myth is similar. This tribe maintained that only the women knew the secret of witchcraft. They had their own particular lodge which no man dared to approach. The girls, when they reached puberty, were instructed in the magic arts, learning how to cause sickness and even death to any man who displeased them.

Paul Radin has pointed out that a parallel fantasy can also be found to the north in the Rio Negro region of north-eastern Brazil. Here the Yurupary dances are associated with musical instruments, taboo to women, sometimes trumpets five to ten feet long, and are the basis of the men's society. The instruments are, of course, phallic and symbolize male ancestors, a sufficient proof that the reversal theme is a fantasy. 'The Mundurucu tell a myth about a primitive matriarchate, the women making their spouses do all the work while they themselves lived in the clubhouse and played the wind instruments. Once, however, the men detected them in the act, took the flutes away from them, and reversed the status of the sexes.'

Altogether the institution of the phallic men's group represents an infantile and unconscious attempt to withdraw from women's company, to create a kind of self-sufficient men's world devoted to male pursuits and partially containing male erotic urges, especially their hostile and power-seeking aspects. As we have seen, the group takes various forms and the rationale varies. There are, however, some primitive cultures which have developed a coherent ideology based on the mana theory, to justify their magical attitudes towards women. These groups are particularly significant as a transitional phase between the simpler forms of magic and the influential misogynist mythologies which have been kept alive throughout human history.

In northern Australia the Murngin organize their rituals around a myth which involves a serpent and not one, but two Eves. In the eternal dream time two sisters made a long journey from the interior towards the coast. One was pregnant and one carried a child. During the journey they killed various animals. Eventually a child was born to the second woman. During their trip the women named clan territories. Finally the sisters came to a water hole with a python in it. When they cooked the animals they had killed over a fire, the creatures jumped off the fire and ran into the water hole. From this they should have realized that the spot was sacred. One of the women went to the well, however, and let some of her menstrual blood fall in, profaning it. The python was infuriated. He spat out some of the water and lunged out of the well. This caused a flood and torrential rains. In spite of spells which they used to check the flood, the women and children were swallowed and spewed up several times by the snake. During this time his trumpet came out of the water hole and played music.

The elaborate ritual which the Murngin have developed about this central myth contains several elements. In the first place, the whole ritual is designed to maintain the rhythm of the seasons. In eastern Arnhemland there is heavy rainfall for four or five months which brings with it high tides, a period which is bad for hunting. The profanation of the menstrual blood for which one of the two Eves is blamed started the main cycle and also marks the beginning of human copulation. Ceremonies mimicking the basic episode and involving the trumpet of the python are meant to hold the flood in check. In this tale of primal magical sin the serpent is openly a phallic symbol of male ancestors, as is his trumpet. The males are thought of as pure, the females unclean and responsible for disaster.

Added to the flood story is the circumcision ceremony which is wound in and out of the ritual and reinforces the dominant phallic complex. The boys who are of an age for circumcision are told the snake smells their foreskins. Hearing the great snake begin to bellow for them through the phallic trumpet, they are terrified. When the men come for them, the women defend them with spears in a mock fight. Once more the castration and assault element of the ceremony is highlighted; poles with a bush at the tip are carried about, the bush symbolizing pubic hair, obviously the amputated organs of the young males. During the ceremony the boys are threatened with spears as if they were about to be killed. Eventually the pure, adult group of males with their symbol of the phallic snake swallows the unclean initiates, who have been associated with women. Eventually the boys are reborn into the ritually purified and symbolically homo-sexual masculine society.

Phallicism is further emphasized by a character in Murngin mythology who uses his penis as an aggressive weapon, equating it with a spear. In one episode his phallus is so large that in coitus he breaks a girl's legs and pierces her heart. Melanie Klein, in discussing the psychoanalysis of male children, has this to say of sadistic phallicism. The boy 'in his imagination endows his own penis with destructive powers and likens it to ferocious and devouring beasts, death-dealing weapons and so on'.

Carrying the phallic myth a step further, the Polynesians, who possessed a priesthood, an organized body of mythology transmitted by rote memory, and, on the whole, a fairly elaborate ceremonial culture, divided the world into two parts; all good was male and all bad female. This did not mean that they saw life in Western ethical terms, but that good mana was male and bad mana was female. The attributes of maleness were light, the sun, the east, secret religious knowledge, the strong right side. Conversely the female was passive, associated with the west, ignorance, the weak left side, darkness and death. The goddess of the underworld was female. In Hawaii she was Pele, the spirit of the volcano sending forth destruction from beneath the earth.

The seat of bad female mana was the genital organ. The vulva was so dangerous that a Polynesian woman of the old school would refuse to sit on a chair for fear a male child might crawl under it. In many cases houses were built on solid platforms to avoid this possibility. That this fear was a castration fear is borne out by a Marquesas myth concerning a woman who caused an eel to bite off her husband's genitals, thereby killing him. Curiously, even among the Polynesians the principle of ambivalence continued to hold good; a woman sometimes, when her husband was ill, sat on his abdomen so that the bad mana of her sex would act as a counter-irritant to the disease.

As a result of this dualistic philosophy the sexes were rigidly separated in most activities. Fishing, housebuilding, planting, canoe manufacture, war and ancestor worship were strictly male activities taboo to women. When engaged in these activities men must keep away from women and not even speak to them.

The paramount chief or king was the visible symbol of beneficial mana which he transferred to the land and the people from the sky – a power dramatized by such phenomena as thunderstorms and heavy surf.

The segregation principle resulted in a multiplication of houses. A wealthy aristocrat would have a men's house in which the males of the family slept during the daytime, carried out male ancestor rites and the slitting of the boy's foreskin at initiation; here the funeral rites took place. It was, of course, taboo to women. There was, besides, a dwelling house for women, not taboo to the husband, where he slept and begot his children. Then there was an eating house for women, since one of the most stringent prohibitions concerned segregated eating. Males and females cooked in separate ovens so that female mana had not the slightest possibility of contaminating the men's food. Finally there was an isolation hut for women at menstruation and childbirth. If a man came in contact with a woman at either of the times, the penalty was death.

In Hawaii, the Polynesian taboo civilization was brought to an end in 1919 by breaking the basic eating prohibition. A strong-minded wife of Kamehameha the Great, after contact with the Europeans, rebelled against being excluded from banquets and parties at which she saw women enjoying themselves. When her son became king she asserted her influence and persuaded him to eat publicly with the women of his family. Although there was a rebellion, the conservative was defeated and the Hawaiian culture fell apart.

The Polynesian theology was elaborated by priests who combined magic with a certain amount of abstract philosophy. However, their discrimination against the female sex was still based on the mana concept. It is in Greek and Judeo-Christian mythology that misogyny is transformed and its magical basis is disguised by an ethical rationalization.

CHAPTER SEVEN

Pandora's Box

The original Pandora never had a box. Most people do not know this. The acquisition of a box is of great psychological interest and fundamentally related to our theme of magical misogyny.

When we seek the older forms of Greek myth we turn to Hesiod the farmer poet who mixed magic, heroic legend and agricultural advice. He is our only source for the story of Pandora; in fact he tells it twice and the two versions do not coincide although they share some details. This has created a great problem for ingenious Teutonic scholars who have spilled a good deal of ink to prove by textual evidence that one or the other tale was not written by Hesiod, that certain lines are interpolations, in short that all sorts of profound difficulties exist which can be discussed indefinitely. This is of course a boon to candidates for a doctoral degree, but recently more literary-minded critics have suggested that Hesiod was a poet and not a German Ph.D. He had a perfect right to tell a story in more than one way and there is no reason why he should not have drawn on one tradition at one time and upon a different one at another. At any rate both stories are relevant to our theme and both contain primitive elements transformed by sophisticated Greek lyrical feeling.

Let us take the version in the *Theogony* first, the shorter of the two. It begins with the theft of fire by Prometheus.

> But the good son of Iapetus again deceived him
> And stole from Zeus the far-reflecting fire
> In a hollow fennel stalk. Then Zeus, the Thunderer,
> Was angry; rage burned in his loving heart
> When he saw the distant gleam of fire among mankind.
> And instead of fire he bestowed evil upon men,

For the Son of Kronos ordered the famed Limping God
To make the image of a modest girl out of earth.
And grey-eyed Athene dressed her and gave her a girdle
And with her own two hands she put a skillfully made
Veil on the girl's head, a marvel to look at.
And around her head Pallas Athene twisted
Lovely wreaths, woven of fresh-blown flowers,
And on her head she put a golden headdress
Made by the famous Limping God with his two hands
To please the Father of the gods. The goldwork
Was very clever, truly a marvel to look at.
It was moulded in the shape of all the land animals
And those of the sea, as many as existed,
All marvellously made as if they lived and cried out.
Now when he had finished the lovely thing
Which was evil instead of good, he brought her
To where the gods and men were all assembled,
She was splendidly adorned by the Great Father's grey-eyed
    daughter.
They marvelled at this snare men could never escape
For it was she who gave birth to the race of women;
From her came this female sex, all manner of women
Who live among mortal men to bring them pain.

In this version the woman made by Hephaistus is not called
Pandora and she is here particularly identified by the remarkable
golden headdress. This fact has caused some critics to suggest that
two different myths are involved. For our purpose this makes no
difference; in both cases a fundamental misogyny is involved which
Hesiod has instinctively seized upon. The consensus is that a headdress in which beasts are depicted suggests that this female figure
has a history which takes us to the Near East where the earth or
fertility goddess seems to have originated and where in early times
primal emotions have crystallized about the image of the woman.
Cybele of Asia Minor and the Cretan goddess, who has been called
the Lady of Wild Things, both have beast attributes. This association is also related to Hesiod's character through the name Pandora
which occurs in the second version of the tale. Hesiod himself says
she was so called because the gods gave her all things. Etymologists,
however, maintain that the name really means all-giving, which is
the usual way of describing the fertility goddess.

Assuming that Hesiod drew upon Eastern tradition current in Greece, why did he make her a symbol of evil? In the first place, this female deity occurs in many forms in different areas. She probably first enters history as Inanna, the Sumerian goddess of love who significantly enough goes down to the underworld and challenges the queen of that realm, Ereshkigal. She eventually causes the death of the male god associated with her, a figure which may be lover, husband or son. The tradition is further elaborated in Babylonia where Ishtar weeps for the death of her lover Tammuz. In Near Eastern tradition Tammuz becomes the spirit of growing things and also of animal increase and the whole story is transformed into a poetic seasonal myth. The same theme reappears in Canaan and probably influenced the Egyptian Isis and Osiris story. In Greece the descent into the underworld reappears in the tale of Demeter and Persephone in which Persephone is an alter ego of her fertility goddess mother and herself becomes a deity of the underworld. In the Persephone story the dying lover has disappeared. Scholars also believe that the Sumerian Inanna was originally an alter ego of the underworld deity Ereshkigal. One more fact also is pertinent. A. M. Kitten has pointed out that a handmaid of Inanna, a sacred courtesan representing the goddess herself, is often called 'the hand of Inanna'. She is a beautiful woman and also a demon who seduced men. We shall hear more of her later in connection with Lilith. The two aspects of the Hindu goddess, Kali, we have already mentioned.

To sum up, around the Eastern fertility goddess, who is considered a prototype of Pandora, there is a cluster of associations. On the one hand she is all-giving and has to do with the growth of grain, fruitfulness, and love; on the other, she is responsible for the demonic seduction of men and the death of her lover and is associated with the earth and the chasm of the underworld. Thus the fundamental ambivalence which we have been tracing all along is once more repeated.

We have suggested earlier that human concepts and institutions are the result of a kind of dialectic, the interplay between the fundamental anxieties common to all men and the pressures of the environment. The Near Eastern civilizations constitute the first great flourishing of agriculture. The wishes and fears connected with the seasons and the food supply were one great influence shaping men's imaginations. Elsewhere the writer has suggested that the connection between woman and the fertility of the fields was not originally a sophisticated poetic analogy. Through the primitive world women have been and still are the gatherers at the nomadic level of society. As has been pointed out in chapter one, there is a good deal of evidence to show that they first collected wild seeds and ground them into flour, and from this activity went on to domesticate grain and improve its yield. It seems reasonable to believe that men would easily attribute a benevolent soil magic to them which would eventually surround the female agriculturalist with religious significance.

The little clay figures of women, found in the earliest village settlements in the Near East, may have been made by either men or women as cult objects to give graphic form to the primal agricultural magician. In any case, men soon took over and male priests shaped the ultimate myths which then naturally reflected the basic male anxieties. The benevolent fertility female who magically causes the grain to grow is also endowed with destructive sexual attributes. Although grain grows from the earth, within the earth is a dark chasm, the womb or vagina, the underworld of death. It should not be forgotten that this same stressing of destructive female mana, this equating of the woman with danger, darkness and earth, is basic in Polynesian theology and something similar also appeared in the traditions of the remote tribes of Tierra del Fuego.

Now let us turn to the second version of the Pandora tale which Hesiod relates in *Works and Days*. It begins as before with the theft of fire.

> For Zeus in anger concealed the food of man
> Because devious Prometheus had tricked him.
> Therefore he devised sorrow and trouble for men.
> He hid fire. But that same good son of Iapetus
> Stole it again for men, from the Lord of Counsel,
> In a hollow fennel stalk, without the god's knowledge.
> Then in anger Cloud-herding Zeus said to him,
> 'Son of Iapetus, cleverer than all other men,
> You rejoice at having purloined fire deceitfully,
> But it shall cause great sorrow to you and future generations.

For instead of fire I shall give them something evil
Which they shall greatly delight in, embracing their own ruin.
So the Father of Men and Gods spoke and laughed loudly.
Then he told Hephaistus, the Master Smith, to mix together
Water and earth and then to put into the mixture
Human speech and strength in order to create
A girl, lovely as any of the immortal goddesses.
He told Athene to teach the creature to weave
And embroider and he ordered the goddess Aphrodite
To endow her face with charm and sensual appeal
Which causes black corrupting passion,
And Hermes, the Messenger and Argos-killer,
Was told to give the thing the mind of a bitch
And a thievish nature. So he spoke and the gods listened.
At once the Limping God made the image
Of a modest girl from earth as the Son of Kronos ordered.
Then grey-eyed Athene clothed her and gave her a girdle
And the goddess, Persuasion, and the Graces hung her
With golden chains and the bright-haired Hours crowned her with
    spring flowers.
Pallas Athene bestowed many coloured ornaments
And the Messenger, Argos-killer, placed in her breast
A talent for lying speech and a thievish disposition.
He did as Zeus, the Thunderer, ordered and gave her speech.
Then the Herald of the Gods named the woman
Pandora, for all the Olympians had given her gifts
To be the ruin of men who work for a living.
Now when this deadly, unescapable snare was made,
The Father sent the swift messenger and Argos-killer
To Epimetheus with the gift. But Epimetheus never heeded
The advice of Prometheus never to accept a gift
From Olympian Zeus, but to send it back
For fear it might bring evil to mankind.
But instead he took her and learned of the evil later.
For in former times men lived upon the earth
With minds free from evil, rough work, and pain
Which the Fates bestow (for in evil times
Men grow old very quickly). But the woman
Lifted the great lid of the jar with her hands,
She let forth gloomy afflictions to give men pain;
Only hope remained beneath the rim of the jar
For the lid was put back before it could escape.
This was the will of the Lord of Counsel,

Herder of the Clouds. But still ten thousand
Sorrows fly about, the ruin of mankind.
For both the earth and the sea are filled with evil.

Although no headdress is mentioned in this version, the garlands
of flowers again occur which in themselves suggest the fertility
deity, and here the name Pandora is specifically mentioned. In the
other version of the myth, there is no specific reason given for the
destructive power of the woman. She is simply called an unescapable
snare and a bringer of pain to men. Here a new element, the familiar
episode of Epimetheus and the jar, is introduced.

Gerhard Fink has pointed out that the splitting of Prometheus in
two was probably due to the influence of another very widespread
myth, that of the two brothers. This ubiquitous tale can be found
among primitive tribes all over North America, South America and
the South Seas. Sometimes, as in North America, one brother is
good, the other bad; one kills the other in a way that reminds us of
Cain and Abel. More often, however, one brother is clever, the
other stupid and inept, as in the case of the Carib version in which
the stupid brother is destroyed by demons and brought to life by
the clever one. Fink however points out an analogy in the relationship between Paris and Hector, the latter being the heroic ideal,
while Paris is betrayed by sex and introduces a woman into the
Greek world who brings about destruction and death. Although
Helen is mortal, her fatefully seductive qualities almost place her in
the category of the love goddess, Inanna.

The most important new element is the jar (Greek *pithos*). The
jar which emerges from nowhere is an attribute of Hittite and
Syrian earth mothers. More than one explicit symbolism may cluster
about it. Jane Harrison, stressing the death goddess aspect, pointed
out that in early Greek tradition, before the building of great tombs,
the dead were buried in large urns or pithoi. One scholar has seen,
in the representations of female figures leaning against jars on
Cretan seals, an image of the fertility goddess bewailing her dead
lover. For Harrison, therefore, Pandora's jar is a bringer of death
and the girl herself a death goddess. There is also another Greek
tradition, related by Babrius in the first century, in which man is
given a vessel containing all the good things of life and because of

his failure to control his curiosity opened the jar and allowed all the benefits to fly back to heaven except for hope. There are also indications that there may once have been two jars bestowed by Zeus, one containing blessings and the other evils, a situation allied to the Biblical story of the Fall. Inherent in all of this is ambivalence, a receptacle containing both good and bad mana. To understand the deepest layer of meaning, a glance at the subsequent history of Pandora is enlightening. She disappears in the Middle Ages and reappears with the Renaissance revival of interest in classical literature. In the sixteenth century it was Erasmus who used the word *pyxis* instead of *pithos* and thus endowed her with a box. In Renaissance art she is naked and shown with a small jewelled casket and for the first time it is referred to as handsome. Dora Panofsky thinks Erasmus was influenced by the tale of Psyche. To this young woman Venus gave a box which she was supposed to take down to Hades in order to bring back a little of Persephone's beauty. The revision stuck and entered European tradition. In Spain it was the 'caja de Pandora', in France 'boite de Pandore', in Holland 'doos van Pandora', in Germany 'buche der Pandora'. Later John Flaxman, Blake's teacher, restored the jar in his pictures but Rosetti brought back the box, which was to enter American literature in Hawthorne's rather coy little tale.

But if all this was founded on Erasmus's mistake, why did he make that particular mistake and why did it take such a firm hold on the imagination of male artists? In 1655 Michel de Marolle commented on pictures of Pandora painted by Abraham van Diepenbeeck as follows: 'It seems as if the painter of these pictures has never represented the subject except holding her box in her right hand, down by that part, which it covers, and from which so many troubles and sorrows have flowed out upon mankind. . . .' Michel de Marolle was born several centuries before psychoanalysis but he instinctively arrived at the psychological explanation of the receptacle just as the painter he discussed instinctively placed the box where it was bound to become a sexual symbol.

Gerhard Fink also writes of the jar as an earth mother attribute which 'seems to indicate that it can also be understood as a symbol for the womb of the earth mother as well as the cavern of the underworld'. For womb we can also read vulva, the old source of evil magic. Fink explicitly brings up the vulgar term 'box' used for the female genital in both English and German, an insight concerning Pandora which Géza Róheim tossed out some years earlier.

The Pandora myth therefore takes its place in the tradition which condemns woman as dangerous because of her sexuality. The Greek poet, however, is already working in an age in which ethical concepts are emerging. What was originally a question of bad mana is now approached more philosophically and with a new rationalization. The sophisticated Greek is no longer a man who admits to a fear of women on superstitious grounds. Hesiod, pondering the problem of evil, fuses old tradition with the concept of All-Father Zeus, whom Aeschylus was also developing into a more rational deity to accord with a more complicated and responsible Greek society. Hesiod's Zeus, however, is still a reflection of the deepest human anxieties. Although he is 'loving' and 'Lord of Counsel' he is also an irascible parent who will not tolerate the desire of his children for the privileges of an adult. Epimetheus is punished because of a heterosexual activity. By taking Pandora as an erotic partner, he is not only destroyed by the evil magic of her genital but also punished by Zeus for acquiring sexual knowledge. It is not really woman's curiosity which results in the opening of the jar (breaking of the hymen) but man's curiosity projected upon her. The penalty for sexual curiosity is ultimately death. In a sense the story of Prometheus has, together with the dread of women, overtones of the same guilt which Freud discovered in the myth of Oedipus.

It has already become apparent that there are strong parallels between Pandora and Eve. The myth of the Fall was destined to be transmitted through the Judeo-Christian heritage and to permeate all of Western culture. It still plays a role in shaping the destiny of women today.

CHAPTER EIGHT

Undone by Sex

The fall of man should rightly be called the fall of woman because once more the second sex is blamed for all the trouble in the world. Psychologically Pandora and Eve are parallel and even perhaps historically related, for it is pointed out: 'And Adam called his wife's name Eve; because she was the mother of all living,' a description with decided fertility goddess overtones. We are not told that Eve had a box, but she had a snake and an apple which also have profound symbolic meanings.

The Paradise myth as told in Genesis is exceedingly complicated, woven of many primitive themes, overlaid with priestly philosophy and patriarchal ethics, and at the same time revealing the fundamental human anxieties which we have been sketching all along.

If we begin with the creation of human beings we immediately encounter a duplication. In I, 26 we are told: 'And God said, Let us make man in our image, after our likeness: and let them have dominion over the fish of the sea, over the fowl of the air, and over the cattle, and over all the earth, and over every creeping thing that creepeth upon the earth.

'So God created man in his own image, in the image of God created he him; male and female created he them.'

This is a generalized account in which it is specifically stated that both men and women are created at the same time. Later in II, 7 we are told that man is made out of dust and put into the garden of Eden which contains the tree of life and the tree of knowledge of good and evil. We shortly discover that there are no women and God proposes to create one for Adam. This second version ties in with the many primitive stories of an early time when there were only men. In chapter four we cited examples of this belief from the

87

culture of the Negritos, the Caribs and the Toba of the Gran Chaco. Significantly, in two of these stories women were created by castrating men or by sadistically cutting a vulva in androgynous entities. The creation of Eve is parallel to these primitive stories. Although the shaping of a woman is transformed into a magical moulding from Adam's rib, the removal of the rib itself has symbolic overtones of castration. Adam and Eve are, in the early part of the story, quite without sexual awareness or sexual desire. The later episodes concern themselves with the invention of sexual intercourse.

Basically this, too, is a theme which appears often in primitive folklore when the primal ancestors are either innocent as Adam and Eve or do not know how to perform the act of love properly. Sometimes these seem humorous. Orphan, who is one of the twin brothers in the folklore of the Trans Fly, New Guinea, invents proper sexual intercourse when he commits adultery with his brother's wife. Before this time his brother had used his wife's armpit. Hortense Powdermaker records another story from the Lesu culture of New Ireland which is interesting because it dramatizes the primitive fear of the wife's 'wound'. A primal couple once lived together with no knowledge of copulation. The husband thought that his wife's vulva was a big 'sore' and he was afraid of it. He asked a medicine man named Kutkut to come and put medicine on the sore. Kutkut came, passed a leaf over the fire, which was standard medical procedure, and invited the husband to go down to the seashore. While he was away Kutkut had intercourse with his wife. We are not told how he acquired this valuable technique but we assume he may have had supernatural qualities. The husband returned and asked if medicine was put on the sore, to which the wife replied yes. The husband saw no improvement, however, and Kutkut was invited twice more to treat the patient. He repeated his first remedy. Finally the husband grew angry and accused the doctor of lying. The doctor also became angry, told the man that his wife had no sore, and asked him why he did not know what to do with a woman. Kutkut then placed the husband in the proper position but the primal innocent still had no idea what to do. The doctor then snatched a hot taro root from the fire and smacked the man's buttocks with it. At this point the husband was galvanized into action. He exclaimed, 'Ah good, very good, wonderful! I like it very much!' From this time on copulation was known in Lesu.

The Genesis account is, of course, highly literary and ritualistic, for it involves three conscious themes: the transition from primitive life to civilization, the coming of death and the acquisition of knowledge. But all, as we shall see, centre around sex. In Genesis the skilful simplicity of style has synthesized all the themes but there are various clues to the primitive prototypes. To begin with, there are two forbidden trees, one of life and one of the knowledge of good and evil. Adam is told he may eat of neither and, in the case of the tree of good and evil, if he does, 'in that day thou eatest thereof thou shalt surely die'. It is significant that Adam does eat of the tree and does not die on the spot as Jahweh promises. Therefore the serpent is telling the truth and the Creator is not. When this sort of contradiction occurs we may be sure that the priest poet has been drawing on various traditions and has not fully amalgamated them, just as Hesiod told the Pandora story with conflicting details. Sir James Frazer was the first to point out that snakes or lizards act as the messenger of a creator entity in a tale widespread in both ancient and contemporary primitive lore which has been entitled 'the perverted message'. Two messengers are sent, the first with the announcement of immortality to man, the second with tidings of death. The first creature either delays or mumbles so that he is misunderstood. In the first case he is overtaken by the second animal; in the second, men understand him to say they will die and they promptly do. An East African version states that the creator came down to earth, addressed all living things and inquired, 'Who wishes not to die?' All were asleep except the serpent, which is why it does not die but renews its youth by casting its skin. The serpent is therefore associated with immortality through this biological attribute and mankind is given a choice.

Frazer thought the Genesis story was related to this folklore theme and conjectured that there might have been two trees, one of life and one of death with man being given a choice. Babylonian sources which predate the Bible also shed some light on this element in the myth. In the ancient Gilgamesh epic, which goes back to Sumeria, the main theme is the quest for immortality. When the Babylonian

Noah takes pity on Gilgamesh and gives him an herb which will renew youth eternally, the hero makes the mistake of pausing to bathe in a pool. While he is doing this a serpent steals the precious herb. In another Babylonian tale, Adapa (equivalent to Adam), the human son of the god of water and wisdom, Ea, has received wisdom but not immortality from his father. His father tells him when he reaches the underworld two gods who have disappeared from earth, Tammuz and Ningiszidu, will offer him the food of death and the water of death, both of which he must refuse. It is interesting to note that the fatal food also occurs in the myth of Persephone, who, by eating a part of the pomegranate, is condemned to the world of death for part of the year. The dangers of eating can have another symbolic meaning as we shall see presently.

To return to the snake, when Adam is beguiled by Eve, who has previously been told the truth by the serpent, the eyes of the primal pair are opened and they 'are as gods, knowing good and evil'. They also learn that they are naked and become for the first time sexually guilty – in other terms, sexual intercourse is invented. It is certainly not by accident that this awareness is brought about by the snake which, as we have shown, is often among primitives an acknowledged phallic symbol. The Hebrews even had a tradition that menstruation was caused by a snakebite. Furthermore the phrase 'knowing good and evil' is basically connected with sex. Robert Gordis, analysing the Hebrew, points out that the word for knowledge often has a sexual significance; for instance, the phrase 'and Adam knew his wife'. Géza Róheim brings up the fact that in the Talmud the verb meaning to eat can also mean coitus. The knowledge imparted by the snake plus the tree is therefore carnal knowledge. It is interesting that the Ashanti of East Africa also connect the snake with the invention of intercourse. In the beginning a man and a woman came down from the sky and another couple came up from the earth. A python also came from the sky and took up his abode in a river. In this early time there was no sex impulse; conception and birth were unknown. The python remedied the situation by making the couples stand face to face in the water. He sprayed a little on their bellies, saying 'kus kus'. Then he told them to go home and couple, which they did successfully and the women conceived.

Gordis suggests that good is heterosexual connection while evil is perversion, sodomy, onanism, etc. This might be the clerical interpretation but not the basic meaning. Rather we have the old ambivalence towards the sex act, knowledge of the good and bad mana inherent in it. Finally, in Genesis, in terms of the supernatural punishment, sexual awareness is related to civilization, for Adam must go to work and till the ground 'in the sweat of his face'. With sexuality, the human family and human society begins with its burden of responsibilities. In the innocent era of the garden of Eden there is no need for repression and all the complicated magic which contains man's anxiety.

The connection between knowledge and sex and the ambivalence inherent in the sexual act is also illustrated in the Gilgamesh epic where the alter ego of Gilgamesh is Enkidu, a wild man who eats grass and consorts with wild animals. Enkidu is a bull man who gives rise to a bull deity. He also seems to represent a conflict between the hunting phase and pastoral and agricultural society, for he leads the cattle astray and makes life difficult for civilized people. He is tamed by a sacred courtesan representing Ashtoreth, the love goddess, who goes forth to meet him and beguiles him with her body so that he couples with her for six days and seven nights. After this 'he listens and opens his ears'. He has become wise, enters the city and takes up civilized life. So far the good mana of the sex act with the fertility goddess is stressed; it is even equated with civilization. Later on, however, Gilgamesh is himself wooed by Ishtar. In this episode the fertility goddess is portrayed as lascivious and evil. She has turned her other lovers into animals (like Circe), she is a door that affords no entrance, a palace that crushes those who live in it, she is like shoes that squeeze the wearer – all, of course, images of the lethal vulva. Gilgamesh flatly rejects her and is punished when she sends the wild bull of heaven against him.

The basic ambivalence was present in Mesopotamian civilization but it was successfully resolved in the worship of fertility; even the death of Tammuz could lead to rebirth, the mother goddess was all-giving and the bull god, as an image of male potency, finally married her. Sacred prostitution in the temple of the love goddess celebrated the beneficial mana of the heterosexual act.

The patriarchal Hebrews would have none of this and were at war with the fertility religion, everywhere present in the land which they invaded. Backsliding took place as the prophets violently denounced both the goddess and the bull who became her mate; in fact Moses angrily flung down the image of the bull calf. The Hebrews practised circumcision with its phallic implication and in fact there is evidence of religious sodomy. The Kedeshim were sacred youths, divine lovers, who were lodged in the walls of the temple until banished by King Josiah in 637 B.C. 'And he brake down the houses of the sodomites that were by the house of the Lord. . . .' In consequence the bad mana of sex comes to the fore with the accompanying emphasis on the evil proclivities of woman.

The whole complex of prohibition of sex with death as a punishment leads us into the oedipal element in the Genesis story. Adam is forbidden by the father god to become sexually mature and to have connection with universal woman, 'the mother of all things', on pain of immediate death. But, as we know from the story, Adam does not die. He becomes instead guilty and afraid. In fact when God calls him he says, 'I was afraid because I was naked, and hid myself.' Adam is not naked, he and Eve have already contrived loincloths of fig leaves. His fear, therefore, is derived from the act itself. He has not died literally but we have already seen that sex and death are closely connected in the deeper layers of the unconscious. Adam has died the death of sex and his symbolic extinction has filled him with the fear of castration. Knowledge of his wife's genital brings with it the danger of punishment by the father as well as the fear of loss of 'life' inherent in the orgasm. We have cited the fact that the dread of women can be dramatized in terms of the phallic woman, whose organ contains the snake which may bite and castrate, an image probably associated with the toothed vagina. Early Renaissance paintings of the Fall depict Eve holding the apple, the snake protruding from a tree beside her. Instead of the more direct image of the dangerous jar or box with which Pandora is shown, Eve is endowed with the menacing appurtenances of the phallic woman.

The complex – sexual intercourse and the coming of death – also occurs in an incest story found in many forms in Polynesian tradition. Maui, who is both a trickster and a primal ancestor, undertakes to gain immortality through symbolic intercourse. Of the several versions with different details, the following is a generalized one which was put together by Edward Tyler. Maui was told he must brave his mighty ancestress:

'Hine-nui-te-po, Great Daughter of Night whom you may see flashing and, as it were, opening and shutting there, where the horison meets the sky; what you see yonder so brightly red are her eyes, and her teeth are as sharp and as hard as pieces of volcanic glass; her body is like that of a man; and as for the pupils of her eyes they are like jasper; her hair is like the tangles of the long seaweed and her mouth is like that of a barracoutu.' Maui boasted of his former exploits and said, 'Let us fearlessly seek whether men are to live or to die forever,' but his father called to mind an evil omen, that when he was baptizing Maui he had left out part of the fitting prayers and therefore he knew that his son must perish. Yet he said, 'O my last born and the strength of my old age ... be bold, go and visit your great ancestress who flashes so fiercely where the edge of the horizon meets the sky.' Then the birds came to Maui to be his companions in the enterprise, and it was evening when they went with him and they came to the dwelling of Hine-nui-te-po and found her fast asleep. Maui charged the birds not to laugh when they saw him creep into the old chieftain, but when he had got altogether inside her and was coming out of her mouth, then they might laugh long and loud. So Maui stripped off his clothes, and the skin of his hips tattooed by the chisel of Uetonga, looked mottled and beautiful like a mackerel's. As he crept in, the birds kept silence but when he was up to the waist, a little tiwakawaka [pied fantail] could hold its laughter no longer and burst out loud with its merry note; then Maui's ancestress awoke, closed on him and caught him tight and he was killed. Thus died Maui and thus death came into the world, for Hine-nui-te-po is the goddess of both night and death. And had Maui entered into her body and passed safely through her, men would have died no more.

Róheim pointed out that this myth reflects the primal scene, with the birds, Maui's siblings, tittering from nervousness. The fish mouth is the toothed vagina displaced upward (in one version he is cut in two by the mouth) and Maui dies in the female organ. In accordance with the phallic tendency, Maui's whole body is equated with the penis. The gift of immortality is combined with the act of intercourse (reproduction) but the penalty of intercourse is the death of the phallus in the vagina, the eternal menace to the male sex.

Géza Róheim wrote, 'Sexual maturity is regarded as a misfortune,

something that has robbed mankind of happiness ... the explanation of how death came into the world is an explanation of the fear
of death, of anxiety.' To this we would add that it is male anxiety
which shapes both the Maui myth and sophisticated stories like that
of Genesis and Hesiod's Pandora legend. As a result the Yahwistic
concept of sin is blamed on the woman. It is she who eats the apple,
experiencing sexual desire with which she seduces Adam.

The connection between woman, sex and sin is thus firmly established in one of the great literary works of all time. The transition is
also made from instinctive magical fear into an ethical code destined
to influence all of Western civilization. Christianity was, of course,
to draw on the basic Hebrew myth and pronounce it literally true in
every detail. But Christianity was also shaped by converted Greeks
and Romans. As Theodor Reik points out, 'Intense misogynist
tendencies that dominated a certain late phase of Greek civilization
transformed the lure of the female body into an organ of danger and
turned the sexual attraction of women into a malicious temptation.'
Side by side with the continuance of misogyny, elements of Roman
civilization to a large extent threw off the supernatural sanctions.

CHAPTER NINE

The Carefree Amorist

> What is the theme of my song?
> A little pleasant indulgence,

Wrote Ovid, pretty well summing up the poetry for which he is remembered. Between the primitive and the Christian world, the Romans at times seem startlingly modern. The urban sophistication of Ovid in particular provides us with glimpses of a relationship between the sexes which is singularly free from darker overtones. The amatory life of this cheerful man-about-town is filled with taking girls to the theatre, paying them little courtesies, enjoying the pleasures of dining in gay company, making signals to a pretty wife behind her husband's back, climbing into bedrooms through the window, suborning servants into taking messages to his love of the moment, gently undressing the quarry once he has reached her bedroom and amusedly allowing for her modest protests. He gives sound advice to the aspiring lover: He must bathe often, brush his teeth, keep his nails clean, dress well but not be too much of a dandy, and he should remember that a healthy tan is highly attractive to the opposite sex.

Both in the famous handbook, the *Ars Amatoria*, and his love songs, Ovid displays a completely relaxed attitude towards women. He tells us that although the male is supposed to do the chasing, the female knows well enough how to make her interest in him evident. He does not regard the other sex as property, as a servant class, as a mechanical means for obtaining offspring, or as surrounded with menacing mystery. Indeed this is practically the first evidence we have of women completely divested of all sexual danger. Women for Ovid were delightfully interesting, their erotic psychology a fascinating study. Above all, and this is what makes him seem so modern,

he insists that they have as much right to pleasure as men and that
mutual delight should be the lover's aim.

> Let the woman feel the act of love to her marrow;
> Let the performance bring equal delight to the two.

This indeed is a male attitude which would satisfy the most demanding contemporary woman. Love to Ovid was a healthy sensual
pleasure with no profound emotional overtones associated with it.
He never reaches the heights or the depths as did stormy Catullus
who was more or less of a *poète maudit*. Also, it must be admitted,
in his work there is little trace of the desire for an enduring relationship. He sings of light love, not of marriage. Ethical values, friendship, constancy and the interweaving of two whole personalities have
no place in his world. This was an ideal which had not yet been
created in the heterosexual relationship. If Ovid was rather a Don
Juan, it was not in the worst sense, that of counting coup, of eternally
proving an underlying doubt. If he enjoyed conquest, it was not a
brutal and cynical triumph; it was rather the outcome of a delicate
game in which both parties were fully aware of the goal. Ovid's
writing is something of a milestone in that it grants women an
equality in the sphere of eros and in a limited way dispels the traditional misogyny. Only in a couple of lines is there a hint of the old
shadow:

> But as for me, let me go in the act of coming to Venus;
> In more senses than one, let my last dying be done.
> And at my funeral rites, let one of the mourners bear witness:
> 'That was the way, we know, he would have wanted to go.'

The image is playful but once more eros and death are equated.
Ovid, however, was man enough to say: It's worth it.

Roman culture, often stamped as decadent and debauched, was
certainly materialistic and carried freedom from repressions to an
extreme. A loss of religious values had, for a sophisticate like Ovid,
removed some of the irrational confusions surrounding the heterosexual relationship. On the other hand the same freedom from
restraints resulted in a devaluation of all relationships and an emphasis on sense pleasure which distorted the personalities of both

men and women. When we turn to the satirist Juvenal, we are shown the other side of the picture. Ovid wrote his best-known poem at about the time of the birth of Christ; Juvenal was active almost a century later when Roman social life had grown more chaotic. The satirist devotes a whole poem to women, whom he excoriates with bitter humour. Juvenal's complaints, however, while they do centre around woman's sexuality and to this extent reflect enduring male preoccupations, have no magico-religious overtones. His is the familiar attitude which discontented writers assume towards the age they live in: the good old days were better. Nevertheless, because both his work and that of his obverse, Ovid, were to have an important influence on the Middle Ages and to be used in a different context, his charges are worth reviewing. In the first place women were not his only target; he was equally merciless towards homosexuals. By Roman times the Greek attitude towards boy love with its educational and military overtones, which carried us back to the organized men's group, had degenerated, if we are to believe Juvenal and many other witnesses, into real cultist pathology. One of his blasts runs as follows:

> 'Remain far off, ye unholy!
> Women remain far off: no females play on our trumpets!'
> So goes the cry, and the orgies blaze like the torches in secret.
> Here's a lad making his eyebrows long with damp soot on a needle,
> Here one taking a swig from a goblet shaped like a phallus,
> Another one fixing his eyes, with a golden net on his hair

And he ends by crying,

> But why don't they follow the Phrygian fashion,
> Cut off the part they don't need? Why in the world are they
> waiting?

The Phrygians were the priests of Attis, self-castrates, and devotees of an Oriental religion of which we shall have more to say. According to Juvenal, men actually went through wedding ceremonies with other men. Juvenal had many other complaints: stingy patrons, corrupt court favourites, bad poets, poets unrecompensed, scholars beaten by their students – everything he saw was a target for bawdy and comic invective. His chief charge against women is adultery: all about him wives were deceiving their husbands wholesale. From what we know from other sources, this was probably true. Matrons frequented the theatres:

> Some of the women pay high for a comic to loosen his codpiece,
> Some like tragedians better. . . .

Another runs off with a sailor:

> She would puke on her spouse, but now she feeds with the sailors,
> Wanders all over the ship, has fun pulling the handropes.

His fiercest attack is upon the Empress Agrippina, as an example of female corruption in high places. He pictures her as slipping off to a brothel where she

> Showed her golden tits and the parts where Britannicus came from,
> Took the customers on, with gestures more than inviting,
> Asked and received her price and had a wonderful evening.
> Then, when the pimp let the girls go home, she sadly departed,
> Last of all to leave, still hot, with a woman's erection. . . .

The charge of insatiability could hardly be more violent. Juvenal goes on to accuse Roman women of affecting Greek manners, lisping in Greek, pretending to be learned. They also treated their slaves and servants brutally when they were displeased with their husbands. The husbands themselves were kept awake all night with their bickering and quarrelling. They spent their husband's money and despoiled their lovers. When caught in bed in adultery they were brazen.

> 'Long ago,' she says, 'it was understood between us
> Perfectly well, you could do what you pleased and no double
>   standard
> Kept me from having my fun, so howl as much as you want to,
> I'm human, too.'

Among their other defects, they drank too much and behaved nastily in public. Juvenal was scathing in his description of paints, creams, perfumes and toilet lotions, high, teased hairdos and beauty treatments.

> Through the last layer of mudpack from the first wash to a poultice,
> What lies under all this, a human face or an ulcer?

Roman matrons avidly took up all the exotic foreign religions which were flooding the city. Pushovers for the castrate priests of Attis, they showered them with presents in return for fortune-telling. They performed any sort of absurd rites required by the cult of Io or of Isis and they even worshipped the dog-headed Anubis from Egypt.

Finally they were good customers of the abortionist. Juvenal suggests the husband himself should pay.

> Give her the dose yourself, whatever it is, never let her
> Carry till quickening time, or go to full term and deliver
> Something whose hue would seem to prove you a blackamoor
> father.

In the light of all this, it is not surprising that Juvenal had bitter things to say about marriage and indeed laid the foundation for a devaluation of this fundamental human institution.

> Surely you used to be sane, Posthumus, are you taking a wife?
> Tell me what fury, what snakes have driven you on to this madness?
> Can you be under her thumb when ropes are so cheap
> And so many?

Finally the last bitter charge of murderess is hurled at the other sex, this time in terms of a mythological allusion.

> Almost every apartment
> Is Clytemnestra's address. In one respect only they differ –
> She used a two-edged axe, our girls toad poison or mushroom.

It is a curious picture of Roman life we get from these two authors, but even from this sampling a confusion of values emerges. Roman men apparently found it hard to make up their minds about women. There was the official image of the virtuous matron, efficient ruler of her own household; there was the mistress who could be everything from the slave girl to the elegant courtesan, to the straying wife or the seductible daughter. That women took the bit in their teeth and often lived lives of their own is evident from Juvenal's testimony. On the whole, in this fairly opulent city culture, women were not feared or hated, except temporarily by a jealous husband or lover, and the heterosexual act, if anything, was overvalued. No real balance in the relationship between the sexes had been achieved, however, and whatever dignity women had been granted was temporary. The empire had no unifying philosophy, and the freedom from repression and superstition which some Romans enjoyed was a two-edged virtue.

CHAPTER TEN

God's Eunuchs

'There be eunuchs which have made themselves eunuchs for the kingdom of heaven's sake.' This statement, attributed to Christ by St Matthew, strikes the keynote of a new sort of misogyny.

With the growth of city civilizations and organized priesthoods, upon the old primitive magic new superstructures arose. Despite the interlude of Greek and Roman rationalism, the unconscious drives were always ready to shape men's thinking. And even the Greeks, as E. R. Dodds points out, 'could describe what went on below the threshold of consciousness only in mythological or symbolical language; they had no instrument for understanding it, still less for controlling it'.

If this was true of the Greeks, it was more so of the mysticisms of the Orient which invaded Rome and contributed their share to the complex influences which was to shape Christian tradition. One of the most important of these, and also one of Christianity's greatest rivals, was the Syrian and Phrygian cult of Cybele, the mother goddess, and the young male god, Attis.

It will be remembered that the mother goddess is connected with Pandora, that in her earliest Sumerian manifestation she causes the death of her son-lover-husband. Her ambivalent femaleness is expressed in the image of fertility and also the dark mother, goddess of the underworld and of death. In her Babylonian form she bewails the death of Tammuz, who is himself dying and reviving vegetation. In Phrygia, where she was called Cybele, as her cult developed and spread to Rome, its mystical orgiastic expression won many converts in a culture which was no longer satisfied with a cut-and-dried state religion, especially in the late imperial era when unrest and pessimism were in the air.

The dark side of Cybele is exemplified by the Phrygian myth. In one version Cybele herself was born from the seed of Zeus or from a stone brought to life by Pyrrha and Deucalion. When she rejected the love of Zeus, he created a bisexual creature, Agdistis, which was made drunk by Dionysus and castrated of its male parts. From the male parts grew an almond tree the fruit of which impregnated a river goddess who gave birth to Attis. Both the now female Agdistis and Cybele fell in love with Attis. The boy's friends sent him to marry the daughter of the King of Pessinus (or King Midas). Cybele and Agdistis both arrived, and drove all the men of the court into a frenzy in which they castrated themselves.

A more literary version related by Ovid explains that Cybele was smitten with mad love for Attis whom the pastoral populations of the Phrygian plateau conceived of as a young shepherd. The jealous goddess demanded exclusive possession of her lovers; anyone who resisted her became insane. Attis was untrue with a nymph. Punished by the goddess, the handsome shepherd emasculated himself in a crisis of mystic fury at the foot of a pine tree and died.

Now it is clear that the basic idea of the myth is not one of self-sacrifice. In the first place, the Agdistis figure echoes the ancient notion of the creation of woman by castration. The latter part of the story in which Agdistis-Cybele drives her lover mad is an example of the demonic and insatiable female sexuality. The castration is no voluntary offering, it is simply an indirect destruction of the male organ by the female; Attis is a victim just as much as Maui.

Why then did the priests of Attis deliberately work themselves up into a fury and castrate themselves on the theory that they thereby attained perfection?

Evidently the original misogynist story was transformed by a second element, that of the need to refrain from sex before any important undertaking because of the dangerous mana inherent in heterosexual intercourse. We have cited numerous instances of continence before hunting, fishing, or fighting for this reason. The idea of impurity is now carried over into the area of religious achievement. The priest must not indulge in intercourse because the ritual he carries out will be invalidated, and when the religious goal is personal, mystical experience, any stain of semen is thought to be an impediment to perfection.

The magical mysticism of the Attis cult therefore derives its strength from a dramatic imitation of a god's action (a common element in all ritual) plus the rationalization that by self-mutilation all pollution of sex is for ever avoided and perfection achieved. To quote Henri Graillot, 'Renunciation ended by transforming the former naturalistic myth. Attis was not killed, Attis was not chastised by Cybele, jealously keeping the beautiful shepherd's love for herself; Attis emasculated himself voluntarily to escape from the desires of the flesh.'

The cult of Cybele was officially recognized in Rome in 204 B.C. St Augustine describes how, in his time in the fourth century A.D., the idol was bathed in the Tiber and dragged along the shore of the river in a boat by aristocratic matrons who pulled the ropes. The priests of Attis, who were called Galli, chanted, leaped and ran, clashing cymbals and tambourines.

At first the eunuch priests were considered abnormal; they lived on the outskirts of the city and were classified on the tax rolls on the same level as prostitutes. As the cult grew in popularity, they were generally accepted and finally revered. Wearing the long robes characteristic of Semitic priesthoods, they danced and sang to the music of flutes and percussion, flinging their heads back and forth, their long hair flying, until they reached a delirious tranced state in which they divined and prophesied. (Trance dancing of this sort is characteristic of many primitive peoples.) The Galli made use of another self-intoxicant which was to be adopted by some Christians – flagellation. They beat themselves and each other as they ran, leaped and howled, and even gashed themselves with daggers.

The public significance of the sect is testified to by Juvenal's sarcastic references. Even frivolous Ovid relates the myth and Catullus, whose passionate nature responded poetically to the terrible poetry in the legend of the dark mother, devotes an effective poem to it. Catullus takes a psychological approach. After narrating the frenzy in the forest and the bloody self-mutilation caused by the goddess, he describes with lyric enthusiasm the orgiastic celebration in which Attis takes part, still in a trance. The delirious horde dances in the forest:

> Where the voice of the cymbal sounds, where the drum re-echoes,
> Where the Phrygian flute sings through its great curved reed,
> Where the maenads fling their ivy-garlanded heads,
> Where the holy of holies is shaken with shrill howling,
> Where, they tell us, the goddess's wandering cohorts
> Used to beat the earth in the dance as they fled onward.

In a long and beautiful passage Catullus writes as though caught up in the ancient magic and the wild exultation. But, identifying himself with Attis, he describes how the rueful god awakens to see what he has done to himself and cries out in terrible remorse:

> I am a woman, I, once a boy, a youth, fill with young manhood,
> I, once the flower of the athletes, sweetly anointed,
> My doorway full of friends, threshold warm in the sun,
> All of my house filled with garlands of flowers
> When I left it, called from my bed by the sunrise.
> And now must I serve as a girl-slave, and priestess of Cybele?
> I, a maenad, only a part of myself, shall I live a gelding?
> Shall I dwell here, in this dress, on cold, green, snowy Ida?
> Shall I linger here in the lofty mountains of Phrygia
> With the forest-dwelling stag and the boar that roams the under-
>   brush?
> Now, now I suffer for what I have done, now, now I lament!

The relentless goddess sends her magical lions once more to drive Attis to fury and herd him back to her service. In Catullus's poem, Attis does not die, for he is a skilful and subtle blend of mythical deity and flesh-and-blood Roman who, in a temporary religious crisis, joins the cult. And in the last lines Catullus expresses his own feelings when he cries:

> Goddess, great Goddess, Cybele, Goddess, Lady Dindymene,
> Mistress, may the fury of all your slaves stay far from my door,
> Drive others out of their minds, drives others to madness!

Catullus could reach the high style, and the power of the myth stimulated him, but with the example of the Galli before his eyes he reacted like the highly sexed male he was. Despite his homosexual poems (which suggest more the Greek type of bisexuality) he was clearly a lover of women. It seems possible, however, that in a time of social distress and disorder, the Galli represented a further step than homosexuality in the flight from women and the responsibilities of ordinary living. As time went on, many Romans began to be stirred by not only the drastic celibacy of the Galli, but also the strange doctrines of the Christians.

While the quotation with which we began the chapter may refer directly to the Essenes, who practised celibacy, some Christian groups were certainly directly influenced by the Galli. A heretic sect, the Valesians, was said to castrate all males who fell into their hands, and the famous church father Origen was a self-made eunuch.

Henri Graillot wrote of the Galli, 'Their burning faith, their ascetic life, their austere disciplines were an efficacious example. Many troubled souls were drawn towards these interpreters of the divine word who appeared superior to other men because they were no longer men, who listened to confessions and examined consciences and gave consolation and divine hope.' The description could easily apply to the early Christian priest.

(A curious Russian group, the Skoptsi, founded in 1757, seems a complete throwback to the priests of Attis. The leader of this Christian sect 'baptized' his converts by castrating them with a red-hot iron. He quoted St Matthew: 'For it is profitable for thee that one of thy members should perish and not that thy whole body be cast into hell.' This group, as the Old Believers, is mentioned by Dostoevski and the adherents were said to have reached the number of 100,000. Parallel to it is the voluntary celibacy of the Shakers and Rappites of the United States. Father Rapp was even charged with castrating his own son for disregarding the taboo against sex.)

There is a similarity between the goddess Cybele with her eunuch priests and the later worship of the Virgin Mary sustained by a celibate clergy. The widespread worship of Mary retained the all-giving earth mother image but removed the dangerous sexual qualities by making her a permanent virgin. And indeed the carefully desexualized figure of Christ is more than a little reminiscent of Attis.

The Catholic Church soon discountenanced actual castration as unfair to voluntary celibates, but the eunuch ideal lived on in Christian tradition in terms of praise of virginity, the rejection of physical pleasure, and the belief that only the unmarried were pure. St Paul made the classic statement: 'It is good for a man not to touch a woman ... but if they cannot contain, let them marry; for it is better to marry than to burn.' In discussing Christian morals, Edward Westermarck made the shrewd comment, 'But the defiling effects attributed to sexual intercourse are also no doubt connected with the notion that woman is an unclean being – regular temporary defilement of a specifically feminine character may easily lead to the notion of the permanent uncleanness of the female sex.' And this is precisely what was achieved by Christian thinking.

If the taboos of early tribesmen seem irrational and excessive, they are always temporary. The primitive accepts his animal nature to the extent that he never completely denies his physical urges even though his anxieties may be in conflict with them. Although the Polynesian philosophy concerning the dangerous nature of the female in many ways paralleled that of the medieval Christians, the islanders never attempted to rule out human reproduction. Why, in the four centuries after Christ, did the rejection of women assume such an extreme form?

Assuming the point of view that social psychological phenomena are the product of a dialectic, latent individual drives are stimulated by the elements in the environment. We know that the late Roman period was a time of unrest and demoralization. Population decline coincided with civil wars and barbarian invasions. More and more foreign peoples were being absorbed into the empire with the result that a sense of cultural unity was destroyed. There was both economic decay and cynicism in the responsible governing class. And we have already cited some examples of social chaos.

In such periods of stress, when the individual feels he cannot cope with his problems, emotional upheavals take place and society resorts to new magic, yet magic derived from the fundamental psychological base. An interesting modern parallel is the cargo cult among the South Sea Islanders who were confused and bewildered by soldiers from a modern technological civilization who swept through the Pacific in World War II. As Margaret Mead describes it, it was called ' "The Noise," in which men shook like leaves in the grip of a religious revelation that promised them all the blessings of civilization at once, without an effort on their part, except the destruction of everything they possessed.' The new idea was fitted into primitive ancestor worship. When the natives had destroyed all their belongings, their ancestors would send supernatural aeroplanes laden with refrigerators, radios and jeeps.

The world in which Christian tradition developed was in the throes of the discovery of abstract thought. Buddhism was preaching asceticism and Nirvana, Roman and Greek pagans were also advocating non-material ideals based on new interpretations of Platonic philosophy. The Greek Orphic cult had already promised immortality as did the death and resurrection philosophy of Mithra; Christianity was to centre its teaching about this promise.

These were the positive elements in the new religion but, in accordance with the instinctive theory of mana, broken taboo, pollution of some sort, must be blamed for disaster and social distress. With so much anxiety centring around the sex function it is not surprising that eros was blamed for the illnesses of the civilized world. The late pagans had thrown off sexual taboos and tended to live for physical sensation. The generation which reacted against this and embraced Christianity had suffered personal traumatic experiences which intensified their rejection of the sexual act and women. St Augustine struggled all his life with a dominant mother whom he unconsciously resented, a conflict which coloured his rejection of marriage. St Paul is a still more interesting example of how individual personality and specific traumas were related to the new movement.

Paul, a Hellenized Jew with a Greek education, was a Roman citizen living in Tarsus. He was unattractive physically, small, somewhat deformed, with poor eyesight. He was also a prey to hallucinatory experiences, almost epileptic in character; in short he was the typical shaman.

A fanatic agent of the Sanhedrin, he was the ringleader in the fatal stoning of Stephen, an early Christian, for heresy. Later Paul had a vision of Christ, fell to the ground blind and was unable to eat or drink for three days. He then rose up, converted, with his vision restored. There is no record of his having any emotional or physical relationship with women. After conversion he associated with the strong and positive Barnabas, then quarrelled with him when Barnabas wanted to add his nephew, Mark, to their missionary expedition. His one enduring male friend was Timothy, who was characterized as gentle and effeminate and whom he circumcised with his own hands. Paul courted martyrdom by bringing an un-circumcised man into the temple and finally achieved it at the hands of the Romans.

From the psychoanalytical point of view, Paul was always strug-gling with father figures, the reflection of the harsh and blatantly male image of Yahweh. In killing Stephen he destroyed a rebel against the patriarch and then, being strongly masochistic, identified with Stephen and with Christ and sought to be sacrificed. Sidney Tarachow feels that after his ambivalent rebellion and also courting of the father god and the symbolic castration in his seizure (loss of eyesight is so regarded), he accepted 'the passive homosexual Catholic Christian solution'. In proof of this we have his resolute rejection of women (even Mary is banished from his theology), his rebellion against Barnabas, and the significant relation with the effeminate Timothy. His circumcising of Timothy has real overtones of the men's group – by this action he allied himself by ambivalent erotic assault with another male. When this intellectual but disturbed person joined the new movement, he contributed further to its rejection of women.

In other words, social distress, grown more intense as society grew more complicated, reactivated basic male anxieties which we have been all along describing. And this is proved by the fact that the myth of the Fall became the central explanation of all evil.

Women ought to wear mourning, Tertullian explains, 'in order to expiate more fully by all sorts of penitential garb that which women derive from Eve – the ignominy, I mean, of original sin and the odium of being the cause of the fall of the human race'. In the same author's diatribe against vanity and love of self-adornment, woman is told firmly, 'You are the one who opened the door to the Devil, you are the one who first plucked the fruit of the forbidden tree.'

In ante-Nicean times, before the Catholic Church had consolidated its rules and regulations, and was picking its way between all sorts of creeds many of which were eventually to be labelled heresy, attitudes towards sex were continually fluctuating but praise of virginity went on unceasingly. Tertullian cried out ecstatically, 'How many are there who, from the moment of their baptism, set the seal of virginity upon their flesh. How many again who by equal mutual consent cancel the debt of matrimony – voluntary eunuchs for the sake of their desire after the celestial city.' One of the few early thinkers who dared to place marriage above virginity was Jovinian, but he was attacked by all the leading preachers of his time and eventually was excommunicated for heresy and blasphemy. The Penitential of Theodore commanded that those who contracted a first marriage should abstain from entering a church for thirty days; a second marriage excluded them for a year; a third for seven years. This type of penance shows clearly that the bad mana of sex was considered detrimental to church ritual, but what can be said of St Augustine's pious wish that all mankind should abstain from marriage so that the human race might sooner come to an end!

Physical drives fortunately proved in most cases stronger than psychic confusion and finally the attacks of the Church simmered down to achieving the two aims of a celibate clergy and surrounding sex in marriage with as many restrictions as possible. The Church also did not cease to characterize women as instruments of the devil.

A celibate clergy was not something which could be brought about with the stroke of a pen. The Nicean council of 325 A.D. merely forbade clergymen to keep women in their houses and only permitted the visits of mothers, sisters or aunts. And indeed many of the early ecclesiastics lived with companions called *agapeta*, spiritual sisters or spiritual wives. The relation was supposed to be chaste but evidently more in theory than in practice, judging by the story of the popular reaction to the Bishop of Autun, St Simplicius. Henry C. Lea writes, 'Even as a layman, his holy zeal had led him to treat as a sister his beautiful wife who was inspired with equal piety. On his election to the episcopate, still confident of their mutual self-control, she refused to be separated from him. The people, scandalized at the impropriety, and entertaining a settled incredulity as to

the superhuman virtue requisite to such restraint, mobbed the
bishop's dwelling, and expressed their sentiments in a manner more
energetic than respectful. The saintly virgin called for a portable
furnace full of fire, emptied it into her robe, and held it, uninjured,
for an hour when she transferred the ordeal to her husband, saying
the trial was nothing to the flames through which they had already
passed unscathed. The result with him was the same, and the people
retired, ashamed of their unworthy suspicions.'

Not all clerics, however, could count on such a miracle to prove
their marvellous self-restraint, and continual complaints testify to
the fact that celibacy was a difficult ideal. Leontius, Bishop of
Antioch, castrated himself and was thus able to retain his agapeta
with a good conscience.

Meanwhile ascetic monks fled to the desert to avoid the sight of
women, at the same time mortifying their flesh by refraining from
washing and encouraging sores and putrefaction. Bathing, involving
the baring of the body, was particularly frowned on by the Church,
since it was supposed to lead to thoughts of lust, and thus Christian
idealism produced an era of medieval filth.

The ascetics who lived as hermits concentrated their whole lives
on the temptations of sex; since they had no other entertainment,
their minds were filled with the drama of their tremendous potency
inflamed by all sorts of dreams or hallucinations sent them by the
devil. St Jerome was one of the most famous of these pioneers of
asceticism. How could anyone find pleasure in a pretty voluptuous
girl, he inquired in one of his diatribes; how could anyone sleep
safely beside a death-dealing serpent? 'Job was dear to God, perfect
and upright before him; yet hear what he says of the devil, "His
strength is in his loins and his force is in the navel." The terms are
chosen for decency's sake but the reproductive organs of the two
sexes are meant.' St Jerome even set out to prove that Mary had
always been a virgin although the Bible mentioned that Jesus had
brothers and sisters. These, Jerome explained, were merely cousins.
His justification for clerical celibacy is revealing. 'A layman, or any
believer, cannot pray unless he abstain from sexual intercourse. Now
a priest must always offer sacrifice for the people, he must therefore
always pray. And if he must always pray he must always be released

from the duties of marriage.' A clearer statement of the evil mana of sex as an impediment to religious success could not be found. St Jerome outdid himself in a much-quoted passage in which he describes his melodrama of temptation in the desert. 'How often when I was living in the desert, in the vast solitude which gives to hermits a savage dwelling . . . how often did I fancy myself among the pleasures of Rome! . . . When I had no companions but scorpions and wild beasts, I often found myself among bevies of girls. My face was pale and my frame chilled with fasting, yet my mind was burning with desire and the fires of lust kept bubbling up before me when my flesh was as good as dead.'

The outcome of all of this denigration of the normal urges towards reproduction, which was supposed to exalt virginity, was the usual human compromise between theory and practice. Only highly spiritual (or highly unbalanced) individuals could accept continence as a way of life. And, of course, intense conflicts were also created. In the words of G. Rattray Taylor, 'In the earlier part of the Middle Ages what we chiefly find is frank sensuality, with which the Church at first battles in vain. Then, as it improves its systems of control, we find a mounting toll of perversion and neurosis.' By 1102 a church council had to state specifically that priests should be degraded for sodomy and anathematized for 'obstinate sodomy.' Since the un-spiritual ordinary citizen was grudgingly allowed to marry, ecclesiastical rules did what they could to pluck the feathers from the wings of eros. 'There was a great spiderweb of regulations whose overriding purpose was to make the sex act as joyless as possible. . . .' Intercourse was to be carried out for the purpose of obtaining offspring only. Those who practised it for pleasure were sinful. Many of the church rules are clearly based on the old magical beliefs. It was considered a sin, for instance, for a menstruating woman to enter a church. A woman who had given birth to a child had to be ceremonially purified before taking communion. Still another instance of persistence of the ancient beliefs concerning the bad mana of women was the superstition that it was inadvisable to sleep with a woman or even to go near a woman's bed during the plague, for this would increase the risk of infection.

In the Middle Ages, therefore, the old magical survivals, plus the enlarged significance of the myth of the Fall, and new psychological tensions tended to stimulate the formation of a eunuch ideal, to intensify the traditional misogyny, and to devaluate the heterosexual act.

In order to appreciate more fully what effect all this had upon the laity we must turn to secular literature and the institution of courtly love.

CHAPTER ELEVEN

The Devil's Mirror

A candid scrutiny of the behaviour of the knights of Teutonic and Celtic ancestry in the eleventh and twelfth century reveals them as essentially the familiar primitive hunter warriors encased in steel suits. They lived by the ethos of the male group, paying lip service to the ethics of the Church. In their attitude towards women they were somewhat like the members of the New Guinea male association, only in some ways less civilized. Wrote Sidney Painter, 'The feudal male was absorbed in war and in the chase. His wife bore him sons, his mistress satisfied his lust. Beyond this women had no place and he had no interest in them. They were freely beaten and in general treated with calloused brutality.'

A good example is William the Conqueror's courtship. This well-known hero had the misfortune, which was however not unusual, to be born a bastard. He proposed marriage to the daughter of Baudouin, Count of Flanders. The lady indignantly refused to be married to a man upon whom lay the stain of illegitimacy. William was furious. He waited at the door of the church which she habitually attended. When she came out after her devotions, he attacked her physically, threw her down and beat her until she promised to be his wife. Important estates came with her, for marriages were arranged on a property basis so that two aristocratic houses might be joined and the ensuing offspring carry on the noble line and inherit the estates. There was also the system of wardship. Unmarried heiresses were granted as wards to nobles whose task was to bring them up and marry them off. In this there could be a profit. Thomas Wright tells us, 'Wards or unmarried girls of property were bought and sold as commonly as if they were beasts.'

No romance, therefore, surrounded the wife. In the old *chansons de geste* when a man's wife spoke up and annoyed him, he hit her on the nose with his fist, drawing blood. Serfs, of course, had no rights and women of this group were treated as property to be used when the noble lord felt the urge. Up to the twelfth century the court prostitute was a recognized institution and most aristocrats had an imposing number of bastards.

As city life developed and a merchant and artisan middle class grew, manners began to be refined. At the same time the Church grew more powerful and continued to impose its antisexual attitude with varying success.

Out of this milieu came the concept of courtly love which, in Painter's view, was a minority movement and mostly a fairly superficial literary convention. The poet of the South of France, the troubadour, would on the one hand be a more sensitive person than the knight whose profession was organized homicide. The troubadour also had more of an education to draw upon; in some cases he probably had some monastery schooling. From the practical point of view, when he entertained at a castle, if the master was away from home fighting, or crusading, as was often the case, it would be worthwhile flattering the mistress. The troubadour therefore set himself to shedding a little grace upon the sexual relationship. In order to satisfy his public, however, and also in deference to the realities of the age, he was not impelled to add much lustre to the marriage relationship. Basically, courtly love is a glorification of concubinage and an attempt to endow it with subtlety and social refinements until it becomes a delicate game. Since the Church forbade concubinage, troubadour poetry, in the South of France, tended to extol a platonic ideal. The lover was supposed to adore his mistress from afar and to do great deeds in her honour, receiving in exchange a smile or a handkerchief to wear on his helmet. The notion that cherishing a pure passion for an often distant fair one made a knight fight better, while it might have little actual truth, was acceptable to the code which ordained fighting as the only acceptable way of life.

At the same time the parallel between the platonically married clergy, the priest and the agapeta, with which the Church had so much trouble, is very strong. In a society where passions were crude and hearty yet in which the priesthood firmly denied one of man's most basic drives, curious sorts of compromise were bound to arise. The make-believe, have-your-cake-and-eat-it-too theory of platonic courtly love satisfied the urge to rationalize, although it is questionable how much it had to do with actual practice.

The contradiction is most apparent in the North of France where Ovid's *Ars Amatoria* was well known. Ovid, who as we have seen made of love a pleasantly sensual but complicated pursuit, could not conceive of the game without its ending in bed. The troubadours had ventured into thoroughly ambiguous situations. One test of the ideal relationship was for the lover and his lady to spend some time naked in bed together with perhaps some caressing of the sexual parts but always stopping short of actual consummation. (We are reminded of heavy and light petting in the contemporary anarchical situation.) The northern poets, influenced by Ovid, felt that somehow the lover and his mistress should contrive to sleep together yet without violating contemporary sanctions. This resulted in still more elaborate gyrations. Chrétien de Troyes, in one of his romances, evolved a curious method of preventing actual adultery. The husband was given a magic potion every night which caused him to believe, when he awoke in the morning, that he had enjoyed his wife. Even this situation had to be resolved and it was done by letting the lover carry off the wife.

If the idealization of women in courtly love is analysed, it will be seen to be only one element in a society in which the dark side of the sexual ambiguity is dominant. Painter himself feels it to have been a minority movement, as we have said. There is little evidence that, as a result, women as a whole were any better treated in the thirteenth and fourteenth centuries. The sweaty, clanking warrior was perhaps induced to bathe once in a while and to learn to dance and sing a love ditty, and that was about all. When it came to plebeian women, the same advocates of courtly love advised immediate rape.

Nevertheless the concept of courtly love might be considered, thanks to Ovid's influence, an example of liberalism in the sexual sphere. It was only a temporary breakthrough but it allowed exceptional females such as Eleanor of Aquitaine, with her court of love, or Marie de France, the talented poet, to contribute something of their own, and for a brief moment male anxiety took second place.

And yet the ever-present disquietude peeps out in some of the courtly romances, too. Two types of women appear in medieval narrative poetry, the unassuming wife who knows her place, and what has been technically called 'the wooing lady'. The latter is a very interesting figure. We find her characteristically drawn in the tale of *Amis and Amiloun* (*Amis et Amile*). This story is first recorded in the eleventh century, an Anglo-Norman French version dates to 1200 and the English poem, which we shall quote, was written about 1330 but is considered to contain some quite early elements. The poem is woven together out of several ancient folklore themes, overlaid with medieval manners and conventions. Basically the tale deals with identical twin brothers who swear an oath always to be true to each other. This, in itself, is a survival of an old Teutonic custom involving an oath and mixing of blood which had nothing to do with actual kinship. We follow Amis, who is only an ordinary knight and who becomes the butler of a duke. The moment the duke's virgin daughter, Belisaunt, sees Amis she is smitten with love in approved courtly fashion.

> When that sche seichte him ride or go
> Hir thoucht hir hert brac awto.

Completely struck down by her passion, she becomes ill and spends a considerable time in bed bemoaning herself. Her mother with practical foresight tells her to get up and go and play in the garden. The sight of nature proves somewhat of a restorative.

> Sche herd the foules gret and smale
> The swete note of the nichtingale.

But presently, as her mother had hoped, she spies the attractive but lowborn knight. She immediately sends her maidens away and boldly makes love to him.

> Sir knicht, on mine hert is brocht
> The to love is al mi thoucht
> Bothe be nicht and day;
> That bot thou wilt me leman [lover] be;
> Ywis min hert breketh a thre
> No longer libben Y no may.

The rather backward Amis objects that he has no money or lands and that he is no match for a duke's daughter.

> And yif we schuld that game biginne
> And ani wicht of al thi kinne
> Micht it undergo,
> Al our joie and worldes winne
> We schuld lese for that sinne,
> Whrethi [Wrathy] god there-to.

Amis appears to think only of the consequences and reacts not at all to the charms of Belisaunt. The panting girl grows very angry at being told to think twice about the consummation of her love and chides Amis harshly, demanding,

> Whether artow prest other persoun
> Other thou art monk other canoun
> That prechest me thus here?

In fact she has no scruples about threatening him, if he refuses her.

> Me love schal be ful dere aboucht
> With pine hard and strong;
> Mi kerchiew and me clothes anon
> Y schal torende [tear] down echon
> And say with ichel wrong
> With strengthe thou hast me to drawe . . .

Poor Amis, faced with a threatened charge of rape, is forced to promise he will act the man, but requests a week's grace. A week later, with no intention of letting him off, she comes to his bedroom. Amis still feebly complains that her father will either kill him or exile him if he finds out, but the rapacious girl is not to be put off.

> That hende knicht bethoucht him then
> And in his armes he her nam [took]
> And kist that miri may.
> And so they plaid in word and dede
> That he wan hir maidenhede
> Er that sche went away.

The erotic couple have been unfortunately observed by the duke's steward. He reveals all to the duke who pursues Amis with drawn sword. Finally, when things have calmed down a trifle, it is agreed that Amis shall fight the steward to prove the accuser is a liar. Amis is in great trouble because he knows he will himself be maintaining a lie and thus is sure to be defeated. He gets a leave of absence and rushes off to find his twin brother, who comes to court, kills the steward in fair fight, and goes to bed with his brother's betrothed. First, however, he sets a naked sword between them, much to the annoyance of Belisaunt. Amiloun gets out of this difficulty by explaining:

> I have swiche a malady
> That mength al mi blod
> And al min bones be so sare
> I hold [dare] nocht touche thi bodi bare
> For al this worldes gode!

In the end Amis returns, gets the lady, becomes the duke's heir, and is gratified to learn that his brother has preserved his wife's honour.

Behind this quaintly motivated story is the old theme of Potiphar's wife which, in turn, can probably be traced back to an Egyptian tale of 1300 B.C. It became a popular episode in Celtic mythology and in the romances takes various forms. Very often the rapacious maiden is a Saracen who jumps into the bed of a crusader – this accorded best with church ethics, for pagans were not supposed to be moral anyway. In Belisaunt's case, everything had to be smoothed over by marriage.

Psychologically, the episode is of course a real pandering to male fantasy with its basic ambivalence. On the one hand the feudal knight enjoyed the idea of being pursued by a shameless but high-born virgin, so flattering to his vanity; on the other, the wooing lady is clearly sexually voracious and dangerous. Though she does not destroy him with her sex organ, she does so symbolically by crying rape and almost causing his death. It is also probable that one of the reasons for the lascivious image of woman as sketched by men is the biological fact that a woman is always capable of the act of love and not limited in its repetition, while a man knows, in spite of masculine boasting, that just so much is possible. Certainly the same apprehensions are behind the image of the wooing lady and that of Cybele who visits castration upon Attis when he fails to give himself up to her exclusively. Even the naked sword episode in *Amis and Amiloun*, although it is ostensibly to preserve chastity, certainly combines the platonic hedging, dreamed up in deference to the Church, and a still deeper fear of contact with the woman's organs, for the castrating blade stands symbolically between the bedmates and the heterosexual act.

Andrew the Chaplain, who wrote on courtly love in the second half of the twelfth century, undertook first the defence of the institution and then in *De reprobatione amoris* proceeded to attack it. One of his arguments needs no comment to point up its primitive character. Love, he said, was harmful to a man's body, for the act of Venus diminished a man's strength. Since it was a sin to diminish the bodily powers given by God, love should be shunned. Worst of all, intercourse shortened a man's life.

While the institution of love was debated, elaborated, and often exaggerated until it had no connection with real men and women, the anti-erotic blasts of churchmen and their attacks upon women did not cease. Most clerical scholars drew upon a stock of material derived from the classics. The Roman cynicism of Juvenal, Catullus and Propertius provided them with a series of charges and epithets while Ovid could be used in reverse as a horrible example. Marbod de Rennes, a French bishop who flourished from 1035 to 1123, wrote a ten-chapter poem in Latin hexameters, the second section of which was concerned with 'the whore' – which in Marbod's eyes meant the whole female sex. He maintained that women came between old friends, separated lovers, set children against their elders, destroyed villages, cities and whole peoples. They did not stop at murder and there was no evil in the world in which they did not participate. He, and those who followed him in the medieval cataloguing tradition, then cited Adam, Samson, Solomon and various stock historical characters as examples of men who had suffered at the hands of women. Marbod rather outdoes himself when he compares woman to the chimaera. This mythical beast had the head of a lion, the tail of a dragon, and its mid-portion was composed of glowing fire. A woman seeks her prey like the lion, scorches it to a cinder with the fires of love, and finally bestows death and destruction like the poison of the dragon.

> O race of mankind beware the honeysweet poison,
> And seductive song and the lure of that fearful chasm,
> O fear the raging flames of that furious dragon!

went the worthy bishop's hymn of hate.

A Benedictine monk, Bernard de Moraix, announced flatly in his poem, *De contemptu mundi*, that there was no good woman on earth. Alexander Neckham, an English monk of the same period who also wrote Latin verses, was of the opinion that woman's sexuality was boundless and often a man was deceived into raising a child which his wife had conceived by some worthless wretch to whom she had given herself out of pure sensuality. Needless to say, all these authors cited Adam, Samson and Solomon as much-abused males and, since the Middle Ages was a time of copying and borrowing, their misogynist treatises influenced many other writers; not to mention the countless sermons preached in village churches, manorial chapels and cathedrals, which must have assaulted the ears of docile congregations every Sunday. On the basis of the myth of the Fall, woman who was basically feared for her sexual characteristics was now gratuitously accused of every vice, a literary convention which also crops up in popular Latin poetry composed by clerks and half-trained scholars who were in and out of holy orders. Such poems often directed their satire towards the institution of marriage. The man who married went like an ox to the slaughter, his wife turned him into a slave or an ass. All the charges formulated by the bishops were picked up and used over and over again. Woman's faithlessness was a favourite subject for comment.

> If you are a man who believes in the word of a woman,
> Believe me, if you do, it's only because she's beguiled you.

Prose works add some fresh images – a woman is the devil's noose, the death of the body and the soul, a stinking rose, a sweet poison. Copying and modifying Marbod, a prose author tells us that woman has the head of a dragon, the tail of a scorpion, the tongue of a serpent, the venom of an asp. Henry II's chaplain, who wrote a *Livre des Manières*, charged that women were expert in using herbs and poisons with which to do away their husbands.

That famous allegory the *Roman de la Rose*, the first half of which is a maze of erotic symbolism and a treatise on courtly love, was continued and finished by Jean de Meung, who wrote from the contemporary misogynist point of view. This author adds to the tirade against the second sex.

> Though you seek her, here there, everywhere
> Every woman is a whore.

Again:

> Woman's like three things, wolf, fox, and cat.
> Wolf, fox, and cat are beasts of prey,
> Cat seeks, fox waits, wolf rends and tears.

Although French and Latin poetry account for the bulk of literary production in the early Middle Ages, the other vernaculars also contributed their share. A couple of choice images from the Italian tells us that 'a woman's face is the devil's mirror' and women's hearts are only good on the outside, within they are like rotten apples.

A Spanish proverb adds to the chorus.

> Who holds a eel by its tail
> And a woman to her plighted word,
> Must admit he has nothing.

The extreme and irrational tradition created in the Middle Ages, through which women were stamped as inherently immoral, destructive and deceitful beings, has had an incalculable influence on later European culture. One of the first literary images to be created was that of Cressida.

CHAPTER TWELVE

'As False as Cressid . . .'

The falsity of women, a theme repeated in the Middle Ages with the monotonous beat of Cold War propaganda in our own age, was rationalized by the story of the Fall with the statement that since Eve deceived Adam no woman was to be trusted. Actually Eve did not deceive Adam; the snake, her informant, as we have indicated, was more trustworthy than Yahweh, who said that Adam would die, but this little fact did not trouble medieval clerical propagandists. It is evident that here, as in other areas, more than one element came into play; upon the fundamental psychological base were added motives of self-interest. The concept of untrustworthiness of women in the sexual sphere on the one hand probably derives from male fear of inadequacy, the infantile sense that the boy's sex organ will not satisfy the female parent, plus the fact that women can perform sexually more often than men, and also from the concept of woman as property. As has been pointed out, the medieval marriage system identified the woman with property; as such all of her services belonged to her owner. The medieval male was touchy and selfish about his private possessions. The greed for material aggrandizement was behind most military activity, including the Crusades, and accounts for a host of brutal and unjust acts of plunder.

It is interesting to note the difference in attitude between the simple hunting and fishing primitive and the primitive encased in armour. Men in the tribal state tend to hold property in common; there is a generalized sense of group ownership. The tribal male therefore is not so concerned that his wife's sexual services should belong to him exclusively. He may lend her to a guest as a matter of courtesy; he may exchange her with tribal brothers in certain ceremonies for magical reasons. Virginity in women is often considered unimportant, as in tribes in which young people indulge in many affairs before marriage or, as in the curious case of Lesu, where the young married women immediately has as many lovers as she can attract, lovers who make a present to her husband.

The desire for a monopoly of female property is borne out by the famous medieval institution of the chastity belt, a metal contraption locked about a woman's middle, which was supposed to ensure her fidelity while the warrior husband was away. Its logical culmination is the Bedouin treatment of female slaves which persisted into the nineteenth century, an example of the brutal excess to which men have gone to insure that female property reach its owner undamaged. The practice of infibulation was carried out on girls before the age of puberty. The edges of the vulva were made raw and sewn together forming scar tissue and leaving only a small opening just large enough for the function of urination. When the slave was sold to her owner, a second operation was necessary in order to make her fit for the purpose for which she was purchased!

A combination of anxieties therefore culminated in the popular notion that women could not be trusted to remain faithful. Actually all the anthropological evidence shows that it is men who have been polygamists and enjoyed the variety of a harem. Polyandry has occurred as an institution in only two or three areas in the world. Man laid down the law in the sphere of eros and then accused women of not adhering to it. Indeed, the element of guilt cannot be ruled out. Having projected its fears upon women, the male imagination then set to work to justify them by creating stereotypes. What use was made of the destructive Pandora-Eve figure we have already seen. We now come to a new character which was created in the Middle Ages, achieved great importance in the fourteenth, fifteenth and sixteenth centuries, and probably has left its traces on subsequent literature in the Western world, that of the fair but frail Cressida.

The story seems to be an invention of the French poet Benoît de Sainte-Maure; it is found in his *Roman de Troie* which was written about 1160. A couple of Latin sources which were drawn upon by medieval writers for Trojan material merely mention three of the characters, calling our heroine Briseide. Benoît gives us a description of the lady in which she is called 'more beautiful and more fair and more white than a lily or than snow on the bough but her brows were joined which a little misbecame her'. Troilus like-wise 'had fair hair, very charming and naturally shining eyes, bright and full of gaiety, none ever had beauty like theirs'. Briseide was the daughter of Calchas, priest of Apollo, who, told by the god that Troy would fall, followed the orders of the deity and deserted to the side of the Greeks. Briseide, left in Troy, threw herself on the mercy of Hector who decreed that she should be allowed to remain in the city in peace. Troilus was the son of King Priam and brother to Hector and Cassandra. Briseide and he were lovers (according to Benoît everyone knew about it), but when Calchas asked that his daughter be sent to him, Priam was quite willing to let her go and scornfully said Troy would keep nothing belonging to a traitor. Troilus and Briseide were grief-stricken and swore to be true to each other. The lady was escorted to the Greek camp by Diomedes, a handsome hulking warrior, the son of a king. He lost no time in making a pass, telling her she needed a knight protector, that he had never had a mistress and that he wished to be her lover. Briseide merely told him it was too soon to think of that. Nevertheless, Diomedes succeeded in purloining her glove.

Briseide quarrelled with her father who defended himself, saying he only followed the orders of Apollo. For a time she clung to her love for Troilus but,

> Fickle and infirm, her feelings were soon changed
> Weak and all inconstant was her heart.

Diomedes captured Troilus' horse and sent it to her but later lost his own. When he next attempted to court her, she twitted him about the loss of his horse but ended by giving him her sleeve. Troilus and Diomedes fought again, with the result that Diomedes was badly wounded. Troilus cried, 'Keep her wholly to yourself now, but she has not yet made an end; she finds pleasure in the trade of love. For if there are so many that somewhat please her, the very innkeepers will have her favours.' Pitying Diomedes because of his wound, Briseide yielded but with a deep sense of guilt, saying to herself, 'Henceforth no good will be written of me, nor any good songs sung.' Troilus, having lost his helmet in battle, was killed by Achilles.

In this first version of the story Briseide's ironical historical fore-sight is significant; Benoît has already marked her as the prototype of unfaithful women.

The poet who gave the plot a full-fledged development was Giovanni Boccaccio, who treated it with a mixture of courtly love and Renaissance feeling in his *Il filostrato* (one struck down by love). Boccaccio was the son of a money-lender who was in love with an unhappily married lady of good family, Maria d'Aquino. Since Maria had left Naples for the summer, Boccaccio was lonely and decided to write a poem in praise of love. He chose the Troilus and Criseida theme, renaming the heroine and adding the character of Pandaro, in this case a cousin of the girl and a comrade of the hero, and henceforth to lend his name to the go-between.

In *Il filostrato* Criseida is won over by Pandaro who tells her of Troilo's passion and in approved courtly fashion insists that the poor lover will die if she does not take pity on him. Criseida's character also conforms to the conventions of courtly love. She is at first passive, then influenced by Pandaro's arguments, but worries about secrecy. By herself, she balances Troilo's important position and his attractions against the danger of being found out and the possibility that Troilo's love is only a passing fancy. She eventually convinces herself by using the standard argument of the period, 'Love that comes from such a friendship is always more welcome to lovers. And let beauty be as great as thou wilt, it is soon stale to the husbands, for they are ever hunting after something new.' After some holding back and a letter or two, she agrees to meet Troilo. She yields im-mediately and from then on Boccaccio indulges in ecstatic and lyric descriptions of youthful eroticism. Criseida in this version is ex-changed with the Greeks for the Trojan hero Antenor and promises, after she and Troilo have nearly died of grief, that she will find a way of returning to Troy. Troilo proposes an elopement which she rejects on the grounds that he would be deserting Troy and ruin his good name. Boccaccio does not allow Diomed to make love to Criseida on the trip to the Greek camp. The poet returns immediately to enlarge upon Troilo's loneliness and misery (and, of course, his own). Criseida has one scene with Diomed in which she does not altogether give in but ends with the words, 'Thou mayest speak to me again; and perchance thy words will be dearer to me than they are now.' When Troilo sees a brooch he has given her pinned on a garment belonging to Diomed he realizes the truth.

Boccaccio's intent in writing *Il filostrato* is to draw a lyrical picture of courtly love with the emphasis on Troilo's constancy. He is therefore not too much concerned with the character of Criseida and rather hurries over her infidelity. The amiable and civilized Chaucer based his charming treatment of the legend on Boccaccio but added a great deal of his own. Extremely erudite, he was fully aware of medieval misogyny and even in his prologue to *The Legend of Good Women*, apologized for having translated the *Romaunt of the Rose* and the story of Criseyde. Moreover, in the character of the wife of Bath, he ingeniously answered the antisexual propaganda of the Church. Chaucer's approach to Criseyde is elaborated in terms of the religion of love; more medieval than Boccaccio, he nevertheless achieves more psychological profundity. She was, he shows us, too suggestible. From the beginning when Pandarus, in his hands a far more subtle character, begins his skilful manœuvres and draws her attention to Troilus, she allows herself to be drawn into loving the handsome knight by a gradual process. She rationalizes and pretends not to see where the affair is leading. First she maintains she will allow him to worship her from afar; when once they have met the relationship is to be Platonic; finally when Pandarus has by a series of devices edged her into bed with her lover she is happy to allow nature to take its course. Again, when she is packed off to the Greek camp in exchange for Antenor, she still honestly believes she will be true to Troilus and will find a way to return. But, never very strong willed, when her father refuses to let her go, she writes letters full of empty promises. Just as she could be influenced by Pandarus, she succumbs to the smooth-talking Diomedes. Her infidelity is motivated in several scenes. She is alone among foreigners with only a disgraced father for companionship. Diomedes is a handsome and plausible warrior. Once more she is talked into an affair. But it should be remembered that she is the pawn of male authority in both camps.

In spite of all the fashionable protestations of both Troilus and Criseyde that they will die of love, in spite of their tears and swooning, neither one does die of love and Criseyde's romanticism cannot stand the pressure of everyday life in an authoritarian male world. Chaucer treats the conventions of courtly love with humour and quaint pedantry, achieving almost a drawing-room comedy. He makes it clear that he feels no primitive compulsion to discriminate against women; he is a spokesman for the religion of love. By his minute analysis of Criseyde's actions he shows clearly that she conforms to a submissive pattern. Criseyde, a creature of her time, is simply all too human.

Even so, Chaucer apologizes for recording her infidelity.

> Bisechinge every lady bright of hewe
> And every gentil woman, what she be,
> That all be that Criseyde was untrewe,
> That for that gilt she be not wrooth with me.
> Ye may her gilt in othere bokes see;
> And gladlier I wol wryten, if you leste,
> Penelope's trouthe and good Alceste.

The tradition which runs from Ovid to the troubadours and to Chaucer reveals the exceptionally gifted literary man sometimes contributing a more civilized outlook towards women in contrast to the compulsive and unbalanced shaman and cleric.

In Chaucer's *Troilus and Criseyde* (and to some extent in Boccaccio) two traditions are in conflict. The first part of the poem makes of Criseyde an ideal figure in the courtly fashion; in the last book she resumes the role created for her by Benoît de Sainte-Maure, that of the eternal whore.

Another gifted writer enlarged upon the tragedy of her guilt, however, and is responsible for emphasizing the sinful side of Criseyde. Robert Henryson, a Scottish poet, wrote a continuation of the story. Both Boccaccio and Chaucer ended with the death of Troilus; both tried to treat Criseyde as sympathetically as possible. Henryson's temperament was far more that of the medieval preacher. Although he made use of classical mythological paraphernalia in his poem *The Testament of Cresseid*, his lines vibrate with the fear of death and corruption. The same spirit which created the dance of death, which cried out against sin and painted the terrors of hell, still lingered in the north in the last quarter of the fifteenth century when Henryson was writing. Although he was dealing with a courtly theme, emotionally he remained in the clerical camp. Out of this anachronistic mixture he succeeded in creating a climax of sombre, tragic intensity. The love poets had recorded Criseyde's infidelity but allowed her to go unpunished. It remained for Henryson to express in artistic form the underlying masculine hostility behind the story.

In the beginning he tells us, Diomed tired of her; his fancy turned to another and he turned her out.

> Then desolait she walkit up and doun
> And, sum men sayis, unto the court commoun.

At last she went to her father, who took her back. In her misery she entered the shrine of Cupid and accused him of sowing the seed of love in her face.

> But now allas! that seid with froist is slane,
> And I fra luifferis left, and all forlane!

Like the protagonist in so many medieval poems, she then falls into a dream in which Cupid calls before him the seven planets in the form of gods and goddesses, Saturn, Jupiter, Mars, Phoebus, Venus, Mercury and Cynthia, all of whom are described in picturesque detail. In this heavenly court Cresseid is accused of blasphemy against Cupid and living "unclene and lecherous". For offending the god of love, Saturn touches her with his frosty wand and decrees immediate punishment:

> Thy greit fairness, and al thy bewty gay,
> Thy wanton blude, and eik thy golden hair,
> Heir I exclude fra thee for evermair.

and adds:

> In mortal neid, and greit penuritie
> Thou suffer sall, and as ane beggar die.

Cynthia, however, adds the most terrible sentence of all.

Thy cristall ene mingit with blude I mak,
Thy voice so deir, unpleasand, hoir [old] and hace [hoarse];
Thy lusty lyre [complexion] ourspred with spottis black,
And lumpis haw [wan] appeirand in thy face.

Wretched Cresseid awakes to find it all true, she is a leper. She
and her father lament the tragic punishment. Finally, since she is of
noble birth, in spite of her deformity she is taken into a hospital
outside the town. Henryson gives her a tragic and beautiful complaint.

O ladyis fair of Troy and Grece attend
My misery, quilk [which] nane may comprehend,
My frivoll fourtoun, my infelicitie
My greit mischief, quilk na man can ammend.
Be war in tyme, approchis neir the end
And in your mind an mirror mak of me.
As I am now, peradventure that ye,
For all your micht, may cum to that same end.

Every day she goes forth with her leper's bell and cup to beg for
alms. One day a company of Trojans which has just made a successful sally from the town rides by. Troilus, who leads the cavalcade,
looks down upon the miserable leper.

Than upon him she kest [cast] up baith her ene,
And with ane blink, it came into his thocht
That he sum-tyme hir face befoir had sene.

He turns pale and trembles.

And nevertheless not ane ane-uther knew.

Troilus drops a purse of gold in her lap.

Then raid away and not ane word he spak.

Cresseid despairs and shortly dies leaving him in her testament a
ring which he had given her. Troilus, learning the end of her story,
buries her sadly. Henryson ends:

Now, worthy wemen, in this ballet short
Made for your worship and instructioun,
Of cheritie I monish and exhort,
Ming not your luf with fals deceptioun.

Artistically Henryson reaches a tragic moment quite beyond the gentle Chaucer. From the psychological point of view the projected hostility dramatizes all the *Walpurgisnacht* which lurked in the unconscious of the medieval and the early Renaissance male, as Henryson destroys poor Cresseid with leprosy.

Because of an ambiguous preface in which Henryson spoke of reading the glorious Chaucer and then seemed to mention another book which contained the end of the story, the *Testament* was attributed to Chaucer and, in spite of the difference in style and tone, was several times printed with *Troilus and Criseyde* as a continuation of the earlier poem. It created the image of Cressid in the sixteenth century, an image which became continually more degraded and which would have shocked the kindly Chaucer if he had known that he was implicated. Skelton referred to Cressid's bad reputation and Turberville in 1567 wrote a poem which emphasized her whorishness. Many other complaints and ballads helped to fix the stereotype; some even pictured her as promiscuous while involved with her affair with Troilus.

In the theatre the theme was popular. A play acted in 1515 has not survived nor has another, played in 1582. When Shakespeare came to write his *Troilus and Cressida*, circumstances combined to make it a less enlightened version than that of Chaucer. In the first place the coarsened stereotype was current and evidently influenced him; in the second place his play is a work of disillusionment which required that the image of Cressid be a symbol of female falsity. The Trojan war is being fought over a whore. Sulky, selfish heroes bicker among themselves while Thersites rails at them all. Even Achilles' victory over Hector is savagely presented. Hector sits resting with his helmet off. Despite his protest that he is unarmed, Achilles unchivalrously strikes him down. Against this pattern of unheroic war, Troilus, who had argued against the sensible suggestion that Helen be given up and peace concluded, himself ironically ends the play fighting with Diomedes who wears on his helmet the glove Troilus had given Cressida.

The story of the lovers is therefore deliberately exploited as a symbol of the general corruption and degradation of the world. Shakespeare is not particularly interested in the psychology of

Cressida. From the first she is drawn as quick-tongued and calcula-
ting. In her witty but waspish exchanges with Pandarus she pretends
to despise Troilus and then through an aside explains that she is
merely being practical.

> Yet hold I off. Women are angels, wooing:
> Things won are done.

Pandarus is a prurient old Peeping Tom deriving a vicarious satisfaction from the intrigue. When Cressida first encounters Troilus she
is forthright in admitting she is ready for an affair. Again, in the
Greek camp, she is happy to exchange quips with the enemy nobles
who are eager to beg a kiss. Ulysses' comment sums her up.

> NESTOR.   A woman of quick sense.
> ULYSSES.   Fie, fie upon her!
> There's a language in her eye, her cheek, her lip,
> Nay her foot speaks; her wanton spirits look out
> At every joint and motive of her body.
> O! these encounterers so glib of tongue . . .

One sympathetic touch is granted her in the scene in which Diomedes begs for the glove given her by Troilus. She hesitates, takes
it back, then grants it with the bitter line:

> T'was one's that loved me better than you will.

Shakespeare's intent to make of her a symbol is underlined by the
device of ironical historical foresight which appeared in Benoît's
poem. Boccaccio omitted it, Chaucer restored it, but Shakespeare
used it twice.

> If ever I be false . . .
> Let them say to stick the heart of falsehood,
> As false as Cressid.

And again:

> Make Cressid's name the very crown of falsehood
> If ever she leave Troilus!

The persistence of the ancient ambivalence of mana in the Middle
Ages is particularly clear when we consider how three significant
medieval works are divided against themselves. The first part of

Andrew the Chaplain's manual of courtly love, *Tractatus de Amore*, is devoted to the erotic religion while the last section is a treatise on misogyny. Guillaume de Lorris allegorizes courtly love in the first part of the *Roman de la Rose* and Jean de Meung attacks women in the continuation. Finally, in Chaucer's hands Criseyde becomes a split character paralleling the double image of the fertility goddess and castrating earth mother. In the Renaissance, however, only the dark side of Cressid's image endures; the stereotype of falsity hardens as another irrationally engendered accusation is pinned on the second sex by the dominant male.

CHAPTER THIRTEEN

Knights without Ladies

In the year 1307 Philip the IV of France arrested all 5,000 Knights Templars within his kingdom and charged them with heresy. This dramatic and shocking episode in medieval history is fairly unfamiliar to any except specialists. Sometimes in digging into the past we begin to feel that some of the most significant actions are buried in the bland discussion of issues and trends in terms of which most history is written.

In this particular case, a brutal power struggle centred around an institution which is important to our theme and, ironically enough, men's defences against women were no defence against greed and political corruption. The order of the Knights Templars is the best example of the men's house surviving in the Middle Ages in terms of the new religious synthesis. For two hundred years it flourished, honoured by kings and popes, and was then wiped out by a ruthless despot.

Monastic orders in general are of course psychologically the descendants of such primitive institutions as those cited in New Guinea, but the Templars were particularly close to the ancient pattern in that they combined the rejection of women with the sadism of warfare. Other similarities will appear in the development of the story.

The Knights Templars (Poor Brothers of the Temple of Jerusalem) originated after the First Crusade during which Jerusalem was captured in 1099. The second ruler of this western oasis in the Holy Land, Baldwin II, felt the need of some sort of protection for the pilgrims who came to the Holy Sepulchre. Since the kingdom was never more than a beachhead and the Moslems were always endeavouring to destroy it, such pilgrims were continually in danger of being attacked and captured. The Templars, in 1118, were an organized group of knights who swore to live in poverty and chastity, obedient to the church and, instead of fighting for the honour of a lady, pledging themselves to eternal warfare against the enemies of Christendom. From merely protecting pilgrims, as their numbers grew, they became the shock troops of the Westerners in Palestine.

Actually the medieval Church took a compromise position towards organized homicide. Priests were forbidden to shed blood although some knightly bishops went to war armed with a mace, claiming that they shed no blood but merely crushed the brains of the Church's enemies. This rationalization could scarcely be applied on a large scale, but the Church had to exist in a world in which nothing was achieved without fighting. The solution of a fighting order which served the ecclesiastical authorities, which submitted to monastic rules but which was not really composed of clergymen, was a brilliant one. Its success was, of course, due to the fact that it was erected upon a sound base of masculine misogyny and sadism. A great many of the crusaders treated the campaigns in the Holy Land as mere bandit forays during which they appropriated land as booty and settled down. Thereafter they lost interest in fighting. At the same time the kings of Jerusalem were hostile to the church authorities; although they were supposed to be holding the kingdom in trust for the Church as the result of a co-operative action of Christian nations, they tended to overlook all this and merely regard themselves as absolute monarchs. There was probably a pious hope in Rome that the Templars might grow into an ecclesiastical army which could be used to dominate the lay aristocracy.

At any rate, having achieved some early successes against Islam, the order was encouraged to the extent that the Pope granted it a constitution, authorized the members to wear a white mantle and allowed its Master, Hugh de Payen, to travel about Europe gathering contributions and recruiting. Wealthy aristocrats were glad to contribute lands and money. Houses were set up in England, France, Italy and Germany for recruitment and administration. Both the King of France and the King of England were on the list of patrons.

A strong partisan of the Templars was the theologian Bernard of Clairvaux. He described the order enthusiastically, saying its members did not hunt or hawk, despised jugglers and wandering minstrels, avoided the theatre, wore their hair short, washed seldom and were always tanned and covered with dust.

The Western beachhead in Jerusalem was, however, continually endangered. It had been conquered in the first place because the Moslem kingdoms were disunited and the Moslem warriors depended on the bow and arrow and lacked the heavy steel equipment of the Europeans. In the decades that followed, however, the Moslems adopted the armament of their enemies and among them stronger and more capable leaders began to arise. They recaptured Edessa in 1144. The Templars at this time were the only effective Western fighting force. Considered the defenders of Jerusalem, the Templars received many gifts from those whose consciences were troubled but who did not wish to endure the hardships of a foreign campaign. At the same time their numbers grew. By the second crusade (organized to defend and extend the Western beachhead in 1146), the Templars were allowed to wear a red cross on the right shoulder and a banner half white and half black. The symbolism of the flag meant that the Templars were white to their friends and black to their enemies.

The Second Crusade, by the bickering and double-crossing which went on among those who took part, demonstrated that the whole enterprise was no more than organized plunder rationalized by religion. A disastrous siege aimed at conquering Damascus failed, probably because one of the leading crusaders was paid off by the garrison. The Templars, however, maintained their record for effective fighting and freedom from corruption.

When Baldwin III was twenty-one he clashed with his strong-minded mother who wanted to split the kingdom with him. Baldwin marched on Jerusalem aided by an army of Templars. Since his mother's partisans deserted her, he entered the city without a struggle. The subsequent action of the Templars revealed that the hopes of Rome had not been realized. Far from being an army which would keep the barons in check, it was beginning to play politics on its own. And indeed the order was growing in strength and gradually beginning to change in character.

Although in the early period of the order some knights entered it only for a time, later it was customary to join for life or only to leave it for an order with stricter vows. Gradually the institution grew more complicated; the houses or presbyteries were supplied with servants and had their own chaplains. The daily life of the Templars was hemmed in by taboos of a traditional magical type. They ate meat only three times a week, did not speak during meals and went to bed still silent. They were supposed to obey every command of the Master as if it came from God. Curiously enough, unlike the medieval laity who always slept naked they were required to wear a shirt and breeches to bed. They were not allowed to leave the house without permission of the Master and their armament was expected to be plain with no gold or silver ornaments. Taboos against women were particularly strong; they were prohibited even from kissing their female relatives.

The courage shown by the Templars was undeniable. The ordinary knight, when he was unhorsed, was carefully preserved by his captor, for the richer he was the more profit there was to be made from him when he was ransomed. Since Templars gave up all their goods to their order and possessed nothing, they paid no ransoms and were generally killed when captured.

Apropos of the phallicism of the medieval fighting man, it is hard to imagine a more monumental symbol than the lance. The technique of lumbering at an opponent and knocking him off his horse with its point was so impractical and so formalized that it is hard to see it as anything but a symbolic penetration with a ten-foot phallus. The absurdity of the whole process is emphasized by the fact that once a warrior was unhorsed he lay prostrate, helpless as a sardine in a can, until he was dragged off for ransom or dispatched with a blow of a poignard by the more mobile man at arms.

In 1161 the whole order was put under the direct control of the Pope at Rome, and this meant that the knights paid no tithes and were permitted to maintain their own churches in which their own chaplains officiated. They had now become an autonomous body, almost a government within governments, a development which always contains the seeds of conflict.

Meanwhile the situation in the East was changing. A generation of crusaders had now been born in the Holy Land. Since they had begun to absorb Eastern ways, a true cultural exchange took place and as the rough Europeans began to dress in silks and satins, eat spiced food, and bathe more frequently, even their religious intolerance weakened. Certain shrines were considered sacred by both faiths, a wonder-working virgin was even worshipped by Christians, Mohammedans and Jews; hatred of heresy was not maintained and, of course, intermarriage took place. Conversely the Moslems became more and more efficient warriors and evidently better administrators, Nureddin united Syria and Damascus, and his successor, the famous Saladin, added Egypt to the gradually consolidating Mohammedan power.

Division of the weakening power of the European invaders increased; the rulers of all four states, Jerusalem, Antioch, the counties of Edessa and Tripoli, were jealous of each other. Alliances were sometimes made with the infidel enemies against Christian rivals. Moreover, with the growth of relationships between Christian and Moslem, trade began to be important, a factor which further weakened enthusiasm for waging relentless war against the non-Christians.

The Templars continued to be fierce fighters but they also quarrelled with the Knights Hospitallers (a rival fighting order), and with the leaders of the Christian states. When at last, after several truces, the peace was broken by Reginald, the one-time king of Antioch, who plundered a Moslem caravan, Saladin struck hard and defeated the European leaders in the battle of Hattin in 1187. The Templars went down bravely and most of their leaders were put to death. Jerusalem was then easily captured.

Not all Templars went to the Holy Land to fight the infidel. As the order grew richer the presbyteries in the various European countries became luxurious establishments in which members of the organization dwelt in comfort. All in all, their number throughout Europe amounted to about 15,000. They were the best equipped military force in the Christian world, their *esprit de corps* was strong, and they held almost as much land as the Church itself. They had become an important political power, even courted by King John of England in his struggle against his barons. Since they were responsible to the Pope alone they could snap their fingers at local church authority and thus they earned the hostility of many important bishops and the other monastic orders. In fact, since they built their own churches and governed them as they pleased, they were accused of defying ecclesiastical rules and bestowing the sacrament on excommunicated individuals. Indeed they were almost above the law.

One other activity added to their wealth. Since they were international in scope with branches in every Western country as well as the Holy Land, they became a repository for church tithes. From this germinal banking operation they went into the business of transferring funds for pilgrims and crusaders from Europe to the Holy Land. As merchants were quick to see the value of this service, the Templars became an institution for the transfer of credit to the East and thus were full-fledged bankers.

In a period marked by struggles between feudal lords and kings who attempted to create a centralized power, the tightly knit organization of the Templars which combined aristocratic, military and financial resources loomed large as a potential rival to the authority of the monarchical state.

The conflict came to a head with the despotic King Philip IV of France who had been instrumental in elevating the weak Clement V to the papacy. Philip, who was always in need of money, eyed the resources of the Templars with greed. He also distrusted their power and professed to believe that they were nurturing a plan to seize his kingdom.

The one-sided conflict which took place is a fantastic example of the way in which primitivism and an essentially modern political struggle were mingled. King Philip, by charging the order with heresy, pressured the Pope into ordering an investigation. In order to make sure that the Templars were condemned the king embarked on a propaganda campaign, aided by the Franciscan and Dominican monastic orders. The charges worked out by the monarch's propagandists, who were themselves monks, are significant for what they reveal of the basic psychological drives in the medieval male celibate. The unfortunate Templars were accused of practising certain rites on the initiation of new members. The new member first stripped naked, was then obliged to spit on the cross and then kissed the officiating Templar, evidently also supposed to be naked, on the navel, the arse and the mouth. The candidate was then obliged to agree to practise sodomy and to worship an idol, variously described.

What is so striking about these accusations is their resemblance to primitive initiation into men's societies. The physical relationship between the neophyte and the officiant reminds us of all the homosexual assaults real or symbolical in puberty rites, and the practice of sodomy takes us back to Malekula. The addition of an idol, while probably pure invention, nevertheless completes the picture of the men's club banded together for its own religious rites, and for its sadistic military activities to the exclusion of women. The dormitory life in the presbytery with its acknowledged food and verbal taboos is entirely in keeping.

King Philip did not wait for the action of the ecclesiastical courts. Since he had a well-organized civil police, he charged the Templars with a secret revolutionary plot and, with an extraordinary efficiency and secrecy which reminds us of the Gestapo, succeeded in imprisoning all the French Templars at one fell swoop.

William Imbert, the head of the Inquisition in France, was a tool of the king and obligingly questioned the Templars with the most extreme tortures. The Dominican order carried these out. To soften a knight up, a cord would be tied around his feet or his hands would be bound behind his back and then pulled over a pulley until he hung in the air. He would then be suddenly released to fall with a crash. Other tortures followed; fire was applied to the feet of the accused, feet and legs were crushed in iron boots or slivers were driven under the nails of fingers or toes.

Under torture nearly all confessed to some or all of the charges. Of the 140 persecuted Templars, six died. Under pressure from the French king, the Pope ordered the Templars tried in other countries. Edward II of England objected but finally ordered trials without torture. None of the accused confessed. In Germany and elsewhere the trials were perfunctory, the accused were not ill-treated and in many cases acquitted. In France, however, the merciless king forced the issue. When the Templars were finally tried in ecclesiastical courts, some of them regained their courage, repudiated their confessions and attempted to defend themselves. Fifty-four were quickly burned, whereupon the defence collapsed. In the end 120 were burned at the stake, some, at the last, protesting their innocence. Pope Clement obediently dissolved the order and its riches passed into King Philip's treasury.

Whether there was really any truth in the charges is doubtful; what is significant is the form they took. Sodomy was probably practised by some of the order and was a natural concomitant of the monastic men's group. Indeed Edith Simon writes, 'Sodomy was not rare in the Middle Ages, and no stigma of effeminacy attached to practices which numbered many adherents among the doughty crusaders and distinguished princes such as (probably) Cœur de Lion and Edward II.' What the brutal tragedy brought to light was the persistence of all the ancient drives in the psyche of the men's group and the contradictions in a Christian rationalization of misogyny which strengthened both passive and active homosexual rejection of women.

The charges against the Templars were also an example of the way in which male anxiety was used for practical purposes to bolster prejudice, for sexual activity and heresy were a standard combination. The word 'bugger', for instance, is derived from the Bogomils, Bulgarian Manicheans, who were so stigmatized by their ecclesiastical enemies. Before long another element was added to the complex of heresy and sex, that of witchcraft, and in this case women were not merely excluded but persecuted, victims of both church politics and male apprehension.

CHAPTER FOURTEEN

The Female Demon

While the fathers of the Christian church carried on and intensified the misogynist tradition on sexual grounds, there was another concept, that of the female demon, which on the one hand has its roots in primitive belief and on the other acquires new life in the late Middle Ages. Although there is no unified line of development, there appears to be a connection between the primitive idea of the female black magician, the Babylonian and Hebrew Lilith, the Greek Empusa, and Lamia, the vampire and eventually the succubus of medieval theology. What unites them is their power to destroy men, either by magically undermining their vitality or by sucking their blood. Sexual seduction may or may not be the method used to gain power over the victim or to drain his potency.

Bronislaw Malinowski stresses the fact that Trobriand witches are far more to be feared than male sorcerers. They are supposed to smell like excrement and are particularly dangerous to mariners.

A witch – and be it remembered that she is always a real woman and not a spiritual or non-human being – goes out on her nightly errand in the form of an invisible double; she can fly through the air and appear as a falling star; she assumes at will the shape of a firefly, of a night bird or of a flying fox; she can hear and smell at enormous distances, she is endowed with sarcophagus propensities, and feeds on corpses.

The disease which witches cause is almost incurable and extremely rapid in its action, killing, as a rule, immediately. It is inflicted by the removal of the victim's insides, which the woman presently consumes. The wizard ... must proceed slowly, and the best he can hope for is to inflict a lingering disease which may, with good luck, kill after months or years of steady labour. Even then another sorcerer can be hired to counteract his work and restore the patient. But there is little chance of combating a witch, even if the help of another witch be sought immediately.

Female witches, therefore, in early and primitive civilizations are especially dangerous and especially skilled in destructive magic. We have already mentioned that one aspect of the fertility goddess is destructive and that even in Sumeria, a representative of Inanna was thought of as a demon, a beautiful and lascivious woman sent to seduce men. In Babylonia she became the original Lilith or Lilu, a night demon. A Babylonian charm refers to

> He whom the handmaid of the night phantom hath wedded,
> The man with whom the handmaid of the night phantom hath union . . .

Indeed the Babylonian charms list a whole series of particularly dangerous female ghosts in whom the sexual functions predominate.

> Or a harlot that hath died in travail,
> Or a woman that hath died with a babe at the breast,
> Or a weeping woman that hath died with a babe at the breast.

Visual evidence, cited by Reginald Campbell Thompson, includes an ancient Babylonian cylinder seal which shows a man copulating with a vampire whose head has been cut off. Thompson writes, 'The idea is I presume to keep off the nocturnal visits of Lilith and her sisters. Just as the prehistoric or early peoples show pictures of their enemies with their heads cut off . . . so will the man troubled by nightly emissions, attributed to Lilith, depict on his amulet the terrors which are in store for these malignants.'

In another charm we find a reference to

> The Lilu, the Lilit, the night Lili,
> Enchantments, disasters, spells,
> Illnesses, evil charms,
> In the name of heaven
> And in the name of the earth
> Let them be exorcised.

A. M. Kitten says this entity is further characterized as the night wraith that has no husband and as an insatiable night vampire.

This is as much information as we get from Babylonia, but the Hebrews, after their Babylonian captivity, brought back with them the names of various demons, among them that of Lilith. In Isaiah xxxiv, 14, the passage, 'The wild beasts of the desert shall also meet with the wild beasts of the island, and the satyr shall cry out to his fellow; the screech owl also shall rest there and find for herself a place to rest,' the word translated in the King James version by screech owl is actually *Lilith*, the night demon. At times she seems to be blended with the Greek Lamia but in the Talmud she begins to acquire a special character because of her affair with Adam. This authority states that Adam after his expulsion from Eden lived with Lilith for thirty years and begot demons. In Hebrew tradition she is believed to kill male children. A spell for exorcising her runs, 'Adam and Eve – Lilith go forth.' The rationalization for her existence is found in the two versions of the origin of men in Genesis. The first creation of men and women is supposed to include Lilith while the second, involving Adam and Eve, is regarded, not as a repetition of the same story, but as second creation of a new race. Still another Hebrew tradition, dating from the tenth century A.D. tells us that Lilith and Adam were made from earth. Adam immediately told her she must obey him. More independent than Eve, however, she replied, 'We are equal; we are made of the same earth.' She then flew up in the air and became a demon which ate children.

Still another Hebrew tale, dating from the seventeenth century, explains that Lilith was created along with Adam and that she tried to attach herself to him but was flung into an abyss. When Adam sinned sexually with Eve, she was let out to become a child cannibal. Still more scandals surround her reputation, for Hebrew lore also records a second marriage which she made with Satan and suggests that she seduced Adam while the snake was performing the same service for Eve. In a sense, therefore, she tends to become the evil *alter ego* of Eve or a projection of the bad mana of the earth mother – significantly, in the Middle Ages she is sometimes called the mother of all things.

It is her cannibal proclivity which links Lilith to the Greek Lamia or Empusa and perhaps this element was borrowed from Greek sources. At any rate the original Lamia was given a specific character by a Greek myth. She was an African queen who lived only for her beauty. She incurred the jealousy of Hera, who killed her children. She was driven mad, became ugly and sought to destroy other women's children. She was also supposed to be able to change her shape.

The story of the Empusa, as told by Plutarch, has a rather psycho-analytical sound. Apollonius of Tyana was famed as a sage and magical expert. A young friend of his, Menippus, met a beautiful woman who said she was a rich Phoenician and had long been in love with him. She invited him to come home to drink with her, hear her sing and share her bed. Apollonius heard about his friend's infatuation and warned him that he was the victim of a demon. Menippus, however, did not take heed and decided to marry the woman. Apollonius was invited to the wedding breakfast. The house was full of splendid furnishings, gold and silver table settings, servants and cupbearers. The sage told Menippus that all was illusion and his bride was a Lamia, a demon able to fall in love and devoted to the delights of Aphrodite, which it used to entice men whose blood it sucked while they slept. The woman tried to check Apollonius but he pointed his golden wand at her forehead and cried, 'Demon, leave this borrowed form!' The gold and silver immediately became light as air and fluttered away; the servants and wine servers vanished and the woman herself turned into a skeleton surmounted by a death's head and fell to the ground. A phantom, half woman, half adder, crawled away.

John Keats, who read the story in Richard Burton's *Anatomy of Melancholy*, contributes a rather baroque description of the Lamia in her serpent form.

> Striped like a zebra, freckled like a pard,
> Eyes like a peacock, and all crimson barred;
> As full of silver moons, that, as she breathed,
> Dissolved, or brighter shone, or interwreathed
> Their lustres with the gloomier tapestries –
> So rainbow-sided, touched with miseries,
> She seemed at once some penanced lady elf,
> Some demon's mistress, or the demon's self.

He goes on to blend female and serpent elements:

> Her head was serpent, but ah, bittersweet!
> She had a woman's mouth with all its pearls complete:
> And for her eyes: what could such eyes do there
> But weep, and weep, that they were born so fair?

Keats calls the young man Lycius and tends to sentimentalize the story. When the Lamia vanishes at Apollonius' stern command the young man is struck down and speedily dies of shock. Love and death were closely interwoven for Keats and thus the Lamia story becomes a perverse fantasy for the expression of his particular talent. The Lamia tradition, on the whole, is responsible for the image of a dangerous demon.

Ludwig Lavater in his treatise *Of Ghostes and Spirites Walking by Nyght* (1572) wrote: 'Lamiae were thought by ancient writers to be women who had the horrid power of removing their eyes or also a kind of demon or ghost. They would appear under the guise of a lovely courtesan or ghost who by their enticing wiles would draw some plump, rosy-cheeked young man into their embraces and then devour him whole.'

Somewhat similar to the Lamia, the vampire embodies a further concept, that of the living dead. Vampires in Slavonic folklore are not predominantly women. A certain sexual element does exist in the sense that the female vampire sucks the blood of a male victim and a male chooses a woman but, on the whole, the concept probably arises from the ancestor worship of the late Stone, Bronze and Iron Age ethnic groups who were converted to Christianity but retained certain beliefs from the past in perverted form. The peoples of Europe and Eurasia who built various stone and barrow graves into which were put elaborate funeral goods are believed to have subscribed to the living corpse concept. In other words, the body maintained a diminished life in the tomb until the flesh had rotted away. Therefore it had to be provided with goods and sometimes recurring festivals took place, feasts which helped provide it with nourishment. Added to this was the idea that the dead might be either harmful or hurtful, might return from the grave in various shapes and either help or attack the living.

The connection between such concepts and the classic vampire belief, in which the body remains undecayed in the grave and even bleeds when wounded, is clear. Instead of returning in animal or spirit form, the living and lethal corpse is able to arise from the grave and suck the blood of living victims in order to continue its twilight existence. The pagan element in the tradition was overlaid with magical Christian concepts such as the common notion that the bodies of extraordinarily holy saints remained uncorrupted. In the case of vampires the converse was supposed to be true, since the bloodsucking menaces were mostly persons who had been excommunicated.

The vampire tradition therefore is not in the direct line of magical misogyny. The Babylonian Lilith, however, who has intercourse with men at night against their will, is more significant. Montague Summers points out that a similar belief is recorded from ancient Mexico about the Civateleo – dead women who compelled handsome young men to copulate with them. This behaviour, of course, is essentially similar to that of the succubus which we shall be discussing in connection with the fifteenth-century witch.

Scylla, Gorgons, Sirens, even the Sphinx could be added to the list of female demons but these assorted monstrosities seem to be no more than incidental products of male fantasy and anxiety and have led to no tradition of importance.

It is the witch who embodies a complete throwback to the most primitive anguish at the same time completely rationalized by Christian theology.

CHAPTER FIFTEEN

'Thou Shalt not
Suffer a Witch to Live . . .'

English witches put beanstalks between their toes and repeated three times:

> Horse and hattock, horse and goe
> Horse and pelattis, ho, ho!

On the strength of this spell they flew off to the sabbat. From the fifteenth century to the seventeenth the belief in organized witch cults flourished in Europe, resulting in some of the most revolting persecution that has ever stained the pages of history. The significance of this activity for our theme is evident for two reasons – the overwhelming majority of the accused witches were women and the whole subject is riddled with sex.

Once again an institutional development in human society is moulded by basic drives and by environmental pressures. Among the latter the position and aims of the medieval Catholic Church play an important role. Curiously, the early Church took the position that witchcraft was imaginary, a heathen illusion fostered by the devil. A synod of 785 A.D. issued the statement that 'if somebody, deceived by the devil, following the custom of the heathen, believes that some man or woman is a striga who eats men, and for that reason burns her or gives her flesh to eat, or eats it, he is to be punished by death'. In other words, the witch burner was to be punished. Another significant statement dating to 900 A.D. explains that 'certain godless women, seduced by the illusions and phantasms of demons, believe and profess that in the night they ride certain beasts in the company of the pagan goddess, Diana, and an innumerable multitude of women and that in the silence and darkness of the night they travel over many lands obeying her commands as their mistress and that on certain nights they are called out to serve her. . . .'

In this document are overtones of the evil earth mother and of course it indicates that survivals of paganism were still extant in Europe. Picking up this clue, both Margaret Murray and Arne Runeberg have developed a more or less anthropological thesis to prove that the witch cult was a widespread anti-Christian religion. Runeberg points out that during the period from the thirteenth to the fifteenth centuries the rise of Manichean heresy became a real threat to Catholic domination of Europe. As a result of persecution, the heretics retreated and continued underground activity in Rumania, Bosnia, southern France and northern Italy. Runeberg holds that survivals of the pagan religions of the Teutons, the Romans and the Greeks, mostly in magical form, existed among European peasants and that these popular beliefs tended to amalgamate with those of the heretics, creating a secret faith with its own rituals. Some of the Manicheans adored both good and evil powers and some were told to profane the holy water and to hate the cross because it tortured Christ, practices which were also followed by the witches.

Margaret Murray goes further. Being under the spell of the rather romantic anthropology of the early twentieth century stemming from Sir James Frazer, she sees the witch cult as a fertility religion complete with killing of the god. The fact that it was generally directed towards destroying fertility and ruining harvests she explains as degeneration. One weakness of this idea is that there was no blanket fertility cult throughout Europe when Christianity spread over Italy, Germany, France and Greece. Greece, it is true, retained the earth mother in the guise of Demeter. Persephone or Diana but the Teutons worshipped predominantly male warrior gods, as did the Celts. Roman religion had some vegetation spirits but laid a great deal of stress upon the Aryan warriors, Mars, Jupiter and Quirinus. Druid priests were male as were Roman Flamines and Teutonic sacred chiefs who carried out sacrifices in the men's house or banqueting hall. The background of pagan religion in Europe, therefore, does not explain a cult predominantly composed of women.

Runeberg's ingenious blending of Manicheans and peasant magic can also be criticized on the grounds that the Church at first made a clear distinction between witches and heretics though it burned both. Heretics *disagreed* with official doctrine and laid the basis of individualism and Protestantism; witches *accepted* all of Catholic dogma and merely reversed it, worshipping evil instead of good mana.

The notion of an actual organized anti-Catholic religion is also not very convincing because it rests upon analogy and ultimately entirely on evidence from witch trials gathered under duress and torture from the unfortunate victims. As Murray admits, 'The actual feelings of witches towards their religion have been recorded in very few cases.'

Finally, as will be seen, the nature of witchcraft as described in ecclesiastical documents includes the wildest fantasy whose character is best illustrated by Hieronymus Bosch at his weirdest. It is true that witchcraft and heresy were eventually blended in Catholic thinking, but it seems likely that the tensions arising from the Church's struggle with dissent triggered the deepest anxieties in a male clergy which had transformed the men's house into a monastery and had equated heterosexual activity with sin. We have already cited the case of the Knights Templars which shows how these same compulsions were ingeniously exploited by self-interest. A still more pertinent example is the story of the Stedingers, the inhabitants of Stedingen, the modern Oldenberg. In 1219 this people quarrelled with their overlord, the Bishop of Bremen, over land taxes and hunting rights. The bishop, when they refused to obey him, proclaimed them heretics and ordered a crusade against them. In some skirmishes they successfully defended themselves against the bishop's hirelings. A quarrel then ensued in which a priest was killed. This enabled the bishop to persuade Pope Gregory to preach a crusade against the Stedingers in 1232. His bull charged them with attending sabbats at which the devil appeared as a toad, a black cat or a half-man, half-cat, and had intercourse with all present. The Templars were also accused of worshipping the devil as a black cat and the more elaborate sabbats described in the fifteenth-century persecution (which we shall discuss later) also included these elements. It is clear, therefore, that the Church was developing standard charges against those whom it considered its enemies long before there was any talk of an organized witchcraft movement. The charges worked effectively against the Stedingers; five bishops united against them and annihilated them.

Many of the fundamental magical practices mentioned in the fifteenth-century records are universal among primitives and only go to show that they continued to be a part of European folk culture (indeed some still persist today). As such they were a part of the background of the ecclesiastic as well as the layman. It is not surprising that church authorities drew on them for their descriptions of sorcery or that accused witches, knowing what was expected of them, also made use of the same superstition in their confessions. That some of them actually believed in magic is also probable. It must be remembered, however, that the interrogators, torturers, and officials of the Inquisition were all men, with opportunities for putting leading questions and elaborating the records. Modern political inquisitions have shown us what satisfactory confessions can be extracted in an atmosphere of hysteria without even using the rack or thumbscrew. It is extremely unlikely that the women of Europe organized and developed a secret cult with branches everywhere. The whole affair has the stamp of male fantasy.

The most important document revealing the real meaning of the witchcraft mania is the *Malleus Maleficarum*. In 1484 Innocent VIII issued a special papal bull empowering two Dominican monks, Jacob Sprenger and Heinrich Krämer, to try witches in northern Germany. Since inquisitors met with some resistance, they composed a handbook, the *Malleus*, and more or less forced the faculty of the University of Cologne to endorse it in 1486. It was also given full legal support by Maximilian, King of Rome. It became the leading text of the Inquisition and went through no less than nineteen editions, being translated into German. This horrifying text, which had a tremendous influence, reveals, with all the rationalizing ingenuity of medieval scholasticism, the alleged facts of witchcraft and prescribes what shall be done about it.

In the first place the *Malleus* proves the existence of witches by pointing out that the Bible states there are devils and that devils can do wonderful things. From this it follows that 'it is useless to argue that any result of witchcraft may be a phantasy and unreal because such a phantasy cannot be procured without the power of devils, and it is necessary that there should be made a contract with the devil by which contract the witch truly and actually binds herself to be the servant of the devil and devotes herself to the devil. . . .'

Six out of the seven chapters of the treatise deal with sex. From the beginning the book states, 'But if it be asked why the devil is allowed to cast spells upon the venereal act, rather than upon any other human act, . . . for the present the reason that has been mentioned before must suffice, namely that the power of the devil lies in the privy parts of men.' The devil acts through incubi, male witches, and succubi, female witches. As we have already pointed out, the succubus seems to be derived from the Lilith of Babylonia, the Lamia, and is even related to the vampire. Richard Burton describes the nightmare as follows in *The Anatomy of Melancholy*: 'Such as are troubled with succubus, or witch ridden (as we call it) if they lie on their backs, they suppose an old woman rides and sits so hard upon them they are almost stifled for want of breath.' The experience often ends in an orgasm. Ernest Jones points out, 'The explanation for these fantasies is surely not hard. A nightly visit from a beautiful or frightful being who first exhausts the sleeper with passionate embraces and withdraws from him a vital fluid: all this can point only to a natural and common process, namely to nocturnal emissions accompanied by dreams of a more or less erotic nature. In the unconscious mind blood is commonly an equivalent for semen.' Thus the basic charge against the witch as a night demon and seducer springs clearly from the experiences of a repressed and celibate male clergy. The *Malleus* goes on, however, to explain, on the basis of the best authority, why women tend to be witches. First comes a resounding quote from St John Chrysostom. 'It is not good to marry. What else is woman but a foe to friendship, an inescapable punishment, a necessary evil, a natural temptation, a desirable calamity, a delectable detriment, an evil of nature, painted with fair colours.' After this blast, which is considered convincing evidence, the handbook goes on to point out, 'wherefore in the many vituperations that we read against women, the word woman is used to mean the lust of the flesh'.

More proof follows. 'Perfidy is more found in women than in

men . . . since they are feebler in body and in mind, it is not surprising they should come under the spell of witchcraft.' And
furthermore, 'she is more carnal than man as is clear from her many
carnal abominations'. Here at last the old magical fear peeps out.
'All witchcraft comes from carnal lust which in women is insatiable.'
'For although the devil tempted Eve, yet Eve seduced Adam.'
Finally a significant paraphrase from Proverbs rounds out the score.
'There are three things that are never satisfied, yea a fourth which
says not, it is enough, that is the mouth of the womb.' Fear of the
female organ could not be more plainly stated.

The worthy inquisitors go on to explain that witches infect the
venereal act by turning men's minds to inordinate passion, by ob-
structing the generative force, by causing abortions, etc. 'More men
than women are bewitched in respect of that action.' On this point
they quote Peter of Palude: 'He says that such obstruction generally
occurs in the seminal duct or in the inability in the matter of erection
which can more easily happen to men, and therefore more men than
women are bewitched. It might also be said that the greater part of
witches being women, they lust more for men than for women.' As
if this acknowledgment of the fear of impotence were not enough,
careful distinctions follow. 'When the member is in no way stirred
and can never perform the act of coition, this is a sign of frigidity
of nature; but when it is stirred and becomes erect, yet cannot
perform, it is a sign of witchcraft.' The manual makes a practical
point which has to do with marriage. 'Impotence caused by witchcraft is either temporary or permanent. If it is temporary it does not
annul the marriage.'

Still more clearly a product of the basic male anxiety is the hys-
terical fear of castration. 'It is asked whether witches can, with the
help of devils, remove the member or whether they can do so
apparently by some glamour or illusion. Since devils can actually do
greater things than this . . . therefore they can also truly and actually
remove men's members.' In other cases the loss of the phallus is an
illusion 'so that it seems to him that he can see and feel nothing but
a smooth body with its surface interrupted by no genital organ'.

Clearly sex repression among a celibate clergy had created fantasies of a most malignant kind. Again and again we are told that

the Church is severely threatened by the witches' organizations. The disturbance surrounding sex resulted in other types of castration fancies. Since the venereal sin was the greatest of all, actual castration was sometimes a help. A certain abbot 'was in his youth greatly troubled by the provocation of the flesh. . . . For a remedy against the affliction an Angel appeared to him one night and seemed to make him an eunuch and it seemed to him in his vision that all feeling was taken away from his genital organs, and from that time he was such a stranger to temptation as if he had no sex in his body.' Another monk, named Helias, was in charge of thirty nuns but began to be troubled by the flesh. He fled to a hermitage and prayed for help. Three angels came to him, one seemed to hold his hands, another his feet, while a third cut out his testicles with a knife. He returned to his nuns 'and never again had a quiver of sex'. Fear of sex was so great that Blessed Thomas when tempted by a harlot seized a lighted torch 'and drove the engine of lust from its prison', after which he had no trouble.

Members of the laity, however, were not so heroic and were content to blame their irrationality on witches. A young man who had lost his member and suspected a certain woman, tied a towel about her neck, choked her and demanded to be cured. 'The witch touched him with her hand between the thighs saying, "Now you have your desire." ' His member was immediately restored.

The wildest story of all, which could scarcely be matched by the primitives of the South Seas, is even funny until we remember that on the basis of such ideas helpless women were tortured and burned to death. 'And what then is to be thought of those witches who in this way sometimes collect male organs, as many as twenty or thirty members together, and put them in a bird's nest or shut them up in a box, where they move themselves like living members and eat oats and corn, as has been seen by many as is a matter of common report? . . . For a certain man tells that when he had lost his member, he approached a known witch to ask her to restore it to him. She told the afflicted man to climb a certain tree, and that he might take which he liked out of a nest in which there were several members. And when he tried to take a big one, the witch said: you must not take that one, adding, because it belongs to the parish priest.'

Most of the ancient beliefs concerning the dangers of women's sexuality which we have seen attributed to them by the primitives turn up in the *Malleus*. They are charged with being able to prevent animal and fruit increase. They are also accused of drying up milking cows, souring milk, spoiling wine, etc., all activities which are traditionally caused by menstruation. It will be remembered that Pliny also stated that a menstruating woman could control storms. Witches were able to create them. A witch who had copulated with an incubus devil for more than eighteen years poured a little water in a hole under a tree and stirred it with her finger, thus causing a storm. She confessed to this act 'after being exposed to the very gentlest questions, being suspended hardly clear of the ground by her thumbs'!

As might be expected, the witch was supposed to derive much of her power from copulating with the devil. 'Witches themselves have often been seen lying on their backs in the fields or the woods, naked up to the very navel, and it has been apparent from the disposition of those limbs and members which pertain to the venereal act and the orgasm, also from the agitation of their legs and thighs that, all invisibly to the bystanders, they have been copulating with incubus devils.'

For descriptions of the sexual orgy of the sabbat we turn to the *Compendium Maleficarum*, written by Francesco Maria Guazzo in 1608. Much of it is a recapitulation of material in the *Malleus* but another twenty-five years of the witchcraft hysteria has added madder details.

In the first place, the whole fantasy of flight, as Ernest Jones points out, is an unconscious symbol of erotic excitation. The method of flight is also significant. The staff, broomstick, distaff or shovel is sometimes said to have been rammed up the anus of the witch, at other times she sat astride it. Once more we have an image of the phallic woman so menacing to men.

The sabbat itself is described in great detail. The group of predominantly female worshippers first greeted the devil, usually by kissing his anus, upon which there was often a second face, in true Bosch style. In the Pyrenees, in a more elaborate ceremony, they kissed his face, his navel, his penis, his anus. The devil himself, or witchmaster, could appear as an old man in black, a young man, a buck, a goat, a dog or some other animal. All the suppressed hostilities towards the bonds of Catholic ritual were expressed in descriptions of the scatological parody said to take place in the nocturnal festival. The celebrants offered pitch-black candles which the devil lit by farting upon them. Water with which they were anointed he created by urinating in a hole in the ground. Dances took place in which the worshippers always moved to the left and danced back to back 'to the sound of a bawdy pipe and tabor played by one seated in the fork of a tree'. A banquet was eaten provided by the devil himself or consisting of a picnic lunch the worshippers had brought along, 'but all who have sat down to such tables confess that the feasts are all foul, either in appearance or in smell, so that they nauseate the most ravenously hungry stomach'. A parody of the mass was often supposed to be carried out, a naked woman's body being used for the altar, the host being kneaded of faeces, urine and menstrual blood upon her buttocks. The grand climax of the orgy took place when the devil personally had intercourse with all present.

Scholasticism went into problems of supernatural sex in some detail. The devil's semen was always ice cold for a good reason. He had none himself and was first obliged to obtain some by copulating with a human male in the form of a succubus. Most curious but psychologically significant were the detailed accounts of the devil's penis. 'The devil has a member made of horne or at least it looks that way. That is why it makes women cry out so loudly.' Another version describes it as half an ell (23 inches) in length, of medium thickness, twisted, very rough and seemingly sharp. Still other versions said it was as long as an ell, sinuous, and twisted in the shape of a snake, or had scales, was cold as ice and burned like fire when it was withdrawn. All agreed that this fantastic instrument caused great pain to the worshippers.

The blatant phallic sadism in all of this makes it very clear that it was the product of the pathological imagination of the medieval male. On the one hand he relished the idea of being obscenely worshipped by a crowd of women, and on the other in his disturbed imagination he expressed his hostility by attacking them with the familiar penis as weapon. We are led back to the Australian trickster whose phallus is so large it breaks a girl's legs and pierces her heart.

So far we have been outlining the relatively minor crimes of fifteenth-century witches. They were also believed to cause disease and death, apart from the general charge of eating young children. As the *Malleus* points out, 'For when a cook of the Archduke had married an honest girl from a foreign country, a witch who had been his mistress met them in the public road and, in the hearing of other honest people, foretold his bewitching and death.' The man immediately died. We are also told, 'But among others there was a well-known gentleman, whom his mistress wished to come to her on one occasion to pass the night; but he sent a servant to tell her he could not visit her because he was busy. She promptly flew into a rage, and said to the servant: go tell your master that he will not trouble me for long. On the very next day he was taken ill and was buried within a week.' Typically both men perished because of a woman's sexual demands.

The attack upon the female sex which took place in the period we are discussing seems to represent a regression to primitive magical fear which is truly astonishing. In its unbalanced character it is far less civilized than the mythological attitudes of the Greeks or the Hebrews. In the past uncomfortable and harassing restrictions had been laid upon women, but the Inquisition destroyed them with sadistic ferocity. The *Malleus* and other sources tell us of the methods used. The witch was to be racked and made to suffer all the tortures prescribed by the law because 'the evils which are perpetrated by modern witches exceed all other sins which God has ever permitted to be done'. Judges could use any sort of deception in order to wring a confession from the accused. Although even a penitent witch was destined to be destroyed, the judge was empowered to promise to spare her. Then a different judge could be brought in who would see to her execution. 'Others think that after she has been consigned to prison, the promise to spare her life should be kept for a time, but that after a certain period she should be burned.' No respect was used towards the person of the poor woman. 'The hair should be shaved from every part of her body. The reason for this is the same as that for stripping her of her clothes; for in order to preserve their power of silence they are in the habit of hiding some superstitious object in their clothes, or in their hair, or in the most secret part of their bodies which must not be named' (but which was obviously handled by the court officers). Their bodies were also examined to learn if the mark of the devil could be seen on their breasts or private parts. In New England in particular it was considered to be a teat or nipple. Still another infallible test arose from the fact that some spot on a witch's body was supposed to be insensible to pain. Professional 'prickers' drove pins into the skin of the unfortunate victim. It was also believed that witches could not weep, hence if torture extracted no tears the accused was automatically guilty.

The tradition of the witch of course lingered on in folklore, and even in fairy tales the same menacing overtones persist. The villainess of the Hänsel and Gretel story is still a child cannibal. Runeberg points out, 'The ghastliness of the woods appears in the language of the tales, above all in the notion of the magic forest. No road leads out of it. It holds a man a captive once he has strayed into it until he has overcome or propitiated the powers operating there.' It might be added that the witch's house is also a trap which destroys the unwary captive. Thus the symbol of the dangerous female organ is spread over both the dark aperture of the wood and the receptacle of the house, an unchanging threat to male virility.

CHAPTER SIXTEEN

The Serpent of the Nile

Despite the aberration of witchcraft persecution, the Renaissance woman, as seen by men, gains in stature. The theatre, which provides a gallery of portraits, shows us many lively, intelligent and independent females. The girls and women who speak for themselves in the Elizabethan plays are not faceless symbols of evil or fantasy images of male self-indulgence. A Portia, a Bess Bridges, or a Duchess of Malfi is a well-rounded figure, outspoken, energetic and far from passive in the erotic relationship. One great character, however, draws on elements of the ancient misogyny and at the same time is a stereotype, an image which becomes a part of western culture – Shakespeare's Cleopatra, the embodiment of the *femme fatale*.

Unlike the case of Cressida, when the great playwright draws the Egyptian queen, the old brutal and magical charges against women are raised to a new level and with rare penetration are dramatized from a psychological point of view which is far in advance of the age.

There are of course many levels in the play. Antony's fall is treated with mythological overtones. He is the last of the divine heroes, identified with Mars at the beginning of the play, and it is also suggested that he stands in a special relation to the semi-divine Hercules. Both he and Cleopatra endeavour to maintain high tragedy in bursts of beautiful rhetoric but their actions always belie their words. Antony is unable to sustain the exalted destiny of a hero because he is a modern man. He has lost his divinity with the increasing secularization of his time. Like most ordinary men he prefers the hedonism of the moment to the heroic commitment; all his great feats lie in the past. Instead of destroying monsters and saving his people, sacrificing himself in the process, he quarrels with Cleopatra in the boudoir. His weakness is clearly stated when it is said that like a boy he pawns experience to the present pleasure.

The framework of his downfall in its broad outlines is, however, the sexually destructive woman. His enemies call Cleopatra a whore and consider him her victim. Caesar describes his demoralization scathingly: 'To tumble on the bed of Ptolemy', and likewise 'To give a kingdom for a mirth . . . to reel the streets at noon.' Pompey is surprised that even news of war

> Can from the lap of Egypt's widow pluck
> The ne'er-lust-wearied Antony.

And further, hoping for his overthrow, brings up the idea of magic. 'Let witchcraft join with beauty, lust with both!' Antony himself remarks, 'I must from this enchanting queen break off' as he vacillates between past glories and present pleasures. Her love is thought of in every way destructive and deeply identified with sensuality. The talk of her women points up the bawdiness of the court. Charmian inquires, 'Well, if you were but an inch of fortune better off than I, where would you choose it?' and Iras answers, 'Not in my husband's nose.' Cleopatra herself says to the eunuch Mardian, 'I take no pleasure in aught a eunuch has.' The famous speech describing Cleopatra's barge of course stresses her irresistible sexuality. Still another element in the outline of the story has ancient overtones. Antony is always presented with a choice between war and Cleopatra. At times he rejects war but when he does go forth to battle, he is beaten. Although Cleopatra has a specific role to play in these episodes, in a more general sense the magic rule applies – abstinence before battle; the men's group should have no commerce with women. Antony expressly disregards this precept when, after the defeat at Actium, he plunges into another drunken feast which is to end with an erotic debauch with Cleopatra. Actually Antony's defection at Actium, his retreat to follow Cleopatra, is never justified psychologically. He tells her, 'My heart was to thy rudder tied by the strings,' but this does not explain his action. He is in the grip of a magic which dooms him to defeat, the evil magic of female sexuality.

So much is traditional, magical and mythological. It is in the character of Cleopatra that Shakespeare reveals new depths of insight. The question is sometimes asked: Did she really love Antony? It is an indication of the rich ambiguity with which she is drawn. In the very first scene of Act One, in which his followers characterize her as a lustful gypsy, she is shown playing the familiar game of tantalizing her lover by asking, 'If it be love indeed, tell me how much?' She does not expect to receive an adequate answer; no woman ever does. The question is born of restless dissatisfaction; it is a symptom of undefined anxiety. Antony finally replies by a spirited defence of erotic indulgence but Cleopatra's response is the aside: 'Excellent falsehood! Why did he marry Fulvia and not love her? – I'll seem the fool I am not . . .' The question is justified, Antony does have a wife, whom he has abandoned, and the image of Fulvia contributes to Cleopatra's other apprehensions. 'I'll seem the fool I am not' is deeply significant. Cleopatra is clearly Antony's intellectual superior. There is no subtlety in his character; all through the play, he is no more than a beefy soldier, a fine hunk of man who appeals strongly to Cleopatra's senses. He knows very well what the world considers his duty but he prefers immediate self-indulgence. He is generous to his followers and capable of rages when he feels he has been betrayed. He deceives himself naïvely when he has lost everything and at the last is able to summon up the courage which his position and his education demand. In contrast Cleopatra is high-strung, fluent as quicksilver, full of second thoughts and calculations, able to entertain two ideas at the same time.

The opening conflict in the play arises from the fact that news of war and messengers from Rome suggest that Antony will leave Egypt. Cleopatra reacts violently. At first she ironically urges him to listen to the messenger, at which point he refuses. When he changes his mind she is furious, brings up Fulvia, and tells him to leave her. The second messenger, however, brings news of Fulvia's death. Antony, who has made up his mind to return to Rome, accuses Cleopatra of being 'cunning past man's thought' and Enobarbus seconds the statement by saying ironically that her sighs and tears are storms and tempests. But is Cleopatra cunning? In the scene in which Antony breaks the news that his wife is dead, we would expect some indications of relief on her part or that she might be tactful enough to show some token signs of sympathy. But she starts the scene by saying she is sick, begins to rail at him and berate the image of Fulvia, and when she hears the news of Fulvia's death there is no change of mood. Without a pause she sarcastically tells him to weep for Fulvia and says his lack of tears show how he will behave at Cleopatra's death. In fact she taunts him unbearably until he lashes out at her and she replies with still more biting wishes for his success when he returns to Rome. This scene does not reveal cunning on her part. Indeed, earlier in the play when she ordered her courtier to go to Antony and 'If you find him sad, say I am dancing; if in mirth report that I am sudden sick,' she was criticized by Charmian, who said it was no way to hold a man. Cleopatra professes to believe it is, but we are not convinced that there is method in this hostility. Indeed her state of mind is best revealed by one particular speech in the farewell scene.

> Sir, you and I must part, but that's not it:
> Sir, you and I have loved, but there's not it;
> That you know well: something it is I would, –
> O! my oblivion is a very Antony,
> And I am all forgotten.

Now the threat of Fulvia (which we begin to suspect was only a club with which to beat Antony) has been removed. If Antony returns to Rome, it is to settle his political interests and maintain his power against aggression on the part of Caesar and Pompey. Egypt's freedom depends upon his success. The separation need not be drastic or final. We begin to realize that there is much more to Cleopatra's outbursts than appears on the surface. And in the line 'Something it is I would, –' followed by a pause and a conventional complaint, her own confusion is revealed. Here she obviously gropes for expression to feelings or thoughts which she cannot put into words.

In the final scene of Act One, still another side of Cleopatra is portrayed and that is her ability to dramatize herself. She sends Antony a messenger every day. When Charmian ironically praises Julius Caesar, Cleopatra savagely threatens to bloody her teeth. In short, she is dramatizing her love in a violent and imperious way.

Whom is she trying to convince, Antony or herself? It will be seen that the question 'Did she really love Antony?' cannot be answered simply even though she announces she would like to 'Sleep out the great gap of time that Antony is away.'

We follow Antony's bargainings, his coldly political marriage to Octavia in order to maintain himself in power. From the mythological point of view this is a further degradation of the hero. Instead of sweeping all before him he is reduced to splitting the territory with the other gangsters. Cleopatra's reception of the news of his marriage takes place in the savage scene in which she beats the messenger. The messenger is of course an unfortunate surrogate upon whom is discharged the hostility which she feels for Antony. That she has behaved compulsively she herself realizes. 'These hands do lack nobility, that they strike a meaner than myself . . .' Later when she greedily punishes herself with more details of Octavia's appearance, she uses an interesting image to describe Antony, 'Though he be painted one way like a Gorgon, t'other way he's Mars.' By the mechanism of projection she describes him in terms of her own ambivalence.

When Antony has quarrelled with Caesar and Pompey, and, back in Egypt, is making ready to war with his former allies, the symbolic action comes to a head as Cleopatra insists on taking part in the sea battle. Enobarbus objects, in an aside, with a soldier's grossness but still echoing, in a sense, the ancient superstition of the men's group.

> If we should serve with horse and mares together,
> The horse were merely lost; the mares would bear
> A soldier and his horse.

When she is told that in Rome they say the war is run by a eunuch and her handmaidens she replies furiously:

> Sink Rome, and their tongues rot
> That speak against us! A charge we bear i' the war,
> And, as the president of my kingdom, will
> Appear there for a man.

It is a part of Antony's vulnerability to destructive female magic that he allows the Egyptian queen to talk him into a sea battle when he is advised that he is better prepared on land.

Why then did Cleopatra 'when vantage like a pair of twins appeared, both as the same, or rather ours the elder', hoist sail and fly?
Interestingly enough, Cleopatra is speechless and has no real explanation after faintly asking for pardon. For once she is completely
subdued. When Antony with a flash of insight tells her, 'You did
know how much you were my conqueror', she merely weeps. Her
defencelessness is one more proof that her action was not calculated.
This was the turning point of Antony's fortunes at which she
destroyed him and, whether she realized it or not, herself as
well.

We have spoken of the ambiguity of Cleopatra's character. What
does she really want from Antony? Does she know herself? She is,
after all, a queen; which means that she fills a man's position. She
is also an emancipated woman; she had another lover before Antony
and in sexual matters she is as free as any male. On the other hand
hers is a second-rate kingdom which has been and is always in
danger of being dominated by Rome. Indeed Rome and Antony,
with Antony sometimes identified with Rome, are the two male
images against which she continually rebels. When Antony leaves
for Rome in the beginning of the play the identification is complete
and her attacks upon her lover express her deeper disturbances. For
this reason, nothing he says satisfies her. Tied to him by sexual
attraction she, at the same time, is a queen; she is superior to him,
aware of a position which supports her masculine protest. Yet she
cannot behave like the man she would like to be; her temperament
and upbringing force her to use feminine devices. 'Music, food of
us that trade in love,' she says at one point, showing clearly that she
feels she must exploit her attractions. From this sense of weakness
springs her pouting and sulking and tantalizing of her lover. She
must always demand proofs of his love although there is no proof
that would ever satisfy her because her own unconscious wishes can
never be clear to her; hence the despairing "Something it is I
would . . .'

Her hostility is expressed both by treating Antony to bouts of
temperament and by smothering him with liquor and sex. She
knows very well what is said of him in Rome and at times she identifies with and exults in his martial prowess yet at the same time does

everything to destroy his greatness and prevent him from retaining his position of power in the world.

Finally in the most revealing speech of all she describes what she did when he was drunk and in her power.

> That time! – O times! –
> I laughed him out of patience: and that night
> I laughed him into patience; and next morn
> Ere the ninth hour, I drunk him to his bed;
> Then put my tires and mantles on him, whilst
> I wore his sword Phillipan . . .

Here, indeed the symbolic image of castration is clearly expressed. The whole passage is in the same tone, for she put a salt fish on his hook, which, though a joke, was also meant to degrade the hero.

With all of these clues in mind, the episode of Actium becomes much clearer. Here she actually speaks of behaving as a man and representing her people in war. She insists on leading the fleet and competing with Antony. Her flight from the sea battle is caused therefore not by cowardice (nothing in her behaviour shows her to be a coward), but from the fierce unconscious impulse to make sure that Antony fails. Having achieved this, she does not really understand why she did it, hence her silence. It is at this point that Antony dimly senses something in their relationship when he says, 'You did know how much you were my conqueror', and indeed he is right although she does not know it consciously. Throughout the whole stormy relationship, however, Cleopatra is torn first one way and then another by her ambivalence. After this very scene, when she has destroyed him, they kiss and once more are lovers. Later, however, she asks Enobarbus if she or Antony is to blame. The soldier takes the stern men's group point of view that Antony has betrayed himself. But Cleopatra by now realizes that all is lost.

She is faced by still another choice, however, when Caesar offers her terms if she will give up Antony. She is offered an out, for Caesar explains he believes she was intimidated by Antony. Once again she shows herself ready to destroy Antony by accepting the deal. And yet when her lover creates a wild but futile scene in which he vows to join battle again, she applauds him and goes back into his arms.

After the last battle, when Antony's Egyptian fleet surrenders, he has reached a point where he blames her for everything, convinced that treachery was prearranged. Actually, judging by Caesar's previous speeches, she is not to be blamed. Fearing his anger, she resorts again to her feminine deceit by sending a message that she is dead and carefully stipulating that she be told how he takes her death. At the very last she again vacillates and sends to tell him she is not dead – when it is too late and he has fallen on his sword. After the duet in the monument (where both are granted all the graces of poetry as they attempt to rise to tragedy), once Antony is dead, Cleopatra is left with her typical indecisions. The only action left which will resolve her conflicts is identification with her lost lover; she can rise to the male dignity of suicide and this after some weakness and hesitation she does. With Antony gone, her comment is, 'Shall I abide in this dull world, which in thy absence is no better than a sty?' Although she has not succeeded in living with him, there is nothing left to live for without him.

All in all, Cleopatra has loved Antony after her fashion, in the only way a highly neurotic woman could love a man for whom passion was balanced with hostility. If, in the long run, she castrated him, poisoning his will, and weaving her sexual magic around him like a net, Shakespeare has instinctively shown us why, by dramatizing her conflicts.

In doing this the playwright has created an image of the modern neurotic woman and essentially preferred all the charges which we shall encounter later when women have arrived at a state of relative freedom in which nevertheless the old difficulties still survive.

Shakespeare's transcendent insight is underlined when we compare his play with Dryden's treatment of the same theme. In *All For Love* there are no psychological shadings. Cleopatra has but one action throughout, to keep Antony with her. She is ready to die with him and does. In fact, by the introduction of the wife, Octavia, and the two children who run to Antony and cry 'Father!' Dryden manages to reduce the action to a kind of bourgeois story of adultery. Antony himself, who sighs, blushes and weeps, impresses us as far more of a pseudoclassical shepherd than a rough old warrior sucked dry by an insatiable woman. Dryden adds nothing to the character of the *femme fatale* because the motivations of his characters are conventional rather than felt. Cleopatra is conceived as single-mindedly and selfishly romantic and the play proceeds by balanced scenes of emotional rhetoric, in the French style, to pit love against duty. In only one speech do we hear an echo of the traditional fear of the sexually dangerous woman. This speech is placed in the mouth of Dolabella, Antony's companion in arms, who says:

> When all the sap was needful for the trunk
> When it went down, then you constrained the course,
> And robbed from nature to supply desire. . . .

In other words, demands upon Antony's potency have destroyed his military valour.

CHAPTER SEVENTEEN

The Bosom Snake

Since John Milton was a theological poet whose experiences with women were publicly unsatisfactory, we should expect him to make contributions to the tradition of misogyny in terms of revealing imagery. He not only does this but also dramatizes the psychological conflicts which ravaged him with startling clarity, conflicts which mirror the larger ones of his time.

On the one hand he was brought up in the Puritan religion, a faith full of the austere intensity of a pioneer movement and still retaining much of the compulsive spirit of the medieval clerical outlook. On the other hand the tradition of courtly eroticism, reinforced by Renaissance humanism, also exerted its pull. He seems to have been a nervous child, afflicted by eye trouble, and very early in life exhibited a talent for verse. In Cambridge he developed a strong attachment to a gay and worldly young man of Italian extraction, Charles Diodati. To him he could write:

> Trust me my joy is great that thou should'st be
> Though born of foreign race, yet born for me.

Throughout his career at Cambridge we learn of his ambivalence towards women. During a vacation he described London girls as follows: 'Here often one may see groups of maidens go by, stars breathing soft flames.' Despite this curiously abstract emotional excitement, in the same letter to his friend he explains that he intends 'to keep far away from the ill-famed halls of the treacherous Circe, using the help of the divine plant of moly'. Moly, he elsewhere explains, is an herb which nullifies enchantment. He also made it quite clear that he shrank from the hearty masculinity of most of his fellow students who ate greedily, indulged in horseplay,

167

and proved their virility in brothels. In short, his passively homo-sexual potential kept him from women and, as we shall see, was translated into a glorification of chastity, an ideal which he combined with Platonism.

Milton, through his contact with the musican Henry Lawes, was drawn into composing the courtly masque of *Comus*. This work in terms of elegant rhetoric quite clearly dramatizes his own feelings. Comus, we are told, is the son of Circe, and like her possesses the power of turning human beings into beasts. The heroine of the piece is the Lady, a virgin who has lost her brothers in the forest. Much is made of the fact that she is a virgin. Now it is a rather striking fact that Milton was called 'the Lady' by fellow students. In the poem Milton's heroine is captured by Comus and his bestial rabble and urged to drink a magic liquid.

> List, Lady; be not coy, and be not cosen'd
> With that same vaunted name, Virginity. . . .
> What need a vermeil-tinctured lip for that,
> Love-darting eyes, or tresses like the morn?

To this invitation to sex, she replies

> Thou hast nor ear, nor soul to apprehend
> The sublime notion and high mystery
> That must be uttered to unfold the sage
> And serious doctrine of Virginity. . . .

After many lines of rhetorical argument, the Lady's two brothers rush in with drawn swords, break the glass and save her from a fate worse than death. Milton's identification with his subject could not be plainer. Although he was writing in the courtly tradition, his theme is chastity and the beastliness of sex. The same image he had used to describe his own temptations, that of Circe, reappears and, in all innocence, the threatened virgin is a girl. It is scarcely far fetched to suggest that the two brothers unconsciously symbolize his Platonic male comrades.

Milton continued to praise virginity and to reject temptation during his trip through Italy, and when his friend Charles Diodati died in 1638, composed a prose epitaph which vibrates with more personal feeling than almost anything else he wrote.

'Because the flush of innocence and stainless youth were dear to thee, because thou did'st not know the joys of marriage, lo, for thee virginal honours are reserved. Thou, with thy bright head haloed in glory, and carrying in thy hand a leafy canopy of joyous palms, shalt to all eternity take part in nuptial songs. . . .' Thus his love for Charles is blended with his own compulsive chastity as he identifies with his friend and both are translated to a Platonic paradise. Milton's biographer, James Hanford, discreetly remarks, 'His concern with chastity and the quality of his friendship with Diodati suggest an ascetic inclination. . . .' Actually his ambivalent nature, his fear of women and sex, taken together with the religious tradition which dominated his mind (he had carefully studied the early church fathers) was pushing him in the direction of celibacy. Yet not quite, for he did not reject marriage. He wrote that celestial Christian songs were 'to others inapprehensible but not to those who were not defiled with women, which doubtless means fornication, for marriage must not be called a defilement'. Yet the sensitive, neurotic, intellectual Milton had evolved for himself a totally unreal image of marriage in which somehow his homosexual Platonic ideal would be achieved and the distasteful aspects of female sexuality avoided. Such psychic confusion was the result of the interplay of his own temperament and the inherited contradictions of Western culture in the sphere of male and female relations.

It is hard to imagine a man less fitted for marriage, yet unaccountably in 1642 he took a wife. Having ridden out to the country to collect a bad debt from a Royalist family of some aristocratic pretensions, he spent a month in Oxfordshire and returned without the money but with the Powells' eldest daughter, Mary, a girl of sixteen. It is quite likely that Milton married on intellectual grounds; as a Protestant he had to defend marriage against its devaluation by the Catholics. A psychologist would also point out that he unconsciously ensured the failure of the enterprise by choosing a girl from the enemy camp. This is exactly what happened. Mary was used to courtly gaiety and after a few weeks of the studious Mr Milton went home to visit her family for a month. Meanwhile the civil war began. Despite letters from her husband directing her to return, she stayed away.

Milton's state of mind can be discovered in the pamphlets in favour of divorce which he wrote from 1643 to 1645. His ostensible purpose was to free mankind from irksome fetters and his real purpose was to express his desire to get rid of his wife. His astonishment at his own behaviour is stated clearly. 'It is not strange though many who have spent their life chastely, are in some things not so quicksighted, while they haste too eagerly to light the nuptial torch.' What went wrong? On the conscious level he tells us clearly that he takes no delight in the heterosexual act. 'That other burning which is but as it were the venom of a lusty and overabounding concoction, strict life and labour, which abatement of a full diet, may keep that low and obedient enough.' He sought for something he could not quite define. 'Since we know it is not the joining of another body will remove Loneliness, but the uniting of another compatible mind.' Groping about intellectually he finally suggests, 'A conversing solace and peaceful society is the prime end of marriage, without which no other help or office can be mutual, beseeming the dignity of reasonable creatures; that such as they should be coupled in the rites of nature by the mere compulsion of lust, without love or peace, worse than wild beasts.'

If he sought intellectual compatibility, why choose a giddy child of sixteen and a Royalist to boot? Quite probably there was something boyish about the scarcely adolescent Powell girl, enough to help Milton overcome his dread of women, but when he was faced with female sexuality, although he was not impotent, his unconscious revolted. Other men have enjoyed the sensual pleasures of female flesh without making too great intellectual demands. Milton, the unconscious celibate, would have been happier in a monastery, but history conspired to make him a Protestant and his torturous mind outdid itself as it rationalized his typically masculine anxiety. Although he speaks of the married pair often enough in his divorce tracts, nowhere does he show any consideration for, or any interest in, the woman's reactions.

As it happens, he seems to have been rather victimized by the Powell family. After the battle of Naseby the Royalist cause was lost and the Powells ruined. Mary was sent back to her husband, in tears and on her knees. It was all a mistake; her mother had come between them. Milton was certainly not ungenerous, for not only did Mary move in but also her mother and sister. Between 1646 and 1652 the poet seems to have adjusted to the bestiality of sexual relations with a woman: Mary bore him four children, dying in childbirth with the last one. It was not a happy household. All evidence indicates that the in-laws were hostile, even though Milton was housing and feeding them, and his three girls may well have been indoctrinated with their grandmother's opinion of their father. In a letter Milton speaks unhappily of 'Persons, though in no other respect commendable, who sit daily in my company, weary me, nay, by Heaven all but plague me to death whenever they are jointly in the humour for it.' It was unfortunate that Milton's basic attitude towards women was intensified by what must have been a nagging chorus. Eventually, after she left his house, he was to sue his mother-in-law. Immersed in a sea of six women, it is not surprising that the poet's eyesight failed and he suffered from indigestion. (The meaning of his blindness we shall discuss later.)

Through the influence of friends in high places and perhaps because of the tolerance of Charles II, Milton got off lightly when the monarchy was restored, enduring only a few months' imprisonment and paying a fine. As he continued to work on *Paradise Lost*, begun in 1660, he tried to use his daughters as his eyes, compelling them to read to him in foreign languages they did not understand. The older ones rebelled, were sent out to learn embroidery, and became lacemakers. Years later a maid testified that they had sometimes conspired to steal the housekeeping money and sold their father's books behind his back.

He married Catherine Woodcock in 1657, apparently after he became blind. She was twenty years younger than himself and died within a year in childbirth. In 1663 his friends found him a third wife, Elizabeth Woodhull, a submissive girl of twenty-four, who functioned as a capable housekeeper and took care of him until his death.

Paradise Lost contains passages which not only release all the spectres in Milton's unconscious, which had accumulated during his relations with so many women, but also repeats certain images which are already familiar to us as a product of the tortured male psyche. When Satan pulls himself together after his defeat and fall from heaven, he sets out on a journey to corrupt the human race and arrives at the gates of hell.

> Before the gate there sat
> On either side a formidable shape;
> The one seemed woman to the waist and fair
> But ended foul in many a scaly fold
> Voluminous and vast, a serpent arm'd
> With mortal sting: about her middle round
> A cry of Hell Hounds never ceasing barked
> With wild Cerberean mouths full loud, and rung
> A hideous peal, yet, when they list, would creep
> If aught disturbed their noise, into her womb
> And kennel there, yet there still lurk'd and howl'd
> Within unseen.

On the other side of the gate stands a shadowy male figure brandishing a dart. The woman explains that she sprang from the head of Satan and was named Sin.

> Thyself in me thy perfect image viewing
> Becam'st enamour'd and such joy thou took'st
> With me in secret, that my womb conceived
> A growing burden.

After the civil war in heaven, she was flung into the abyss with the rest of the rebels.

> At last this odious offspring whom thou see'st,
> Thine own begotten, breaking violent way,
> Tore through my entrails, that, with fear and pain
> Distorted, all my nether shape thus grew
> Transformed: but he my inbred enemy
> Forth issued, brandishing his fatal dart
> Made to destroy. I fled and cry'd out *Death!*
> Hell trembled at the hideous name, and sigh'd
> From all her caves, and back resounded *Death!*
> I fled; but he pursued (though more, it seems,
> Inflamed with lust than rage), and, swifter far,
> Me overtook, his mother, all dismayed,
> And, in embraces forcible and foul,
> Engendering with me, of that rape begot
> These yelling monsters that with ceaseless cry
> Surround me . . .

The horror of sex and women could not be expressed more elaborately and more in accordance with analytical findings. In the first place, the female image combines explicitly the roles of mother, wife and daughter (and no doubt mother-in-law); fear of incestuous desires towards the mother and also the daughter are clearly symbolized. The female figure also combines the aspects of the phallic woman (since she has the lower parts of a serpent endowed with the poisonous sting of sex) with the castrating dogs' heads which we have also met in Eskimo mythology and in modern psychoanalysis. Milton's passive homosexuality both pictures the female genitalia as a loathsome kennel for hellhounds and punishes the composite female image for being a sexual threat by deforming the lower half of her body. If this were not enough, death is made to issue from the same menacing orifice. Finally, in accord with Christian tradition, the whole monstrous nightmare of female sexuality is labelled Sin. We are reminded of Karen Horney's testimony concerning the fantasies of her male patients. Through this fantastically intricate symbolism Milton's personal drives mingle with and shape his intellectual rebellions, in turn triggered by the conflicting political and religious trends of his period.

The marital relations of Adam and Eve in the great Protestant epic dramatize the basic conflict aroused by the sexual act. The couple came together

> Straight side by side were laid; nor turned, I ween,
> Adam from his fair spouse, nor Eve the rites
> Mysterious of connubial love refused.

In other words this was the pure, unreal and idealized fantasy of sex which Milton entertained before facing the brutal facts of marriage. More light is shed on it when Adam innocently asks the archangel Raphael what is done about sex in heaven. In defiance of tradition that heaven is sexless, Milton permits the angel to blush. Why should a sinless and guiltless angel blush? Especially in the light of what follows?

> 'Let it suffice then that thou know'st
> Us happy, and without Love no happiness.
> Whatever pure thou in the body enjoy'st

(And pure thou wert created) we enjoy
In eminence, and obstacle find none
Of membrane, joint, or limb, exclusive bars.
Easier than with air, if Spirits embrace,
Total they mix, union of pure with pure
Desiring . . .'

Such airy, celestial fornication translated means therefore that angels enjoy the pleasures of physical union raised to a high degree and without the usual inefficiency of mortal sexual organs. Why did Raphael blush? Was it because even in this fantasy Milton's unconscious had supplied a homosexual content?

When the character of Eve-Mary has made Adam-Milton eat the apple and thus taught him what heterosexual bodily passion entails, the poet tells us that, when they awoke next morning after the fall, and rose up, innocence had left them.

So rose the Danite strong,
Herculean Samson, from the harlot-lap
Of Philistean Dalila, and waked
Shorn of his strength; they destitute and bare
Of all their virtue.

The image is peculiarly strained; it applies to a man and Milton stretches it clumsily to describe the primal pair. Once more Milton's unconscious betrays him. He is saying that after sexual knowledge the man feels castrated. That the Samson image had a deep meaning for the poet is borne out by his last important work, *Samson Agonistes*, in which his religious ideas, his intellectual rebellion and his own sexual problem are fused in a most significant synthesis.

In the first place the blind hero is chosen to accord with Milton's blindness. We have mentioned before that loss of eyesight is believed by analysts to be a symbol of castration; we have encountered the situation before in the case of St Paul. Ancient and primitive mythology bears out this interpretation, equating the eyeballs with the testicles and loss of sight to loss of virility. James Hanford, the discreet biographer, points out that modern medical analysis of Milton's affliction (which he described minutely) indicates it was probably glaucoma, a disease which is more and more being connected with psychogenetic disturbance. In other words, Samson starts out symbolically castrated, as was the poet, by the women in his life. Samson of course was symbolically castrated by Dalila when she robbed him of his strength, his virility, by cutting his hair. And Samson, like his creator, chose a woman from the other camp. The interchange between Samson and Dalila, which occupies a good part of the play, goes back to the relation with Mary, to which is added all the accumulated hostility towards the other women in the poet's life.

> ... into the snare I fell
> Of fair fallacious looks, venereal trains,
> Softened with pleasure and voluptuous life;
> At length to lay my head and hallowed pledge
> Of all my strength into the lascivious lap
> Of a deceitful concubine, who shore me,
> Like a tame wether, all my precious fleece ...

We suspect that, for Milton, his strength was his chastity and he never forgave Mary for whatever female arts she used to win him over for, when Dalila appears and tries to win him back, he attacks her immediately.

> Out, out, Hyena! These are thy wonted arts,
> And arts of every woman false like thee –
> To break all faith, all vows, deceive, betray;
> Then, as repentant, to submit, beseech ...

When Dalila excuses herself not very convincingly by saying that the Philistines brought pressure to bear upon her (as did the Powells upon Mary) he answers he no longer trusts her.

> If in my flower of youth and strength, when all men
> Lov'd, honour'd, fear'd me, thou alone could hate me,
> Thy husband, slight me, sell me, and forgo me ...

Finally, when the woman reiterates that she loves him, all the accumulated rejection of female sexuality is flung into the line:

> But love constrained thee; call it furious rage
> To satisfy thy lust ...

It is perhaps true that Milton had personal justification for his complaints against women, but it is also true that he got himself into these situations and his own compulsions account for most of his woes. What is important is the manner in which the great Protestant artist revived some of the basic misogynist imagery in Christian tradition and once more charged women with castration. Milton was able to accept his symbolic physical affliction as a martyrdom in the cause of religion just as he sublimated his earlier passive homosexuality in Platonic idealism, and in each case produced poetry of great value. His hostility towards women, however, he could never resolve and he, too, subscribed to the legend of the dangerous second sex.

CHAPTER EIGHTEEN

'By G—d, I Will Have Her!'

'Women, then, are only children of larger growth; they have an entertaining rattle and sometimes wit; but not solid reasoning, or good sense, I never knew in my life one that had it or one who reasoned or acted consequently for four and twenty hours together. . . .'

'A man of sense only trifles with them, plays with them, humours and flatters them, as he does a sprightly forward child; but he neither consults them, nor trusts them with serious matters; though he often makes them believe that he does, which is the thing in the world that they are most proud of. . . .'

'Women are much more like each other than men; they have in truth but two passions, vanity and love; these are their universal characteristics.'

These often-quoted generalizations of the suave Lord Chesterfield, as Gordon Allport has pointed out, contain familiar expressions of prejudice which are habitually used against an out-group. Just as some Europeans used to say that all Chinese looked alike, so the eighteenth-century gallant generalizes about women, insisting they all think alike. His condescending description is similar to the image which the die-hard segregationist applies to the Negro or the white-man's-burden imperialist to a colonial people. We are reminded of the Bushman and Pueblo myths in which men and women are treated as belonging to separate tribes.

It might be objected that Chesterfield knew what he was talking about, that his characterization of the woman of his time had a factual basis. Actually it makes no difference, for the women of the past have been as men have made them. Under male dominance women have always accepted the roles which men have created for

177

them. Having reduced them to the role of submissive dependents, men then criticized them for being submissively dependent. Having forced them into a position in which they could only achieve their ends by indirection or subterfuge, they were branded by men as false and untrustworthy. Thus the situation is parallel to that of the Negro who, after being deprived of educational advantages, is then called ignorant and unintellectual by the white supremacist.

Chesterfield's remarks are symptomatic of male attitudes in the age of reason. In many ways this was a period parallel to Roman times; there were very few sex repressions as far as the physical activity of sex was concerned, and religious sanctions had little weight. The amorous game, described by Ovid, is carried to new lengths and the stereotype of the Don Juan is born. At the same time there is a tendency to repress any evidence of strong emotions; relationships between the sexes are often reduced to elegant formality.

Though it is true that the old magical misogyny does not appear on the surface, the frantic rutting on the part of the gallant is as extreme in its way as the preoccupation with celibacy in earlier times. The male who has to prove his maleness by the continual performance of the sex act with as many partners as possible is expressing a deep insecurity. In some ways it appears as though this type of behaviour harks back to the phallic phase in which men do not really accept the other sex, in other ways it reveals a hidden fear of impotence.

The Don Juan is described by Otto Fenichel: 'After having "made" a woman he is no longer interested in her, first because she, too, has failed to bring about the longed-for relaxation and second because his narcissistic need requires proof of his ability to excite women; after he knows he is able to excite a specific woman, his doubts arise concerning other women ... an unconsciously homosexual man, for example, may be aroused by sexual contact with women but not satisfied; he then vainly seeks satisfaction in more and more sexual activity.'

The uninhibited fornication of the gallant, taken together with a repression of strong emotion in the sphere of sex, reveals both a profound disturbance in the unconscious and a deep hostility. The

medieval male expressed his apprehension by cries of sin and philo-
sophies excluding women, the gallant his insecurity by a mono-
maniacal effort to dominate all women with his phallus.

A pattern of cynical sexuality is already established in Restoration
England and is reflected in the plays of the period. When the
sophisticated rake is not paying well-turned compliments, he is
utterly callous. Here, from Congreve's *Love for Love*, is Tattle
talking to Miss Prue, a rather retarded rural sexpot, whom he has
come within an inch of seducing in an earlier scene.

> PRUE: ... And I know you may be my husband now if you please.
> TAT: O fy miss! who told you so, child?
> PRUE: Why my father. I told him that you loved me.
> TAT: O fy miss! why did you do so? and who told you so, child?
> PRUE: Why! why you did, did you not?
> TAT: O pox! That was yesterday, miss, that was a while ago. I have been
> asleep since; slept a whole night and did not so much as dream of the
> matter.
> PRUE: Pshaw! O but I dreamed it was so though.
> TAT: Ay, but your father will tell you that dreams come by contraries,
> child, O fy, what, we must not love one another now – pshaw! that
> would be a foolish thing indeed. Fy! fy! you're a woman now and
> must think of a new man every morning and forget him every night.

Congreve's amusing caricature is symptomatic of social reality
and the following from George Farquhar's *The Inconstant, or The
Way to Win Him* satirizes the fashionable attitudes of one sex towards the other. Oriana and Young Mirabel are bound by a marriage
contract which Mirabel finds irksome.

> YOUNG MIRABEL: ... I never heard of a man that left an inch of his
> honour in a woman's keeping that could ever get the least account of
> it. ... I tell thee, child, there is not the least occasion for morals in
> any business between you and I, don't you know that of all commerce
> in the world there is no such cosenage and deceit as in the traffic
> between a man and a woman; we study all our lives long how to put
> tricks upon one another. No fowler lays abroad more nets for his
> game, nor hunter for his prey, than you to catch poor innocent men.
> Why do you sit for three or four hours at your toilet in a morning?
> Only with a villainous design to make some poor fellow a fool before
> night. What are your languishing looks, your studied airs and affecta-
> tions but so many baits and devices to delude men out of their liberty

and freedom. What d'ye sigh for? what d'ye weep for? what d'ye
pray for? why for a husband: that is you implore providence to assist
you in the just and pious design of making the wisest of creatures a
fool, and the head of creation a slave.

ORIANA: Sir, I am proud of my power, and am resolved to use it.

YOUNG MIRABEL: Hold, hold, madam! not so fast – as you have a variety
of vanities to make coxcombs of us; so we have vows, oaths, and protestations of all sorts and sizes to make fools of you, as you are very
strange and whimsical creatures, so we are allowed as unaccountable
ways of managing you. And this, in short, my dear creature, is our
present condition; I have sworn and laid briskly to gain my ends of
you, your ladyship has patched and painted violently to gain your
ends of me: but since we are both disappointed, let us make a drawn
battle and part clear of both sides.

Here we are dealing with the brittle relation between persons of
quality in which marriages are arranged in order to repair the rake's
squandered fortune or to further the parents' material ambitions.
Here, too, is the first formulation of the facetious yet nevertheless
unconsciously meaningful concept of 'the battle between the sexes'.
It gives rise to stereotypes we still have with us, that of the capricious
and inexplicable woman who can never be understood by the clumsy
but down-to-earth male.

The gallant's attitude towards the courtesan or demimondaine, a
type which accounts for a large percentage of his affairs, can be
wholly brutal. John Wilmot, Earl of Rochester, writes of his mistress:

> See the kind seed receiving earth
> To ev'ry grain affords a birth:
> On her no showers unwelcome fall,
> Her willing womb receives them all.
> And shall my Celia be confin'd?
> No, live up to thy mighty mind
> And be the mistress of mankind.

These same rakes of the Restoration, Rochester, Buckingham and
Sedley, were compulsively inclined to outrageous behaviour which
either shocked the general public and got them into gaol or antagon-
ized the king and banished them from royal favour. This urge to
self-destruction combined with more profound pathological drives
is recorded by Anthony à Wood, an Oxford historian writing in
the 1690s. 'Sir Charles Sedly Bt., sometime of Wadham coll.,

Charles, Lord Buckhurst (afterwards Earl of Middlesex), Sir Thomas Ogle, etc., were at a cook's house, at the sign of the Cock in Bow-street, near Covent Garden, within the liberties of Westminster; and being all aflame with strong liquors, they went into the balcony, joining to their chamber window, and putting down their breeches, they excrementized in the street. Which being done, Sedley stripped himself naked, and with eloquence preached blasphemy to the people. Thereupon a riot being raised, the people became very clamorous and would have forced the door next the street open.' The upshot was that they were taken before a magistrate and all fined, Sedley's share being 500 pounds. 'And he made answer that he thought he was the first man that paid for shiting.' Sedley refused to pay the fine but friends begged the money from King Charles.

Towards the middle of the eighteenth century the cynical and aggressively exhibitionistic behaviour of the rake began to be sick-lied over with the sauce of sentimentality secreted by the rising bourgeoisie. Richardson's Mr B still clings to the old habits until halfway through the book where he is suddenly overcome by Pamela's impregnable virtue, pious sentiments, and remarkable resistance to physical abuse. He then abruptly turns into a man of sensibility and an ideal husband. His activities as a rake throw some light on the attitudes of the gallant. He is always ready to drag her behind a door, kiss her and put his hand in her bosom. When she escapes and complains of his attempts, he is furious. He calls her a foolish slut and tells her to 'cease your blubbering' or he cries, 'Get out of my presence, hussy! I can't bear you in my sight.' At the same time he says, 'I tell you she is a subtle, artful gipsy, and time will shew it you.' He does not scruple to hide in her room and creep into bed with her. Pamela, however, has a convenient habit of faint-ing in such crises which saves her, although if it were not for the exigencies of the plot fainting would do her little good. When the housekeeper takes her part, Mr B threatens to throw her out of the window and cries, 'Say no more, Mrs Jervis; for by G–d I will have her!' All such attempts are described by him as 'innocent freedoms' or 'playful romping'. Because of the social distance between master and servant, he treats her efforts to avoid seduction as impudence and grows more and more angry as she guards her valuable virginity.

All his advances show a compulsive, hostile need to dominate which dehumanizes the girl and makes of her a thing to satisfy his obsession. Although he does apparently take time off to go hunting, most of his waking hours seem to be spent plotting to prove his masculinity, and both Pamela and her parents are convinced that once this is accomplished, Pamela will be cast off. Hence she must preserve her bargaining advantage at all costs, and the chase goes on, the satyr panting at her heels while tear-drenched Pamela is half the time on her knees begging for mercy and half the time delivering moral lectures or scheming, on her part, to foil his latest plot. Indeed Pamela, with a flash of psychological insight, reflects, 'If ever he had any kindness towards me I believe he now hates me heartily. Is it not strange that love borders so much upon hate? . . . And how must this hate have been increased, if he had met with such a base compliance after his wicked will had been gratified.'

Mr B lies, abducts Pamela and holds her prisoner in one of his estates, deceives her parents, plots to fool her with a sham marriage ceremony, and allows her to be tyrannized over by a housekeeper who is no better than a procuress. Finally when Pamela has tried to climb a wall to escape and she is bruised and battered by falling bricks, her little heart 'going pit a pat' all the while, Mr B gains access to the MS in which she has been steadily writing down all her adventures and analysing her feelings. He is so overcome by her impeccable sentiments and her failure to harbour any resentment that the miraculous rebirth takes place and the story becomes very tame as Pamela deals with the problems of having risen in the world.

Though in Richardson's novel the hero is fanatically determined to subdue only one girl, he has had other mistresses and the whole pattern is applicable to the man of many conquests. Casanova, one of the most famous Don Juans, has recounted all his adventures and very likely exaggerated them. From his point of view he was God's gift to women and all of his conquests were only too delighted to be the recipient of his attentions. If the other side of the story were told, it is probable he would not appear in such an amiable light. Though many of his mistresses were actresses or dancers, and there was a tradition of promiscuity in the theatrical circles, many of his victims must have felt exploited and destroyed.

While pathological excess may seem monstrous and alien, it is often a key to weaker drives which are fairly generally present. In order to explore more deeply the unacknowledged motivations of gallant, it is worth while examining the case of the controversial and legendary Marquis de Sade. The man himself is a symbol of all that was hidden beneath the polished exterior of the Age of Reason and his novels have influenced later writers whose attitudes are significant for our theme (including Baudelaire and Swinburne).

Although the public image of Sade is that of a fiend and his name has been borrowed to designate a specific sex deviation, recent investigation and literary criticism has shown him to be a fantastic mixture of genius and neurosis. The very violence with which he was persecuted in his own time proves that his actions and his writing infringed upon the most sacred taboos of the age and hence that he held the mirror up to all that it wished to disclaim and suppress. It is only by virtue of the psychological tolerance of today that enough impartiality and insight have been achieved so that he can be rationally discussed.

Sade's life span runs from 1740 to 1814; it both covers the period in which the affairs of the rake were veneered with sighs and sentimentality and overlaps the French Revolution in which reason and violence negated each other in a social holocaust. He was related to the French royal family and he tells us himself that as a boy he was made to believe that he was a superior person to whom nothing should be denied. His father was cold, formal, and always in debt. The boy was rejected by his parents and raised chiefly by a grandmother and an uncle. The uncle was an abbé notorious for keeping two mistresses, a mother and daughter. The pattern of rejection is exactly parallel to that in the life of Casanova, the archetypal Don Juan. In Casanova's case, the parents came from a lower social strata. Facts seem to indicate that cold relationships between parents and children helped to form the gallant. Both Casanova and the Marquis de Sade, like the rakes of the Restoration, had a penchant for self-destructive acts. Thus rejection set up emotional repressions which were to result in violent or excessive behaviour, particularly in the sexual area.

Donatien de Sade was taken out of school at fourteen, a sensitive

and important pubertal age, and put in the army where he served
with distinction during the Seven Years War with Germany. By the
age of twenty-one he had already seduced and abandoned a young
girl of good family. The circumstances of his marriage were also
disturbing. His father was bent on marrying him into a family with
money; the daughter of a judge was selected. Just when the engage-
ment was entered into, Sade was begging another girl (from whom
he had already contracted venereal disease) to marry him. Her family
was not considered good enough by Donatien's father and, although
the young man wrote letters full of real despair, his mistress does
not seem to have been faithful. He therefore bent to his father's will
and married Renée de Montreuil, tall, clumsy and badly dressed,
whom he was to characterize as 'too prudish and cold'. In fact he
much preferred her younger sister.

The young Marquis de Sade was about five feet two, plumpish,
round-faced, with blue eyes, blond hair and a small mouth. Four
months after his marriage this exquisitely courteous, refined-looking
young man was in trouble with the police for some excess committed
in a *petite maison*. This was what used to be called in the old gutter
press 'a love nest', an apartment or cottage in or near Paris. To these
Sade brought girls lent him by brothel keepers. Sade's early reputation won him the constant surveillance of Police Inspector Marais,
who reported that he had five or six *petites maisons*. The trouble in
1763 seems to have been a complaint from one of Sade's girls which
was hushed up. Inspector Marais told the brothel keepers not to
supply him with girls. Sade continued to draw his women from the
courtesan class and from the theatre and the opera, whose per-
formers were always accessible. He was arrested later in 1763,
apparently for his treatment of women, and wrote an almost tearful
letter to the chief of police promising to reform. Finally, by appealing
to the king, he was released under a kind of house arrest in the
Montreuil country château. Here he amused himself by organizing
amateur theatricals. Finally, allowed to return to Paris, his amatory
career continued under the disapproving eye of Inspector Marais
and included an involvement with a courtesan named Colette who
cost him a good deal of money. From her he moved on to Mademoi-
selle Beauvoisin, one of the famous kept women of his time. He

passed her off as his wife and went to live with her in his château at La Coste. Beauvoisin, who made a career of ruining men, managed to spend most of his wife's dowry and helped him to antagonize his in-laws and his uncles. The scandal lasted about two years and was followed by one of the episodes which helped to ruin Sade's life.

In 1767 as he was walking on the Place Saint-Victoire, a thirty-seven-year-old Alsatian woman, named Rose Keller, asked him for money. He convinced her she should go with him to one of his *petites maisons*. There are two stories concerning what followed. The woman, aided by a good deal of public indignation which clustered about her, managed to create an atmosphere of horror. She maintained he undressed her, tied her face downward on a bed, beat her several times with whips and sticks and dropped hot sealing wax on her wounds. A surgeon's report, however, indicated that she had merely been beaten with a knotted cord. Sade himself maintained that she knew for what purpose she was to be used and that he had stopped the whipping when she asked him to. All in all, it seems probable that what Sade did was no more and no less than he had been doing all along but in this case the woman saw a chance to exploit him by making a public scandal. The unconscious sadism of the community seized on the episode with hypocritical indignation. Sade's father-in-law tried to get him out of gaol but was handicapped by hostilities between himself and other justices. Once more Sade had to appeal directly to the king as a relative for a royal licence of amnesty. This was granted on condition he stay away from Paris and reside in his château. Then Sade performed the most perverse act of his life. He went to the convent in which his sister-in-law Louise was living, abducted her, lived with her for a while, and returned her to the convent in 1772.

This aroused the undying enmity of his mother and father-in-law but strangely enough not that of his wife, who stood by him in all that was to follow. The second and only other sexual episode for which Sade was prosecuted took place in Marseille in 1772. Sade and his valet visited a brothel in Marseille and provided themselves with two girls. The marquis and the valet beat the girls and fed them candy containing aphrodisiacs. The girls claimed they were frightened when the marquis took a nail-studded, bloodstained parchment whip from his pocket. The whip was not used, but the girls were encouraged to give the marquis and the valet 800 strokes apiece with a twig broom. After that the valet had anal intercourse with the master, who performed the same act on the girls. Unfortunately the doctored candy made the girls sick. When complaints were made, Sade fled the country. Although the girls were never very sick and soon recovered, the marquis was condemned to death *in absentia* for murder and sodomy. The first he had not committed, the second was not a capital offence. The judge was the same magistrate who had condemned him before. At this point his in-laws were anxious to have him prosecuted. His mother-in-law intercepted his letters and helped see to it that he was captured in Chambéry, Savoy, where he was imprisoned. The following year he escaped to Switzerland where he was joined by his wife, who had broken with her family. From then on, with a sentence of death still hanging over his head, he lived in his château at La Coste, got in trouble with chambermaids, went to Italy, came home, and was shot at by the parent of another one of the maids.

In 1777 his mother-in-law had him arrested and he spent a year in the worst dungeon which could be found in Vincennes, without exercise, books, proper food, or anything to keep his mind busy. He almost lost his reason and began to suspect his wife of betraying him. At the end of a year his case, thanks to his wife's efforts, was reheard and the punishment altered to a fifty-franc fine. He was not released, however, for the implacable mother-in-law secured a *lettre de cachet* from the king which meant he was to be kept in protective custody.

He remained in Vincennes for the next ten years while his wife took care of the estates, and worked for his freedom. After a time, however, she became an invalid, retired to a convent and lost touch with her husband and the world. Sade's prison years were spent writing a series of extraordinary novels and plays (many of which are lost), an outlet for an intense mental activity. He was transferred to the Bastille in 1784. In this period the marquis had become completely disillusioned with all conventional ideas and was a wholehearted revolutionist; in fact much of his writing expressed is violent criticisms of the society whose polished façade and inner corruption were both to be blown apart by the hurricane of revolution.

In 1789, eleven days before it was stormed, Sade was transferred from the Bastille to an insane asylum at Charenton and the following year was released by the Constituent Assembly. After thirteen years of prison he had grown very fat, was almost blind in one eye, and had no means of support. His wife refused to see him. He was later separated from her, and there are various begging letters on record. For a time he lived with Madame Quesnet, an actress with a son, who was separated from her husband. Sade seems to have become domestic. He tutored the boy and looked after him as he had never done his own children. He seems to have been fond of Quesnet and she of him, for she remained friendly with him to his death.

In this period he had some success with his plays, mostly comedies in verse, and his novels were published. He was active in the revolutionary movement, becoming a speaker for the Section des Piques, and later the president of a tribunal. From this arose the greatest irony of his life. His father and mother-in-law, who had been instrumental in keeping him in gaol for thirteen years, were accused and tried by his court. Sade, who was firmly opposed to the death penalty, voted to pardon them. For this he was put in gaol during the Terror for moderationism.

Sade, a genuine humanitarian, who had hoped for great things from the revolution, was disillusioned by the Terror. As a result he wrote his most bitter and terrible novel, *La Nouvelle Justine*, in 1792. After ten months of ghastly prisons – one had windows which looked out upon the guillotine where more than 1,800 prisoners were executed – aided by Madame Quesnet's efforts, he was released. For the next few years he struggled with poor health, living by small literary jobs. When Napoleon became dictator, the uncompromising ex-marquis wrote a satire against him and Josephine in which he expressed his hatred of dictatorship. *La Nouvelle Justine* was burned by order of the new government and Sade himself gaoled for the third time. Since Napoleon had no intention of ever freeing him, he was declared insane and transferred once more to the asylum at Charenton where he was to spend the rest of his life.

Thus Sade was imprisoned by three governments, twice on charges which are a credit to him and have nothing to do with the legend which branded him a monster. Fat, white-haired, but indomitable, thanks to an intelligent asylum director, Sade was able to keep himself going by organizing a theatre in his mad-house. He wrote plays which were acted under his direction by his fellow inmates and sometimes by actors hired from outside. His productions were so successful that many visitors from the town came to enjoy them. The jealousy of the head doctor (who branded him not mad but vicious) put a stop to this pioneer work in psychodrama. The faithful Madame Quesnet continued to visit Sade until his death in 1814. Sade, an uncompromising atheist, had requested that his grave be sown with acorns so that the spot would become forest growth and disappear, but the authorities gave him a Christian funeral and firmly planted a cross where he was buried. Perhaps they wished to keep his ruthlessly critical spirit from walking.

Sade's literary work is an amazing mixture of insight and rationalization. He found depths of perversity in himself which he determined to face and as a result there was nothing in his experience or his dream world that he shrank from recording. His own age and those which followed never forgave him for setting down on paper the most terrifying fantasies, in short releasing all the repressed wishes which he rightly understood were basically human. Much of his work was therefore a kind of instinctive pioneering in depth psychology. Since he had had the worst of three societies, his searing iconoclasm spared no human institution and he wove his cultural criticism in and out of his sexual fantasies.

Justine, the most famous of his novels, is sufficiently characteristic to illustrate the panorama of the gallant's unconscious. Sade was influenced by Fielding and Richardson and, indeed, *Justine* is a kind of nightmare obverse of *Pamela*. In the beginning Justine and Juliette, aged twelve and fifteen, are left orphaned by the death of their father and mother. Although theirs is a well-to-do banking family, their father was ruined just before his death. Juliette immediately chooses the path of vice and, by peddling her wares shrewdly, in fifteen years has an income of 3,000 French pounds a year, owns a fortune in jewellery and three houses. Justine, who is the resolutely virtuous Pamela type, like Richardson's heroine, spends most of her time on her knees begging to be spared. She, too, sheds oceans of tears and is never without a pious sentiment upon her lips. Her fate is not that of Pamela, however, for she is horribly treated by everyone she meets and is never spared by the assorted satyrs into whose hands she falls.

From the very beginning when she goes to a wealthy man to ask for work and is immediately propositioned she gets a lecture on the impracticality of virtue. After securing a position in the house of a miser, she finds that her master expects her to commit a robbery. When she virtuously refuses, as a reward she is thrown in gaol and unjustly charged with robbery. A gun moll of the period, the wicked Dubois, burns down the gaol and helps Justine to escape.

Inducted into a gang of robbers, she is first beaten and treated to sexual indignities. Heart-of-Iron then insists on deflowering her. He suggests anal intercourse if she wishes to remain technically a virgin. Before this can happen the mob catches a young merchant and plans to murder its prisoner. Justine virtuously helps him to escape and flies from the robbers in his company. He rewards her by taking her into the forest, hitting her over the head, violating her in the way suggested by the robber, and taking her money.

It is one of Sade's ironies and also in deference to his favourite sex deviation, that she retains her technical virginity until well on in the story; after that we lose track of the various things which have been done to her. Befriended by a homosexual aristocrat, she refuses to be a party to poisoning his aunt and, of course, ends by being blamed for the crime. Meanwhile her pious clichés have been answered by the count with the most scathing attacks on religion. Before she escapes from him she is bitten by his vicious bulldogs while she is helpless and tied to a tree. She next falls into the hands of a sadistic doctor-schoolmaster who amuses himself by beating his students and sodomizing his daughter. Justine, when she endeavours to save the daughter from becoming a subject for dissection, is branded with a hot iron and driven out.

Seeking refuge in a monastery, Justine falls into the hands of four monks, all of aristocratic family, who keep prisoner a harem of girls with whom they practise every perversion including flagellation, fellatio, sodomy, coprophilia and various forms of torture. Like

Pamela she is driven to climb over a wall but it does her little good, for she next falls into the hands of the Comte de Germande who practises the usual sodomy combined with group perversions in which he employs some of his pages. His final refinement is opening the veins of both Justine and his wife. Justine escapes during the confusion caused by his wife's death.

In one of the later episodes Justine rescues a man she finds lying by the road after he has been beaten. He takes her to his castle and turns out to be a counterfeiter who has a private torture chamber where he practises inhuman brutalities upon his sister. He is described as possessing an outsize phallus, as long as Justine's forearm, and much is made of the pain it causes when it is driven into the unfortunate women.

By the end of the story Justine is on her way to be executed for murder, robbery and arson (none of which crimes she has committed) when she meets her sister, Juliette, with a fashionable paramour, who is staying at an inn. After Justine has told her sad story, Juliette befriends her, uses her connections to have her freed and takes her home. During a thunderstorm in which Juliette is frightened, Justine runs to shut the window and is hit by a thunderbolt which enters her right breast, disfigures her body and kills her. Sobered by this judgment of God upon the virtuous, Juliette decides to think of the next world and enters a nunnery. Sade's final mocking comment runs, 'May you be convinced with her that the only true happiness is found by reposing upon the bosom of virtue, and that, if, in ways which we cannot fathom, God allows it to be persecuted on earth, it is to indemnify it in Heaven with the most flattering rewards.'

All through the book every one of the calloused monsters who assaults Justine justifies himself in the most cynical terms. The parade of types includes aristocrats, monks, law officers and pillars of the community who are shown to be on the same level as the criminals who appear in the book, a type of assault on society which was to be used later by Bertolt Brecht. Sade tells us quite plainly that the world is utterly monstrous and deserves to be destroyed. It was – but he found the new one to be no better and was thus impelled to introduce some of the horrors he had witnessed during the

Terror in *La Nouvelle Justine*. His attitude fluctuates between a desire to reform society along anarchistic lines and complete cynicism. The sadism in his work, it is true, is compulsive and unpleasant; *Justine* is as monotonous as *Fanny Hill*, but redeemed in spots by its intellectual ironies. Sade, as analyst A. Besnard points out, was quite consciously working out his own ferocious impulses in terms of fantasy; in fact he said that setting them down on paper was his only consolation for his miseries.

Despite his pathology, we must remember that his career of conquests was that of the typical gallant. He said himself that he was very often fond of ugly women of good character with whom he could talk with no thought of sex but after getting all he wanted from a woman who attracted him, he detested her. 'What need for the heart to have a role in the situation in which only the body plays a part?' This split between emotion and sexual expression is what we have indicated as typical of the Age of Reason. Geoffrey Gorer, citing Sade's beating of the Keller woman, so much older than himself, feels that the episode reveals a hostility towards his mother. We also note that Sade's libertines often possess huge penises and inexhaustible potency; they are fountains of semen. This kind of exaggeration is, of course, related to fears of impotency while the huge phallus, used as a weapon against the female body, takes us back to the phallic phase in male development.

Sade's most profound expression of antagonism to women, which no doubt also derives from his observation of his libertine contemporaries, may stand for all that is unexpressed in the behaviour of the gallant. It is a speech put into the mouth of the Comte de Germande, the perverse murderer of his wife. When Justine tries to soften the count's heart towards the unfortunate woman, he tells her that women have everywhere been treated as beasts and, if they were not meant to be dominated by men, they would not have been created weaker. He goes on to say that woman is 'a miserable creature, always inferior to man, less handsome than he, less ingenious, less wise, disgustingly shaped, the opposite of what could please man or delight him. . . . A creature sick three quarters of her life, unable to satisfy her husband whenever nature compels her to produce a child, sour of disposition, cross-grained, imperious, a tyrant if you give her leave and base and grovelling in captivity, but always false, always nasty, always dangerous. . . .' And finally, 'a creature as far from man as man is from the forest monkey, so that it is a question if it could have any pretensions to being human or whether such pretensions can be reasonably respected.'

This, then, is how the gallant really felt about women.

CHAPTER NINETEEN

The Beast with the Indolent Air

My soul, do you recall that thing which we once saw
    Upon a mild and sweet spring day:
Where the path turned aside, there on a pebbly bed,
    A loathsome carrion lay.

There like a lecherous woman, legs in the air,
    Burning and sweating poisons
With cynical disdain it spread its belly
    Full of putrid exhalations.

*   *   *

– And nevertheless, you, too, shall match this dung,
    Twin of this horrible infection,
Starlight of my eyes, sunlight of all I am,
    My angel and my passion!

So wrote Baudelaire, associating love and sex with death and decay.

In the nineteenth century the sophisticated urban man became increasingly introspective, increasingly aware of his inescapable links to the second sex, and less and less able to see her as a human being, so preoccupied was he with his own emotional outpourings.

The mood of romanticism had its ties with the past. Rejecting the surface commonsense approach of the age of reason, it went to the Gothic for its cult of terror. It even revived the idea of sin, mostly in reverse by dabbling in satanism and including blasphemy on its list of perverse pleasures. Apparently the upheaval of the French Revolution and awareness of social injustice elsewhere continued to disturb the nineteenth-century psyche. It is noteworthy, too, that many of the poets reacted to industrialism which was rapidly blasting the countryside, degrading the working class, and manufacturing new fetters for the human spirit.

We have the feeling that in earlier ages it was easier to reject women, to escape from them. The medieval man had his monasteries and his warrior groups. The image of the gallant is never that of a homebody. We see him drinking with his fellows and calling for women when it suits him. In the nineteenth century, the house, the room, the family closed in. Men are constantly aware of women and write love poems to them; seldom, however, achieving the awareness and insight of such an exceptional human being as Chaucer.

Of course it is true that we seldom have a detailed idea of just what went on among the less literate and articulate members of society. On the whole, however, there was probably more overt brutality towards women, more pietistic moralizing, also used to keep them in their place, and, among those who had social aspirations, a good deal of aping of the aristocracy. It is the dominant group, and the artists who are accepted by this group, which sets the pattern for the intellectual and emotional forms which characterize a period.

From the past therefore the concept of sex as sin, the *femme fatale*, and Don Juanism were available for the expression of male anxiety. The so-called decadent romantic writers were able to add cruelty, decay and a mortuary atmosphere to their image of the relationship between the sexes. Just as Baudelaire is reminded by his angel and his passion of a decaying corpse with its legs spread, so in many cases the ambivalence of sexuality is dramatized with a ghoulish pleasure, the repugnant side uppermost. The nineteenth-century man was, of course, no longer able to rationalize his reactions in terms of magic; instead he sanctified his perverse thrills in the name of art.

Significantly enough, three characteristic figures who maintained a kind of chain of influence, Poe, Baudelaire and Swinburne, seemed to have been shaped by the same sort of family tensions. Poe and Baudelaire hated their stepfathers while Swinburne's relationships with his own father were extremely hostile. In the case of Baudelaire, we know that, as the child of a marriage of convenience, his mother lavished an overabundance of affection upon him in his earliest years only to marry a second time, rejecting her

son and lover for a military man who really aroused her mature
eroticism. This pattern, which is repeated in the case of several
other writers whom we shall discuss is what Frederic Wertham has
labelled the 'Orestes complex'. He lists the main characteristics:
'excessive attachment to the mother image; hostility against the
mother image, a general hatred of women; indications of homosexual
potentialities, ideas of suicide and emotional disorder based on profound feelings of guilt'. In *Dark Legend*, Wertham describes a case
of matricide resulting from this complex of forces. The writers we
are dealing with exhibit some if not all of the characteristics just
listed; above all, hostility towards women. As Wertham also remarks, 'One cannot hate without fear.' It is probable that an Orestes
complex is the exciting cause for the literary misogyny we are about
to discuss but that the fundamental dread of women is also present.
All the three poets just mentioned have been accused of impotency
or at least sexual weakness by their biographers and thus, together
with a sense of rejection by their mothers, these writers also had to
struggle with a sense of inferiority in relation to the second sex.
Exceptional as these writers were both in temperament and in
individual unhappy experiences, their gift of expression was so great
that they interposed their vision between men and the living,
breathing women of the nineteenth century.

Poe's marriage of the Gothic horror tradition with his own
peculiarities is exemplified by his fondness for corpses and grave-
yards. Although the Gothic novelist Mrs Radcliffe was a great
popularizer of mouldy skeletons, in Poe's hands the tradition is connected with love. He speaks of 'The vault of thy lost Ulalume', he
sings of Annabel Lee, 'In her sepulchre there by the sea', and again
he tells us in 'A Paean':

> But she is gone above,
>   With young Hope at her side,
> And I am left with love
>   Of the dead who is my bride. –

More explicitly charnel is 'The Sleeper'.

> My love she sleeps. Oh, may she sleep,
> As it is lasting, so be deep!
> Soft may the worms about her creep!

In a whole group of stories the hero is no sooner married than his wife dies. In the tale 'Ligeia' the wife dies, the hero marries a second time only to find his new companion soon moribund. In a series of trances and returns to life she subtly changes and finally rises up, his lost Ligeia. His reaction is one of horror. Again in 'Morella' the husband pathologically longs for his wife's death. She obligingly expires in giving birth to a daughter whom he loves but cannot bring himself to name. Finally when she is almost grown up he has her baptized. Just as she is named Morella, after her mother, a sepulchral voice cries, 'I am here.' The girl dies at once and the mother's tomb is found to be empty.

In these peculiar episodes there is both a strong death wish projected towards women and a fascinated dwelling on returns from the tomb which seems to have overtones of necrophilia. These are expressed more clearly in 'The Fall of the House of Usher'. Here, when the Lady Madeline has been buried by her brother, the young man becomes a prey to gloomy misgivings, fearing that she was buried alive. Sure enough she returns. '– But then without those doors there DID stand the lofty and enshrouded figure of the Lady Madeline of Usher. There was blood upon her white robes, and the evidence of some bitter struggle upon every portion of her emaciated frame. For a moment she remained trembling and reeling to and fro upon the threshold, then, with a low moaning cry, fell heavily inward upon the person of her brother, and in her violent and now final death-agonies, bore him to the floor a corpse, and a victim to the terrors he had anticipated.' The return-from-death theme is here spelled out in terms of a grim parody of sexual connection in which the semi-decayed and dying woman destroys the man in her embrace. The image is not unlike Baudelaire's in the poem quoted at the beginning of the chapter.

Poe, however, has more explicit horrors in store. The tale 'Berenice' starts off with a clear expression of apprehension towards the woman from which it is named. 'During the brightest days of her unparalleled beauty, most surely I had never loved her.... And *now* – I shuddered in her presence, and grew pale at her approach; yet bitterly lamenting her fallen and desolate condition, I called to mind that she had loved me long, and, in an evil moment, I spoke to her of marriage.' Despite the fact that she had been 'transformed' by epilepsy, the hero of the story marries her. One day she stands before him, emaciated and with dull eyes.

'I shrank involuntarily from their glassy stare to the contemplation of the thin and shrunken lips. They parted; and in a smile of peculiar meaning, *the teeth* of the changed Berenice disclosed themselves slowly to my view. Would to God that I had never beheld them, or that having done so, I had died!' By evening the poor woman is obligingly dead of epilepsy. Apparently she is buried somewhere in the yard, and the hero has a spell of amnesia. He awakens with a sharp cry ringing in his ears. A servant enters. 'He told of a wild cry disturbing the silence of the night – of the gathering together of the household – of a search in the direction of the sound; – and then his tones grew thrillingly distinct as he whispered to me of a violated grave – of a disfigured body enshrouded, yet still breathing, still palpitating, still *alive!*' The narrator's clothes are bloodstained, he sees a spade leaning against the wall. With a shriek he seizes a box lying on the table beside him. It slips from his hands and falls open, disclosing dental instruments, 'intermingled with thirty-two small, white and ivory-looking substances that were scattered to and fro about the floor'.

In this fantasy, Poe has managed to mingle the return-from death theme with the most aggressive sadism. But even more significant is the image of the teeth which Poe has dredged up from his unconscious – clearly the old chimera of the *vagina dentata*, here thanks either to American prudery or Poe's own psychological censorship, displaced upward.

All this might be waved away as literary posturing, but literary postures are dictated by the writer's compulsions. With the facts of Poe's own marriage in mind, fantasy is reflected in actuality. There is no doubt that he chose to marry a child because, by this device, physical connection could be avoided. Ironically, Virginia's death from tuberculosis reproduced Poe's favourite situation of the dying mistress.

We know that Baudelaire became deeply interested in Poe's work and spent a good deal of time translating it. Both felt themselves to be isolated rebels, mistreated by society. Much of their irresponsible behaviour was intended to punish their families and especially their mothers, but we must not forget that they were also insecure in their masculinity. Poe was able to avoid the test of phallic virility by his choice of a wife and in fantasy by killing off his mistresses. For him a beloved woman was a dead woman. Baudelaire's psychological mechanism ran to projection and also to some extent to sadism. If he could not dominate his loves with his penis, he could endow them with all the hostile feelings that were burning in his own heart. His favourite feminine image is a cold, indifferent, cruel beauty. In one strangely revealing poem he pours out his aggressions against his own mother, couching them in terms of her hatred for him, expressed in a blasphemous prayer.

> Would that I had brought forth a knot of vipers
> Rather than to have nourished such a mockery,
> Cursed be that night of ephemeral pleasures
> In which my womb conceived to punish me.
>
> Since Thou hast chosen me from among so many women
> Only to be my sad husband's shame,
> Since I cannot toss this unnatural monster,
> Like a rejected love letter, into the flame
>
> I fling back again the hate Thou hast heaped on me
> Upon this cursed instrument of all Your spite,
> I will soundly twist this miserable tree
> So that its poisoned buds shall never sprout.

Further on in the same poem, the poet's wife expresses herself with equal ferocity.

> And when I have tired of these impious farces,
> My strong and fragile hand will know how to part,
> With its nails, long as the claws of Harpies,
> His flesh and rip a pathway to his heart.
>
> Out of his breast I'll tear the ruddy heart,
> Like a young nestling that quivers and beats,
> And as fodder for my favourite animal
> Scornfully I'll fling it at his feet.

The predatory feline image is a favourite one.

> She stares at me with the eyes of a subdued tiger . . .

And again:

> Come, lean on my heart, you deaf and cruel soul,
> Adored tiger, beast with the indolent air,
> I long to plunge my trembling fingers lingeringly
> In the thick mane of your heavy hair.

And in a poem to a cat he tells us he sees his loved one reflected in the beast whose cold piercing glance wounds like a dart. Since we know that his mistress was the fairly illiterate and stupid Jeanne Duval, the image thus projected upon her comes out of his own need to find her dangerous and cruel. Actually he bored her with his poems and his fantasies and, judging by her scorn of him as a lover, his lack of virility. In return he had to punish her by writing of the poison which flowed from her eyes or the implacable winter of her disposition. He could also punish her by reduction and distortion in terms of revolting images.

> Blind and deaf machine, fertile in cruelty,
> Useful instrument, drinker of the world's blood.

A still stronger dramatization of repugnance occurs in the following:

> When she had sucked the marrow from my bones
> And languorously I turned to her with a kiss,
> Beside me suddenly I saw nothing more
> Than a gluey-sided leather bag of pus!

This has a familiar ring and indeed St Odo of Cluny in the tenth century had already written, 'How should we desire to embrace what is no more than a sack of dung!' Thus the curiously perverted catholicism of the nineteenth-century decadent makes use of the tradition of the Middle Ages and testifies to the strength of this early formulation of rejection.

Baudelaire was not without his sadistic side. The quarrels which arose between him and Jeanne Duval were bitter and continuous. He could not bear to be with her yet he continued to martyrize himself by clinging to a vision of the poor woman to which she had no relation and which must have only bewildered her. Once he became so enraged that he struck her, causing her to fall and split her head on a table. Although this violent episode resulted from a moment of extreme exasperation, there are other proofs of hostility.

He was fond of making shocking statements such as 'I consider that women are domestic animals which ought to be kept locked up in captivity; they should be well fed and cared for and beaten regularly.' The same sentiments appear in his poetry. To punish Madame Sabatier for being too lighthearted he wishes

> To make in her astonished side
> A wound both wide and deep.

And elsewhere he addresses one of his loves as follows:

> I'll strike you without malice
> Without hate – a butcher's stroke!
> O rock that Moses smote
> And from your eyes will gush
> The waters of your suffering
> To moisten my Sahara . . .

We know, too, that he was attracted by the Don Juan theme, for in 1853 he talked of writing a libretto for Meyerbeer and actually got as far as sketching in a fragmentary scenario. For him Don Juan was to be the archdandy, the great individualist or, in other words, the isolated romantic hero far above the common herd in taste and originality. Actually the solipsism of this type of character accounts for the failure of so many projected romantic poetic plays. Just as Byron's Manfred can do nothing but soliloquize, so the Don Juan is aware of only his own sensations. Thus the evidence we have been presenting shows clearly that the nineteenth-century decadent was farther than ever from any conception of women as people. In Baudelaire's sonnet the great seducer is not dragged down to hell by the Commendatore's statue but instead is allowed to retire to the classical underworld. He is presented to us aloof, proud, destructive, and wrapped in his neuroses like his creator.

> When Charon had received the obola due him
> As Don Juan descended to the stream below,
> A dark beggar, eyes proud as Antisthenes',
> Seized the oars and vengefully began to row.
>
> Showing their hanging breasts through their open robes
> A group of women writhed under a black sky
> And like a herd of victims offered for sacrifice
> Behind him they set up a long wailing cry.

Sganarelle laughingly demanded his wages,
From the riverbank all the wandering dead
Saw Don Louis point out with trembling finger
The brash youth who had mocked his white head.

Shivering in her mourning, thin, chaste Elvire
Near her faithless lover who had been her spouse
Seemed to be begging one supreme smile from him,
Burning with the sweetness of his first vows.

Upright in his armour a great stone soldier
Tended the tiller which cut the black tide,
But the calm hero, leaning on his rapier
Stared at the boat's wake, nor looked to either side.

Swinburne, who translated Baudelaire, and who, more than any
other critic, was responsible for interpreting nineteenth-century
French literature to a prudish Victorian English public, was more
pathological than either Poe or Baudelaire. He was apparently first
made aware of his peculiar disposition when he was introduced to
Sade's *Justine* by Richard Monckton Milnes, who had an extensive
library of erotica. Swinburne wrote a long letter in which he professed to find the horrors described in a novel funny but added, 'A
schoolboy set to write on his stock of experience, and having a real
gust and appetite for the subject in him, may make and has made
more of a short sharp school flogging of two or three dozen
cuts—'

Fron then on, Swinburne was obsessed by flagellation; in letter
after letter to intimate friends he dwelt on such masochistic experiences. He makes it quite clear that his taste for pain was developed by the floggings he received at Eton. To Charles Augustus
Howell he wrote in 1865, 'I want you to compose for me a little
dialogue (imaginary) between schoolmaster and boy – from the first
summons "Now Arthur (or Frank or Harry) what does *this* mean,
sir? Come here" - to the last *cut* and painful buttoning up – a rebuke
or threat at every lash (and *plenty* of them) and a shriek of agonized
appeal from the boy in reply. I want to see how like real life you
will make it. Write this – and you shall have more of my verses – a
fair bargain. Describe also the effect of each stripe on the boy's flesh
– its appearance between cuts.'

Swinburne continued to write all sorts of privately published or unpublished flagellation literature, an early story in which a lady kills her page by flogging, *The Romance of the Rod*, *The Whippingham Papers*, etc. Edmund Gosse, who maintained that the poet had never had any physical relationship with a woman, describes a naïve attempt at a cure worked out by his friends. Ada Isaacs Menken, who was at the time playing in *Mazeppa's Ride* in London, was introduced to the poet in hopes that her hearty and generous femininity would have some effect. She lived with Swinburne for a time but confessed that her mission was never accomplished. After admitting that Swinburne used to visit a brothel where he was flogged, Gosse remarks quaintly that such activity had nothing to do with sex, the poet was so high-strung that he needed pain to release his tensions. Wrote Gosse, 'I believe that the generative instinct was very feebly developed in Swinburne. . . .' Translated from the Victorian, this would mean he was weakly sexed. The editor of his letters mentions persistent oral tradition that he was an active homosexual. In fact one bawdy poem seems to be a confession.

> And what when seen by girls in front
> Was but a lank limp tassel
> Becomes, though puny near a c——,
> Gigantic near an a——hole.

Swinburne was therefore fixed at an infantile level of masochistic flagellation, which was combined with a certain visual sadism – his letters show that he enjoyed the idea of watching flogging. He was personally grotesque, a small man with a big head, rather like a marmoset. Unskilful at athletics, he had various reasons to feel inferior in relation to women. The censorship of his age required that his poetry be publicly heterosexual and as a result he created images of women which are patently counterfeit but always coloured by sadistic associations.

As with Baudelaire and the medieval homilists, the feline images present. He describes Semiramis whose lips

> Curled like a tiger's that curl back to feed;
> Red only where the last kiss made them bleed.

Again:

> As one who hidden in deep sedge and reeds
> Smells the rare scent made where a panther feeds
> And tracking ever slotwise the warm smell
> Is snapped up by the sweet mouth and bleeds
> His head far down the hot sweet throat of her –
> So one tracks love, whose breath is deadlier.

A complicated version of death by means of the female mouth whose symbolism we have abundantly explored in earlier chapters.

The other telltale image, that of the snake, is also used.

> Thou has a serpent in thine hair;
> In all the curls that close and cling;
> And oh, that breast flower!
> Oh love, thy mouth, too fair
> To kiss and sting!

'Faustine', which in its day was considered shocking, is really a composite of fantasy images which create a sadistic phallic woman, of the sort with which we are already familiar.

> She loved the games men played with death,
>   Where death must win
> As though the slain men's blood and breath
>   Revive Faustine.
> Nets caught the pikes, pikes tore the net;
>   Lithe limbs and lean
> From drained-out pores dripped thick red blood
>   To soothe Faustine
>
> *   *   *
>
> What sterile growth of sexless root
>   Or epicene?
> What flower of kisses without fruit
>   Of love, Faustine?
> What adders came to shed their coats,
>   What coiled obscene
> Small serpents with soft stretching throats
>   Caressed Faustine?

If the decadents created a picture of woman as a beautiful, frightening, disgusting or menacing animal on which to hang their dreams and nightmares, and if in many cases their own deviant personalities account for the imagery, nevertheless their contribution to the stereotype of the *femme fatale* was not unrelated to the prevailing attitude of the romantic nineteenth-century novelist or philosopher. Man's doubt concerning his own masculinity seems to become more troubling to him as Western civilization grows more complex. Although the members of the second sex with whom he lives are sometimes in the position of private property, sometimes status symbols, sometimes idealized out of all reality, he continues to project his dissatisfaction with himself upon them. If the world is out of joint, women, as usual, must bear the major share of the blame.

CHAPTER TWENTY

Broad-hipped and Short-legged Race

Germany, in the nineteenth century the home of philosophy, gave birth to a philosopher who rationalized his misogyny in curiously personal ways. It is impossible to separate Arthur Schopenhauer's life from his ideas concerning women. As in the case of nearly all the nineteenth-century figures we are discussing, emotional relationships with his mother were intense and disturbed.

Madame Schopenhauer was married without love, as she wrote in one of her letters, to a man twenty years older than herself, a man whose gloomy, irascible temper she endured for twenty years. Although she maintained that she did her duty, the atmosphere of the home could scarcely have been warm and gay. When Arthur was nine a sister was born and the boy was sent away to a business friend of the family in Le Havre. He lived with him for two years and during that time he learned French. This clear-cut rejection in favour of a younger child certainly left its mark on Arthur Schopenhauer. His father, who may have committed suicide, died in 1805. His mother then left for Weimar without saying good-bye to her son, excusing herself by letter, and set up a salon in which she was able to exercise her social and literary talents. Goethe, the arbiter of Weimar cultural life, was in a difficult position at the time because he had just married his housekeeper. Madame Schopenhauer accepted the housekeeper, secured the protection of Goethe, his patronage for her popular novels, and achieved a position in intellectual circles.

Arthur, who had been forced into business by his father against his will, soon gave up his position and followed his mother to Weimar where he undertook further humanistic studies. His disposition was, however, already crusty and combative. He considered his mother silly and superficial and when he came to dinner managed to insult her literary friends. She, on the other hand, made it quite clear that he irritated and upset her. They agreed to live apart.

When he reached his majority, another source of friction arose, for his mother made difficulties about turning over his inheritance. Arthur Schopenhauer then spent some time studying in Göttingen. He returned to his mother's house in 1813 to find a thirty-three-year-old poet, Müller von Gerstenberg, living in it. The poet was on terms of 'platonic' familiarity with his mother.

Arthur, who had already resented her literary flirtations and opposed the possibility of a stepfather, quarrelled bitterly with the *cavalier servente* and accused his mother of having an affair with him. Madame Schopenhauer wrote her son a letter, as she always did when she had something unpleasant to say. He had made it plain she must choose between him and Gerstenberg. She chose her amorous poet and in the remaining twenty-four years of her life she never saw her son again. The whole episode strongly reinforces the interpretation that he longed for his mother's love and could not forgive her for bestowing it on someone else – in short the Orestes complex.

Schopenhauer had already written his first philosophical work, *The Fourfold Root of the Principle of Sufficient Reason,* which his mother could not understand and made fun of. He told her furiously that his work would live when her frivolous but very popular novels were forgotten. He was right, but belief in his own genius did not compensate for his personal unhappiness. It is clear that any chance of a successful relationship with a woman was poisoned by emotional patterns now deeply imbedded in his unconscious. While living in Italy he had an affair with a certain Teresa, toyed with the idea of marrying her, but eventually decided against it. Something of his sense of sexual inferiority (he was not an unattractive young man) is betrayed by an anecdote concerning Byron. Once, walking with Teresa in Venice, he saw the dashing Byron ride by. He had a letter of introduction to him from Goethe in his pocket. Teresa cried excitedly, 'There goes the English poet!' Schopenhauer never used his letter for fear that Byron would 'put horns on him'.

In 1818 Schopenhauer wrote his masterpiece *The World as Will and Idea*, only to be further frustrated by the closed corporation of the academic world which icily ignored his book. For most of his life he was to meet this sort of rejection because he was not a university professor, and as a free-lance philosopher was viewed with jealousy by the university faculties who considered philosophy their private monopoly.

In 1821 a very strange episode took place. Schopenhauer, then living in Berlin, was developing a series of phobias and one of them was a hatred of noise. He was disturbed by loud chattering and discovered that the anteroom to his apartment had been invaded by a group of women who lived in the building. They maintained they had been given permission to use the room; when he ordered them out, a seamstress refused to leave. There are two versions of what followed. The woman charged that he hit her with his fist, beat her with a stick, threw her down, trampled upon her and caused permanent injury. The philosopher said that he had his walking stick in his hand but that all he did was put his arm around her waist and twice push her out. Schopenhauer was taken to court and won his case. The implacable seamstress carried it to a higher court, got the decision reversed, and forced him to pay her five thalers a month for the rest of her life. This experience was not calculated to improve the philosopher's relationship with the other sex.

His illness in 1823 in Munich was also ironically in keeping with his other unfortunate experiences with women – it is generally considered to have been syphilis. The attack was severe and resulted in temporary paralysis, fainting spells and numbing pain. When he recovered he seems to have been prematurely aged. It was about this time that he began to develop his ideas concerning polygamy and polyandry which he was to elaborate in later books.

Back in Berlin, in the period from 1824 to 1831, Schopenhauer again toyed with the idea of marrying, this time an actress, Fräulein Medon, with whom he was having an affair. After a long period of summing up her virtues and defects he of course ended by avoiding the altar. About this time his eccentricities increased. A phobia concerning being robbed caused him to keep loaded weapons always near him and to hide his more precious possessions. A morbid fear of infection made him lock up the mouthpiece of his pipe for fear someone might use it. He would not allow himself to be shaved because he was afraid of the barber's razor.

The latter part of his life was passed in Frankfurt, where at last he received some recognition for his contributions to European thought. In one of his later books, *Parerga und Paralipomena*, published in 1851, he included the 'Essay on Women' which sums up his reasoned denigration of the second sex. Schopenhauer repeats all the clichés which had been accumulating in Western tradition and justifies them on bad biological and worse psychological grounds. He begins with the generalization that 'women exist, on the whole, solely for the propagation of the species. . . .' From this it follows that 'just as the female ant after fertilization loses her wings which are superfluous and actually dangerous to the business of breeding, so after bearing one or two children a woman generally loses her beauty, probably for the same reason.' Women being thus shaped (presumably by natural selection) to preserve themselves and their young, 'the only calling that really claims their attention is love, making conquests and everything connected with this, toilette, dancing, etc.' Nature works in other wondrous ways. 'Being the weaker, they are dependent by their very nature not upon strength but upon slyness and from this arises their instinctive aptitude and ineradicable tendency to lie.' All in the interest of preserving the species, we discover, 'Perjury in a court of justice is more often committed by women. . . .' The same incubators of the race are 'childish, frivolous and shortsighted', they have no feeling for the arts, and their sole aim is to achieve importance by mastering men. Schopenhauer concludes, 'Therefore the *sexus sequior*, the second sex, is inferior in every respect to the first; their infirmities should be treated with consideration; but to show them great reverence is extremely ridiculous.'

Far more revealing is the famous passage in which he displays distaste for the female body. 'It is only the man whose intellect is clouded by his sexual impulses that could give the name of *the fair sex* to that undersized, narrow-shouldered, broad-hipped and short-legged race.' Still more significant are his arguments for polyandry.

'A woman is capable of gratifying two or three vigorous men simultaneously without suffering in any way.' Since there are twice as many men as women, several men should keep one woman. This is not the argument of a man who feels himself normally potent and fully masculine. Indeed, other statements show his distaste and disillusionment with the sex relation. 'He who marries young is tied later to an elderly wife; he who marries in youth acquires venereal disease and in age has to wear horns.'

On the other hand, quite illogically, Schopenhauer also advocated polygyny on the basis that it would reduce prostitution and also reduce women to their true and natural position as subordinate beings.

Apart from the very clear references to his own unfortunate experiences, the more compulsive motives shaping Schopenhauer's appraisal of women include a definite feeling of sexual inferiority; the belief that women are sexually insatiable and the knowledge that men's capacity for erotic action is limited. Although he undoubtedly was driven by normal impulses, satisfaction was evidently attended by psychological revulsion. 'Most men fall in love with a pretty face but find themselves bound for life to a hateful stranger, alternating endlessly between a workshop and a witch's-kitchen.' His biographer, Vivian McGill, also points out, 'He felt keenly the "abomination" and taboo element which clings to many of the facts of sexual relationship in both savage and civilized societies.' He also dwelt upon the carnal sin of Adam and Eve as a serious and significant historical fact.

Disturbed by these unconscious revulsions, it is not surprising that his thinking became fantastic when he considered the possibility of marriage. Using the familiar beast-of-prey image, he maintained that those who sympathized with women would succumb to the same fate as the keeper in the zoo who sympathized with a lioness defending her cubs – and was eaten. He even went so far as to maintain that 'nature' in the course of evolution had provided men with whiskers to conceal their emotions from their enemies while women needed no such protection because they were instinctive deceivers.

The absurdity of Schopenhauer's amateur biologizing, coming

from a man who had demonstrated his talent for abstract thinking, demonstrates how in the area involving the second sex irrationality continued to reign. The Middle Ages had its myth of sin; now, in the nineteenth century, pseudoscientific mythology was called in to confuse the issue.

CHAPTER TWENTY-ONE

The Femme Fatale

Even such a scientific observer of the human species as Honoré de Balzac, who captured with uncanny omniscience every detail of the corrupt and commercial Restoration society in which he lived, was not without his romantic side. His philosophy was mingled with occultism, and in the mysterious character of Vautrin, the chief villain of the *Comédie Humaine*, demonic forces seem to lurk. In short, in some aspects of his work which are mystical and irrational we can trace his inner compulsions. It seems likely that, in common with the other nineteenth-century writers we have been discussing, his ambivalence towards his mother was intense. Stefan Zweig describes her as follows: 'She had completely neglected her son during the decisive years of his development, suppressing his childish affection for her, deliberately destroying his confidence in himself and trying to keep him at arm's length in humble subjection.' The fact that he formed a liaison with the amiable Madame de Berny when he was twenty-three and she just twice his age (and the mother of nine children) shows pretty clearly that he longed for maternal love and did not find it at home. It is a tribute to his masculinity, however, that this love affair lasted for ten years and gradually tapered off into friendship.

Whatever catalytic to misogyny may have existed in the Orestes situation, we must not lose sight of the fact that Balzac's novels reflect a keen mind and that, like other exceptional artists, he possessed more than ordinary insight.

While the English romantics were aware of the ugliness of the industrial revolution and the cruelty of wage slavery, Balzac was more impressed by the poison of money. For the new bourgeoisie of which he became the Homer, money was power, money was the measure of everything. For this reason his novels are concerned with business, with finance, with the beginnings of advertising and with the corruption of the press. Avarice raises the story of Eugénie Grandet to something like tragedy; Goriot's daughters reject every human sentiment as they drain their father dry of his last cent; César Birotteau is abandoned by everyone when he becomes a bankrupt; everywhere Balzac paints for us a mad squandering of fortunes in which money is the supreme symbol of status. It is natural therefore that he should have much to say about bought women. Although the *grandes courtisanes* appear in all of his novels, his first important work, *La Peau de Chagrin (The Wild Ass's Skin)*, written in 1830, achieves a multiple symbolism which has relevance to our theme. In it he both draws the *femme fatale* and her opposite and reveals that the stable heterosexual male's fantasies concerning the second sex were, in this period, not so unlike those of the decadents we have just been discussing.

The Wild Ass's Skin is frankly a fairy tale and an allegory. It is divided into three parts, the first of which is concerned with Raphael de Valentin's decision to do away with himself after throwing away his last franc at the gaming table. Since he intends to wait until night to commit suicide, he wanders into an antique shop which, in Balzac's hands, is magnified into a mirror of all cultures and civilizations, a kaleidoscope of achievements in terms of the graphic arts which to the disillusioned young man are 'like a poem without end'. To him, however, all is vanity until he encounters a mysterious old man, the owner of the establishment, who, when he hears of Raphael's decision, ironically offers him a talisman. This is a wild ass's skin, burnished to a brilliant sheen, on which are engraved Solomon's seal and an inscription promising the owner anything he wishes for. There is a price, however, for with each wish the skin shrinks and with it the lifespan of the owner. Raphael seizes the skin and wishes for a saturnalian orgy. No sooner does he leave the shop than he encounters two friends who announce they have been searching all over for him, for he is to become the editor of a new, and venal, review which is to support the government. They are about to take him to a banquet given by its founder, a businessman said to have gained his millions by murdering his best friend during the Revolution.

At the banquet are all the leading lights of cultural and intellectual Paris. As the eating and drinking proceeds, Balzac exhibits them in all their cynicism, ribaldry and venality; in fact when this particular chapter was first published, apart from the novel, the characters were named for well-known personages. When the company is sated and thoroughly drunk, it is invited upstairs where the demimondaines come to meet the diners; 'the seraglio offered seductions to all eyes, and pleasures for all caprices'.

Balzac's attitude towards the *grandes courtisanes* is no different from that of Baudelaire. They are considered to be heartless and destructive yet it is quite clear that they outshine legitimate wives. The *femme fatale* may be dangerous but the domesticated woman is a bore. 'In Paris alone do we meet such creatures whose candid faces mask beneath a brow as pure and tender as the petal of a daisy the deepest depravity and the subtlest vice,' Balzac tells us melodramatically.

From the perspective of the present there is considerable irony in the gusto with which the French writer dwells on the 'depravity' of the type of woman whom he considers necessary to his way of life, the woman who has obviously chosen her 'depraved' role because it is expected of her and provides a living. But he goes on to say she is 'A picture of cold corruption, voluptuously cruel, thoughtless enough to commit a crime, strong enough to laugh at it, a species of devil without a heart, who punishes warm and tender souls for experiencing the feelings of which she is deprived.' Balzac, as always, is concerned with a moral view of society and here as usual he stresses the role of money. The courtesan cries, 'I haven't a mania for perpetuity nor much respect for the human species, seeing what God has let it come to. Give me millions and I'll spend them; I will not keep a penny for next year. Live to please and reign – that is the teaching of every pulse in my body.'

Though strongly male-oriented, Balzac is after all a good novelist and for a moment he has insight enough to let the dangerous sex speak for itself. 'To give yourself all your life to a hated being; to bring up children who abandon you and say thank you when they break your heart – those are the virtues you expect from a woman! And then, to reward her for her self-denials, you try to seduce her and heap sufferings on her; if she resists you compromise her. What a life! better be free and love those who please us and die young.' The courtesan is, of course, describing the results of the *mariage de convenance* system by which women are divided into two groups, the faithful and obedient and the 'depraved'. This, therefore, is a general picture of the seductive woman in the microcosm of Paris shown us at Taillefer's banquet. The plot moves into its second phase with the story of the woman without a heart narrated by Raphael to his friend to explain why he had been ready for suicide.

In this tale there are touches of Balzac's autobiography. Raphael describes a typical nineteenth-century patriarchal father: 'If I tried to show him a soft and tender feeling he treated me like a child who had said a silly thing. I dreaded him far more than you and I ever feared a schoolmaster; and to him I was never more than eight years old.' Left penniless by this demanding parent who had great ambitions for his son, and aristocratic connections, Raphael took the last of his money and rented a cheap room from a woman with a young daughter in an obscure part of Paris. Here he set out with rigid economy to work on *The Theory of the Will*, a philosophical work which of course reflects Balzac's own ideas. At this point Raphael was tended by his landlady's daughter, Pauline, who brought him his meals and looked after his room. Pauline was the typical angel of purity familiar to us from sentimental nineteenth-century engravings. Her father had been an army officer supposedly captured on one of Napoleon's campaigns. Since her mother could not afford to educate her, Raphael undertook to instruct her and soon taught her various domestic skills, including how to play the piano. He always, however, treated her as a sister. When the young man had almost completed his treatise he fell in with Eugène de Rastignac, a dandy and a good-natured Gascon, who introduced him to the gay life of Paris. Through him he came to love Countess Fédora who was rich, fashionable and unattainable. The countess, a different type of *femme fatale* from the *grande courtisane*, was the completely frigid woman, who gave herself to no one, who allowed her would-be lovers to wear themselves out with palpitating devotion and then tossed them away. It is interesting that although Raphael and his friend speculate upon the reason for this, it is never disclosed. Balzac, writing from the apogee of male egotism, seems to consider it a part of woman's original sin that Fédora did not respond to the charming Raphael. Her crime was apparently a self-protective egotism which, in the light of the customs of the period, seems quite justified. 'She was standing erect, and replied to my look with a commonplace smile, the odious smile of a marble statue, seeming to express love, but cold as stone.'

Raphael's passion ran its course; he disclosed his love and was cast off indifferently. When he cried out that he would die for love she replied, 'But it seems rather difficult to die at a woman's feet, for I meet dead men everywhere.' It appears that Balzac is half satirical, half caught up by the romanticism which follows, for Raphael decides to perish of excess because Fédora refuses to love him. The whole fine flower of absurdity inherent in the *femme fatale* idea is exposed. Since the countess had warned Raphael that she had no intention of falling in love with him, there is no valid reason to stigmatize her as a woman without a heart. Indeed her lover has nothing to offer except his egotism and his great capacity for feeling. That he should decide to destroy himself by excess because he is frustrated is not Fédora's fault. Although the countess is not drawn as a sympathetic character, neither is Raphael, the young man of talent who believes himself irresistible, subject to tantrums when crossed. Yet, despite Balzac's insight into Raphael's egotism, we have the feeling that he considers Fédora rather a monster. Faintly, like the horns of elfland, we hear echoes of the code of courtly love. Cressida was obliged to take pity on Troilus because he was dying of love. When Fédora refuses, she arouses all those anxieties which sit deep in the male and are always externalized as distrust of the sex which possesses different and dangerous organs of procreation. Raphael cried, 'That woman is killing me! . . . I am mad, sometimes I feel the madness surging in my brain.' Egged on by Rastignac, he spent every cent in debauchery up to the last few francs wagered at the gaming table in the beginning of the story.

At the end of his autobiography Raphael wishes for two hundred thousand francs a year and, when a notary appears to announce that he has inherited a fortune, the skin shrinks. Now that he can actually see his death approaching if he indulges any of his appetites, Raphael's romantic gesture of suicide is abruptly abandoned. The last part of the story concerns itself with his efforts to wish for nothing, simply to vegetate in order to prolong his existence.

Surrounded by his new luxury, he lives the life of a machine. His old family servant, acting as butler, shields him from the world, allows no one to see him and discreetly arranges all his activities. Ironically, to illustrate the allegory, although he possesses the means to indulge any whim, if he allows himself to desire anything, he commits slow suicide. Jonathas, the old butler, makes the mistake of arranging for an evening in the theatre. In the box next to Raphael sits a beautiful and fashionably dressed young woman; it is Pauline. Her father has miraculously returned loaded with money; the angelic landlady's daughter has blossomed into a breaker of hearts. Balzac works the Cinderella magic deliberately, for he has earlier made it clear that Raphael is such a snob that he cannot be stimulated by a woman unless he sees her lapped in luxury. Pauline cannot hide her passion. 'The movement of the sleeve that covered the arm showed that the body was palpitating with the beating of her heart.' She and Raphael shortly throw themselves into each other's arms. The concept of the good woman, the converse of Fédora, is now elaborated in Pauline. All during the time when Raphael had been a poor boarder she had sat up every night painting screens so that she could charge him almost nothing for his food. In addition she paid for his laundry and cleverly placed five-franc pieces where he would think he had mislaid them. When he kissed her, she cries, 'Let death come now, for I have lived!'

After his marriage to Pauline, Raphael throws the talisman down a well, but when the gardener recovers it, he discovers that it has shrunk until it is now only six inches square. All efforts of scientists, whom he now employs, to stretch it are in vain. Wildly, he indulges in another night of love with Pauline and wakes up feverish, with a tubercular cough. With his usual egotism he deserts Pauline to go and live in a sanitorium in hopes of husbanding his life.

The character of Pauline is one of absolute self-abnegation. She is ready to do anything for Raphael; she is, in short, pure male fantasy. As Raphael has remarked earlier, 'Superior men need women of Oriental natures, whose sole thought is the study of their needs. . . .' Since all men consider themselves superior, the definition pretty well covers the ideal woman. Even though Balzac maintains some perspective in regard to Raphael, he is painting the prevailing attitudes of his time and the reader is convinced of the author's fondness for 'the true wife in heart and flesh and bones who will let herself be drawn hither and thither where he goes who is her life'.

Strangely revealing, however, is the way in which the fairy tale has finally worked around to equating the heterosexual act with death. Balzac the moralist is busy showing that the society which enthrones appetite and excess is destructive; Balzac the male has placed even the adoring ideally angelic female Pauline in the position of destroying Raphael by her sexual appetite. And indeed this is how the story ends. Raphael returns home and one night the banished but yearning Pauline appears in his bedroom. He tells her the truth, and she, mistakenly selfless to the end, tries to commit suicide, thinking this will save him. Raphael manages to burst into the room, tries feebly to take her sexually once more and, failing, 'At the last moment, furious at his own weakness, he bit her in the breast. Jonathas, terrified by the cries he heard, rushed in, and struggled to tear his mistress from the dead body to which she clung in a corner of the room. "What do you want?" she demanded. "He is mine. I have killed him." '

And thus despite the realistic and allegorical levels on which the book is written we are left with an image of a woman hovering over her prey like a homicidal female spider.

Interestingly enough, in the latter part of the nineteenth century in France the twin movements of naturalism and symbolism seem in retrospect to be even more romantic in some respects than the forthright storytelling of Balzac. The choice of the sordid subject by the followers of Zola, although it was justified in the name of truth, nevertheless leads us back to Baudelaire's aesthetics of pain and decay. Although Huysmans with his *Marthe*, Edmond Goncourt with *La Fille, Elisa* and Zola with *Nana* all may have felt they were creating sociological documents, there is a strong presumption that darker drives impelled them to paint women in the most sordid aspects possible.

J.-K. Huysmans' novel is clearly misogynist. The female protagonist is drawn as an unintelligent slattern who stifles her lover's poetic talent. Huysmans, who thus started his career with a novel of squalour which was suppressed by the censor, is extremely significant in relation to the further history of the concept of the *femme fatale*, for he not only was the direct descendant of Baudelaire and Poe but he even carries us back to the witch-hunts of the Middle Ages.

A glance at his family reveals the same picture we have sketched so many times. His father, a mediocre Dutch painter, died when Huysmans was young and was replaced by a stepfather, a Monsieur Og. His mother had two girls by this husband. The boy resented the second marriage and felt himself rejected in favour of the girls.

After being banished to a school he did not like, as a teenager Huysmans sought his first sexual experience with a middle-aged prostitute. Unlike Balzac's more successful solution, this search for maternal love was only disillusioning. Two liaisons which followed were unhappy. Huysmans lived with an actress who bore a child which was not his and which he was obliged to support. The ménage was sordid and poverty-stricken. Later he lived with a factory girl who died tragically. This was the period of the war with Prussia, in which Huysmans played a small part. The disturbances of the Commune followed and finally the Third Republic was born. Social upheaval seems, as usual, to have produced psychosexual disturbances; satanism flourished and in Paris there were actually groups which reconstructed a dilettante parody of the Black Mass or witches' sabbat. It was in this atmosphere that literary decadence as a conscious movement was born and Huysmans' *À Rebours* (which is generally translated *Against the Grain* but which really means *In Reverse*) became its manifesto. The young novelist had spent several years freeing himself from the school of Zola, and was now striking out in a new literary genre which bears the clear imprint of his growing neuroticism.

À Rebours has no plot, it simply deals with the opinions and exotic experiments of des Esseintes, a jaded and sophisticated aristocrat who retires to his country house to exploit his bizarre tastes. Huysmans used the eccentric Count Robert de Montesquiou as a basis for his character but obviously endowed him with his own feelings and fantasies. A sexual obsession runs all through the book. We are told at the beginning that the hero is jaded: 'He had contributed to the fortunes of those agencies which for a fee supply dubious gratifications, finally sick and satiated with this repetitive indulgence, these identical caresses, he had plunged into the lower depths thinking to stimulate his exhausted senses and hoping to revive his erotic desires by the exciting contrast of poverty.' We are also told that he invited his guests to a mortuary feast in which the food was black, black candles were lit and the table was served by naked black Negresses – all this in mourning for a temporary loss of potency. Thus once again sexual weakness appears as a cause for feelings of inferiority in relation to the other sex. A description of a painting by Gustave Moreau of Salome which Huysmans hangs in des Esseintes' house is full of misogyny. 'In this she was altogether female, obedient to her passionate cruel woman's temperament; active and alive, the more refined the more savage and the more hateful the more exquisite; she was shown awakening man's sleeping passions, powerfully bewitching and subjugating his will with the unholy charm of a great venereal flower sprouting in sacrilegious beds and raised in impious fields.'

Despite the purple writing, the emotional and physical rejection of the female is powerfully expressed. Such images were to grow even more violent. In the course of developing his decadent tastes, 'surexciting' his senses, des Esseintes cultivates weird and menacing flowers. After working among them he has a dream which is the epitome of lurid symbolic decadence. In the dream a repulsive woman attempts to embrace him. 'He made a superhuman effort to disengage himself from her embrace but with an irresistible movement she seized him and clung to him, and haggardly he saw the savage Nidulanium blossom yawning under her open thighs and bleeding from its sabre-like blades. His body touched the plant's hideous wound, he felt himself dying and awoke with a start, choked, crazy with fear, sighing, "Ah, thank God, it's only a dream."'

Thus in the visions of the Paris decadent the vulva appears as a menacing, bladed wound just as in the folklore of New Guinea or South America. *À Rebours* institutes the disordering of the senses in search of metaphysical experience which was also to be exploited by Rimbaud. From this Huysmans moved on to an actual attempt to investigate contemporary witchcraft. He became friendly with various crackpot characters who believed they were involved with succubi. Among them was a defrocked priest, Joseph Antoine Boullan, who presided at orgies and who insisted he had intercourse with celestial entities. Boullan was also convinced that satanist enemies were constantly attacking him. There is a strong presumption, but no proof, that Huysmans did actually attend a Black Mass. He seems to have been convinced of occult influences, for after writing *Là-Bas* he complained of feeling cold presences passing over his face and resorted to burning a special diabolical incense and muttering charms to protect himself from supernatural dangers.

Before discussing *Là-Bas* it is interesting to note that in Huysmans' art criticism we already find an identification of women with satanism and a thoroughly disturbed attitude towards the female body. Discussing Degas, he praises this painter's pastels of bathing women in a way that shows him to be approaching closely to Schopenhauer and also to Baudelaire and his medieval forebears.

Degas, he said, chose to draw the proletarian woman: 'A creature whose vulgar figure and coarse features lead to continence and arouse horror.' But Degas was even more perceptive than this; there were to be found in his pastels 'a series of froglike and simian poses inherent in even the young and beautiful woman. . . .' In fact his works 'glorify disdain for the flesh as no artist since the Middle Ages has dared to do . . . by the revelation of the damp horror of a body which no bathing can purify'. Having thus characterized women as ugly, revolting and impure, Huysmans goes on to contemplate the paintings of Félicien Rops which included scenes of fantastic eroticism and satanism. Elaborating on these themes, Huysmans tells us that woman 'is, to sum up, the great vessel of iniquities and crimes, the charnel house of poverty and shame, the one who

truly guides into our soul the embassies delegated by all the vices'.
He quotes Tertullian to the effect that witches are generally women.

Huysmans novel, *Là-Bas*, consisted of an interweaving of two
themes. Durtal, the hero of the story, a writer, is retelling the
history of Gilles de Rais, the medieval satanist who slaughtered and
raped hundreds of children in his attempts to summon up the devil
and who, when caught, dissolved into penitence and tears and was
executed in such an aura of piety that even the parents of the mur-
dered infants wept for him. Interspersed with these chapters from
the past are the narrator's discussions of contemporary blaspheming
cults and a liaison with a Madame de Chantelouve who eventually
takes him to the sabbat. Madame de Chantelouve was probably
inspired by a real character, Berthe de Courière, a half-mad creature
who fed consecrated wafers to her dogs. The fictional Chantelouve
is drawn as an insatiable mysterious woman who woos the narrator
by letter. After the first physical relation Durtal reacts against her,
summing up his feelings in the phrase 'Women are only good when
not possessed.' The Black Mass proves to be a dilettante recreation
of the rites described in the *Malleus*. A nude woman forms the altar,
various blasphemies are carried out and an erotic orgy takes place.
Durtal is repelled by the affair and drags Chantelouve away. When
they enter a café and ask for a drink, they are ushered upstairs to a
private room. Here Chantelouve falls upon Durtal and practically
rapes him, revealing to him 'depravities that he had never even
imagined which she spiced with the furies of a ghoul and suddenly,
when he succeeded in escaping, he trembled for he saw fragments of
consecrated wafer in the bed.'

Thus Huysmans has returned completely to the disturbed image
of the female created by the Inquisition in the fifteenth century.
That this had for him a more profound meaning than mere dandyism
is proved by the fact that in 1895 he was converted to Catholicism.
He had reached religious faith by the indirect route of first exploring
sin and his explanation of his sincerity was the same as that developed by Dostoevski, that only by experience of evil could real
sainthood be achieved.

We have shown that all during the nineteenth century traditional
imagery from the past continued to help shape the concept of the

femme fatale through which the constant apprehensions of the male were expressed. Another curious reaction, however, which reached its finest flower in Anglo-American culture, is what has been named Victorian prudery, in essence an effort to desexualize the female completely by splitting her into two concepts.

CHAPTER TWENTY-TWO

The Bell-shaped Woman

The Victorian woman had no legs; they were replaced by 'limbs' and, eventually, covered with many petticoats and crinolines, they disappeared entirely. The bell-shaped creature which resulted wore padded upper garments which effectually concealed the mammary glands. Since undergarments were always hidden away and considered unmentionable, all trace of the dangerous organ with which men had never succeeded in coming to terms was banished from the public consciousness. It was Captain Marryat who, when he visited America, recorded the fact that even the legs of pianos were in some cases covered with crinoline pantalets.

Nakedness, of course, was terrifying, almost as reprehensible as in the Middle Ages. New England missionaries, as early as 1820 when they came to Hawaii, could not wait until they had covered the seductive Polynesian female form with long flowing holokus. The Reverend Bingham wrote, 'Degradation and barbarism, among the chattering and almost naked savages, whose head and feet and much of their sunburnt swarthy skins were bare, was appalling.'

Along with this attempt to deny the visible evidence which identified women as female, went an emotional and intellectual desexualization that was positively fantastic. Women were supposed to be so sheltered from girlhood that they were never to suspect the 'facts of life' existed. A fairly liberal writer in *The Westminster Review* of London states in 1851, 'In men in general, the sexual desire is inherent and spontaneous and belongs to the condition of puberty. In the other sex the desire is dormant, or non-existent till excited; always till excited by undue familiarities. . . . Women, whose position and education have protected them from exciting causes, constantly pass through life without being cognizant of the promptings of the senses.' The author goes on to say, 'Nature has laid many burdens on the delicate shoulders of the weaker sex: let us rejoice that this, at least, is spared them.' A real fear of eros is betrayed by the statement that if women were aware of their physical needs and potentialities, 'sexual irregularities would reach a height of which, at present, we have happily no conception'.

In order to protect women, therefore, the compulsive desire to censor literature (still with us) reached remarkable proportions. It was Charles Dickens who ventured to satirize it in the repeated demand of Mr Podsnap, 'Would it bring a blush of shame to the cheek of a young person?' – the young person being the teen-age Georgina Podsnap. Since the young person's mind was supposed to be a *tabula rasa* we wonder how she was to know when she ought to blush. Such contradictions however are typical of a wholly irrational situation. Anglo-American literature in the mid-nineteenth century was kept pretty much under control but, the continental tradition being franker, there was always danger from abroad, especially from the horrifying details of naturalism. Alfred Lord Tennyson, who himself was thought to have gone too far in the *Idylls of the King*, spoke out bravely against Zola in the following stanza from 'Locksley Hall Sixty Years After', denouncing an age which

> Set the maiden fancies wallowing in the troughs of Zolaism –
> Forward, forward, ay, and backward, downward too into the abysm!

The image of the good woman therefore was 100 per cent pure. To quote Tennyson again, as he described her in *The Princess*, she was

> No angel, but a dearer being, all dipt
> In angel instincts, breathing Paradise,
> Interpreter between the gods and men,
> Who look'd all native to her place and yet
> On tiptoe seem'd touched upon a sphere
> Too gross to tread, and all male minds perforce
> Swayed to her from their orbits as they moved
> And girdled her with music.

Coventry Patmore went further and, in his long poem on wedded love, called her *The Angel in the House*.

If, in other ages, men ran away from women, the Victorians made a cult of the Home. A lecturer on the insipid songs of Mrs Felicia Hemans described 'the true office of the bard; to decorate the homely threshold, to wreathe flowers around the domestic hearth'. The pure, ethereal, bell-shaped creature who glided about, with no visible legs, as if on wheels, presided over the home with its over-stuffed furniture and its loaded whatnots and heavy velvet curtains, elevating men's minds when they came back from the marts of trade. Indeed her identification with the home is interestingly des-cribed by John Ruskin, the arbiter of the taste of his time.

Ruskin's essay 'Of Queens' Gardens' begins by explaining: 'It is the woman who watches over, teaches and guards the youth; it is never by any chance the youth who watches over, or educates his mistress.' This he proves by roving vaguely over the courtly love of the Middle Ages. Although he appears to be establishing a connection between Victorian idealization of women and the courts of love, he conveniently forgets that the troubadours were dealing with flesh-and-blood lovers who never denied their physical urges, even if they debated what to do about them. Ruskin's knight and mistress are as vague and sweetly spiritual as the figures in a Pre-Raphaelite paint-ing. Ruskin's ideal woman, he tells us, 'is protected from all danger and temptation. The man in his rough work in the open world must encounter all peril and trial. . . . But he guards the woman from all this; within his house, as ruled by her, unless she herself has sought it, need enter no danger, no temptation, no cause of error or offence.' As the majestic periods roll on we learn that a man should know all things thoroughly but a woman only enough to sympathize with her husband's pleasures. In the snug nest she has created for him, 'So far as she rules, all must be right or nothing is, she must be en-duringly and incorruptibly good. . . .' Again: 'What the woman is to be within her gates, as the centre of order, the balm of distress and the mirror of beauty . . .' is something which to a modern mind seems totally unreal. In Ruskin's world, the Victorian, after driving a hard bargain, paying his workers less than a living wage, and de-nouncing the Chartists as dangers to law and order, goes home to his wife for solace since 'All that is dark in him she must purge into purity.'

A final image is truly revealing. 'This is the true nature of the home – it is the place of Peace, the shelter not only from all injury, but from all doubt, terror and division . . . and, wherever a true wife comes, this home is always around her . . . home is yet wherever she is; and for a noble woman it stretches far around her, better than ceiled with cedar or painted with vermilion.'

By his symbolism Ruskin has thus robbed the womb of its terrors and by ignoring the organ at its mouth, it is both the woman and the home at the same time, a refuge into which the anxiety-ridden male may creep and forget all his troubles.

In Ruskin's philosophy the woman is on the one hand a servant in her husband's house and, on the other, his moral arbiter. A lady novelist, Mrs Sarah Stickney Ellis, who knew her place, offers us a more abject formula. 'It is the privilege of a married woman to be able to show by the most delicate attentions how much she feels her husband's superiority to herself . . . by a respectful deference to his opinion, and a willingly imposed silence when he speaks.'

In a relationship so far removed from the flesh, all expression of passion was theoretically taboo. Here is how Charlotte Yonge, a best-selling novelist and the acme of piety and propriety, allows one of her heroes, Louis Fitzjocelyn, to propose:

'If you would have me, I would do all I could to make you happy; and it could be such a joy to my father – and to me.' Fitzjocelyn later explains his proposal more fully to a friend. 'I could not meet anyone half so good, or whom I know so well. I look up to her, and – yes – I do love her heartily – I would not have done it otherwise.'

When we realize that thousands admired the purity of Miss Yonge's sentiments, wept over her death scenes, and considered themselves elevated by her moral precepts, we begin to feel that the Good Woman has turned into a wraith, a kind of disembodied allegory.

Yet large families of children saw the light of day in both Victorian England and America. It is difficult to picture the secrets of the ideal intimacy. The husband, who would never have dreamed of viewing his wife's naked body, crept into a dark bedroom to perform an animal duty. The wife endured her part of the operation in a sort of coma, apparently pretending that nothing was happening. The slightest sign of life on her part would have been a humiliating admission of depravity. The male Victorian's apprehensions were thus soothed by refusing to admit that his wife was a party to the act, by turning it into mere masturbation and pretending she was not there. As a result, a tradition of frigidity in women arose which has provided more than one generation of psychoanalysts with a copious clientele.

We have already seen that Balzac drew a sharp line of demarcation between the good woman and the 'depraved' but exciting courtesan. In Victorian culture the split was sharper and the contrast more intense. When any reference was actually made to eros it was habitually associated with animality, with the 'brute' in man. As Tennyson put it in Darwinian terms in *In Memoriam*:

> Arise and fly
> The reeling Faun, the sensual feast;
> Move upward, working out the beast,
> And let the ape and tiger die.

But the imperious brute was there and, as in other periods, its owner created a class of women to satisfy it. The anonymous author writing on prostitution in *The Westminster Review*, who was inspired by a moral purpose, nevertheless begins a lengthy apology for speaking of 'so dismal and delicate a matter' only overcoming his qualms 'with pain, reluctance, and diffidence'. He furthermore goes on to make it clear that he shares the customary fear of sex. 'Sensual indulgence, however guilty in its circumstances, however tragic in its results is, when accompanied by love, a sin according to nature, fornication is a sin against nature. . . .' Prostitution, of course, brought filth into the sanctuary of the affections and brought man down to the level of the brute. All this preamble was thought necessary before going on to describe the condition of women who had not had the good fortune to be born into middle-class families and provided with all the opportunities of living up to the public ideal of purity. The author goes on to point out with some indignation that it was considered discreditable for a good woman to know of the existence of her sisters in sin. Throughout the article the most significant point made is the unspeakable brutality with which these women (who were not supposed to exist) were treated.

'No language is too savage for these wretched women . . . they are outcasts, Pariahs, lepers . . . they are kicked, cuffed, trampled on with impunity by everyone. . . . They seem to be considered far more out of the pale of humanity than Negroes on a slave plantation, fellahs in a pasha's dungeon.'

The image of the British courtesan bears no relation to the handsome kept women described by Balzac. Again and again the writer refers to 'the curses, the blows, the nameless brutalities they have to submit to from their ruffianly associates of the brothel and the saloon'. He also points out that if they are mistreated or cheated, it is useless for them to go to court because they are so discriminated against that their word would never be taken against a man's; their evidence would be disregarded. As a result, 'Gin alone enables them to live or act; without its constant stimulus and stupefaction they would long since have died from mere physical exhaustion or gone mad from mental horrors.' The writer estimates that there were, in 1850, 8,000 to 10,000 prostitutes in London and says that in New York there were said to be as many as 12,000. These are fairly shocking figures, particularly stark after the moralizing which has just been quoted, the dream of purity which the Victorian cherished as a public image. The author of the article has no illusions; he writes, 'The extent to which the frequentation of brothels is carried among all classes and professions and even among the married . . . is little suspected by the public at large. On this topic some frightful disclosures have, from time to time, had to be hushed up; though not soon enough to prevent an astounding glimpse of the hideous iniquity within.'

Yet the writer is honest enough to quote a number of biographies and case histories of prostitutes, both full- and part-time, which show clearly that the majority of these unhappy women, often seamstresses, were simply not paid enough to keep them and their dependents alive and consequently had to eke out a living by satisfying the urges of the Victorian male, wearied of the purity of his home.

The author of the article is rather at a loss how to cure the evils of prostitution. He finds the government supervision of the French a lesser evil than the hypocrisy of the British and shows that many prostitutes give up their trade when provided with a better way of making a living. His final suggestions are typical of the age. He remarks that if boys at school were not allowed to use licentious language and to indulge in 'coarse and vulgar habits' there might be a chance of keeping them chaste before marriage. 'Is it not certain that all of the delicate and chivalric which still pervades our sentiments towards woman may be traced to *repressed* and therefore hallowed and elevated passion.' In other words, Ruskin and more Ruskin. Instead of seeking a more anxiety-free approach to sex, the typical Victorian solution was to deny its expression completely.

A physician, William Acton, who wrote a standard work on prostitution which went into a number of editions, expressed a completely resigned attitude. 'I regard prostitution as an inevitable attendant upon civilized, and especially close-packed, populations. When all is said and done, it is and I believe ever will be ineradicable.'

Acton, for all his medical approach, draws an equally harsh picture as that presented by the contributor to *The Westminster Review* 'The rouged and whitewashed creatures, with painted lips and eyebrows and false hair, accustomed to haunt Langham Place, portions of The New Road, The Quadrant, the peristyle of the Haymarket Theatre, the City Road, and parts of the Lyceum were the most prominent gangs of this description in London. They were watched by persons of their own sex purposely to prevent their abstraction of the lodging house finery, and clandestine traffic with men. These wretched women, virtually slaves, though nominally free, with bodies and time no longer their own, were restricted for the convenience of their real proprietors to certain beats or parades and from year's end to year's end might be observed on the same side of a particular street.'

Dr Acton explains that the brothel keeper provided them with food, lodging and clothes and was careful to keep them in debt so that they could never free themselves. If they became diseased they were driven into the streets with taunts and curses. When not working, they lived in the brothel. 'During the day . . . dishevelled, dirty, slipshod and dressing-gowned in the kitchen where the mistress keeps her table d'hôte, stupid from beer or gin, they swear and chatter brainless stuff all day, about men and millinery, their own schemes and adventures and the faults of others of their sisters.'

Acton's description of the kept woman, equivalent to Balzac's *grande courtisane*, is equally uncompromising; despite his medical attitude, male hostility peeps out. 'She is a sort of whitewashed sepulchre, fair to the eye but full of inner rottenness – a mercenary human tigress albeit there exists at times some paltry bull dog nursed in the same Bohemian den who may light up all the fires of womanhood within her – some rascally enchanter who may tame her at the height of her fury, when none else human may approach her, by whispering or blows. Exigent of respect beyond belief, but insufferably rude, she is proud and high-minded in talk one moment, but not ashamed to beg for a shilling the next.'

Acton further pointed out that seduction was blamed on women; men could not be punished for it without witnesses but the law could always be used against women because the woman was the consenting party.

Woodhull and Claflin's Weekly added a few details concerning prostitution in New York. If the prostitute 'is seen to stop and talk to a man, to prevent arrest she gives the patrolman $3 to $10 a week. Police captains and police sergeants demand $20 to $30 when these officers need money. Wine is furnished them when wanted and they are accorded the privilege of frequenting without charge such inmates [of the brothel] as they may select.'

The ambivalent attitude towards women in the nineteenth century is thus carried almost to the point of caricature by the Victorians. It will be remembered that in ancient times the fertility goddess was divided into the beneficent great mother and the dark, sexually dangerous earth mother. In the Middle Ages, when sex was frantically denied, the great mother image was saved by making her a virgin; her sexual processes simply did not exist. The Victorians after a lapse of some centuries brought her back as the bell-shaped angel who, to all intents and purposes, by means of a conspiracy of silence, also produced young by parthenogenesis. Men publicly refused to contemplate the horrors of her femininity. On the other hand, the woman who was all eros was degraded to the role of hired instrument of pleasure and the male's extreme hostility towards her was expressed by physical brutality, exploitation and indifference to her sufferings. Thus the split concept, virgin and prostitute, was born.

This retrogression to a situation less relaxed than, for instance, that of the Renaissance is hard to explain. It appears that the basic male apprehensions we have been tracing were somehow reactivated. There are, of course, so many historical variables, we can only conjecture how the discontents of civilization have been increasing the tensions in the human psyche. Although the Victorian Age was for England and for the United States (except for the Civil War period) a time of relative economic stability and industrial expansion, emotionally and intellectually there was conflict in a number of areas. To begin with, a revival of religion after the rationalistic indifference of the eighteenth century took various and contradictory forms, and such individuals as Charles Kingsley and John Henry Newman went through various phases and struggles with their consciences. Faith was lost and found, the emotionalism of the dissenters was carried to the orgiastic extremes of revivalism, especially in the thirties in America. Opposed to it was a Church of England piety which, today, strikes us as rather conventional, a desire to feel appropriately rather than experience actual feeling. On the one hand when the old literal interpretations of the Bible were challenged by Darwinism and the new sciences of anthropology and psychology, the champions of conservatism felt threatened and fought back. On the other hand 'muscular' thinkers accepted evolution, equated it with free competition and free trade, and could believe with Kingsley that Englishmen pleased God by inventing, importing and exporting and had been commanded by Him to replenish the earth and subdue it.

Although the social and economic equalitarianism of the French Revolution had been stemmed by reaction, the spectre of the Terror was not easily forgotten. It was brought back by the short-lived Paris Commune and kept alive by workers' movements. The Chartists, as early labour organizers in England, were a threat and, in Germany, Karl Marx was spinning a philosophy which called again for revolution. Although the bourgeoisie was in power, its leaders knew that its emergence had toppled the feudal order. What if the working class should grow strong enough to make its bid for dominance? All of these fears and tensions were wound in and out of the relationship between the sexes. An interesting example of this interaction occurs in a review by Lady Eastlake of *Jane Eyre*. Jane was, of course, an early symptom of revolt against the public image of the Victorian woman. Instead of quietly fading into her submissive place, an eternal spinster, as the governess heroine of many other novels of the period did, Jane asserted herself as a passionate human being and even aspired to the affections of her employer. The aristocratic critic saw something else in the novel. 'There is throughout it a murmuring against the comforts of the rich and the burdens of the poor. . . . We do not hesitate to say that the tone of mind and thought which has overthrown authority abroad and fostered Chartism and rebellions at home, is the same which has written *Jane Eyre*.' Lady Eastlake was speaking for the male world. If the male Victorian had put woman in her place as a virgin and prostitute so that he could deal with the changing values and the challenging conflicts of his era, he was bound to react strongly when, for the first time in history, she made a determined effort to rebel.

Among all the contradictions of the nineteenth century, therefore, the appearance of the New Woman, bent on shattering the image of the virgin and the prostitute, and actually demanding a change in the laws which imprisoned the second sex, was a culminating blow to male security.

Before discussing further masculine reactions to this change in attitude on the part of the submissive sex it is important to sketch certain representative individuals who heralded things to come whose pretensions were to arouse new terrors in the male soul.

CHAPTER TWENTY-THREE

The Natural Right to Love

'The Queen is most anxious to enlist everyone who can speak or write to join in checking this mad, wicked folly of Woman's Rights, with all its attendant horrors, on which her poor, feeble sex is bent, forgetting every sense of womanly feeling and propriety.' So wrote bell-shaped Queen Victoria in 1860, apparently feeling no contradiction in the fact that she herself was filling a man's role.

Actually in 1792 Mary Wollstonecraft's *Vindication of the Rights of Woman* had blown the first trumpet in the battle for freedom. Her ideas and activities were combined with social radicalism which, in turn, was compromised by the Terror of the French Revolution. The seeds of revolt therefore lay dormant during the rise of bourgeois conservatism until a new generation of women was ready to carry on.

Three of these rebels, each emerging from a different background, and each of a different nationality, will give some idea of the stamina it took to stand up and defy a male-dominated world. Both George Sand and George Eliot felt the need to take male names, in order to compete with the other sex in the field of fiction. In the United States Victoria Woodhull, on the other hand, triumphed through her femininity and skilfully used men to help create her public personality. All three women, although their interests and their styles differed, were fundamentally in agreement in their effort to assert their right as women to legal, sexual and emotional freedom.

To begin with George Sand, born Aurore Dupin in 1804: She was the daughter of Colonel Dupin, who came of a land-owning family of some pretensions. Her mother had been a dancer, had had affairs with other members of the Napoleonic army, and made a love match with the colonel, who must have been a man of remarkably liberal ideas to have married her. She was faithful to him for eight years until he was killed in an accident. Aurore (who had been begotten out of wedlock) became a bone of contention between her Bohemian mother and her father's aristocratic mother. The old lady never failed to stress Sophie Dupin's dubious past. Little Aurore rebelliously sided with her mother. After many quarrels, the child was put into a convent while her mother went off to live a free life in Paris. The convent was run by English nuns, from whom Aurore learned to speak English and drink tea. She also received a good literary education. Although she never became an orthodox church member, a youthful crush on one of the nuns helped to channel her emotions into vague, romantic piety.

When she left the convent she went to live with her grandmother on the estate at Nohant where, for a girl, she had unusual freedom. She lived a horsey outdoor life and wore men's clothes when she went hunting. She was friendly with the village doctor who allowed her to become his assistant. Working as a volunteer nurse, she acquired a matter-of-fact attitude towards the human body which sometimes shocked her lovers in later life. She read Rousseau, whose ideas filled her with a new enthusiasm she somehow managed to blend with her personal emotional religion.

When her grandmother died, her mother took her to Paris, but she had neglected Aurore for too long; there was no real bond of love between them. In addition her mother was possessive in a rather paranoid way and obsessed with the idea of marrying her off. When Aurore objected she threatened to lock her up in a convent again.

While staying with friends of her mother's in the country, Aurore happened to meet Casimir Dudevant, a long-nosed young country squire, the natural son of a baron. Since his father recognized him Casimir lived with the family and had been given a generous settlement although he had no claim to the paternal acres. Casimir was kind to the rather troubled young Aurore and asked her to marry him, without first consulting her mother, an unconventional step which pleased her. It was his last.

The pair were married in 1822, Aurore became pregnant immediately and her son, Maurice, was born on the estate at Nohant where the young couple had settled. The Dudevants were mismated physically, or at least Casimir was an unskilful lover, for he wrote to his wife, 'Your senses seem proof against all attempts of mine to rouse them.' Aurore herself later explained bitterly, 'Men do not know what is fun for them is hell for us. . . . Nothing is more frightful than the terror, the suffering, and the disgust occasioned in a poor young thing as the result of being violated by a brute. We bring them up as saints only to dispose of them as fillies.'

Although Aurore was not living in Victorian England, the nineteenth-century denial of sexual knowledge to women had shaped her education. She was to suffer from this erotic failure, which seems to have been traumatic, all of her life.

Casimir was inadequate in other ways. No more than a country squire, his interests extended to shooting, drinking and local politics – not to books. His wife had a feeling for literature and a flair for writing. She was evidently more intellectual than he and was bored by provincial life.

They got on each other's nerves, quarrelled and began to drift apart. On a trip to Bordeaux she met a young lawyer with whom she fell in love. The couple went through crises of idealism and platonic vows. There were emotional farewells and chaste kisses. Unfortunately, when, on a second trip to Bordeaux, they met again, Dudevant surprised them in each other's arms. Aurore fainted. Casimir was briefed on the Platonic aspects of the affair, and urged to rise to heights of understanding. This he attempted not very successfully. He began to feel he was losing his wife and took to drinking.

Although Aurore and Aurélien de Sèze, her Bordeaux admirer, continued to exchange passionate letters, Aurore got it into her head that he had turned to other women for physical fulfillment. On a trip to Paris she met a student of natural science in whom she had had an interest some years earlier. All of a sudden she had her first affair, spending considerable time travelling about with her lover, Stéphane. When she returned home she was pregnant and in a few months gave birth to a girl. When Aurélien heard about the affair he was dazed. Casimir continued to drink and become involved in business deals in which he lost money.

Aurore rationalized her behaviour by a vague reference to a higher authority. 'I neither could, nor wished to act save in harmony with a law which is superior to the customs and opinions of the majority.'

Casimir, ejected from her bedroom, solaced himself with his daughter's nurse and his wife's maid. By this time he and Aurore tacitly went separate ways. Aurore, to mitigate her boredom, was writing a novel. She still thought in pietistic terms. 'It was desperately important for me to seek in God the answer to my life's enigma, the knowledge of my real duties, the justification for my secret feelings.' Aurore's God was scarcely that of the Catholic Church, however, but rather a deity fashioned from her own emotions, which remained with her all of her life. Whatever she did was justified because it was in some way sanctioned by her private theology.

By this time she was dreaming of a more glamorous and sophisticated existence. Although she had visited Paris, she had never entered its intellectual circles. There was Victor Hugo, there was Honoré de Balzac and countless other men of letters whom it would be thrilling to meet. There were new ideas in the air; François Fourier was elaborating his theories of Utopian socialism into dreams of colonies, self-supporting, equalitarian, based on formulas involving numbers and colours. But in the doctrines of Fourier and also those of the other important radical social philosopher, Saint-Simon, there was talk of equality between the sexes and the Right to Pleasure. It was beginning to seem as if the God of Aurore Dudevant had intuitively been aware of what was going on.

In 1830 a young man with curly blond hair and a pink and white complexion, Jules Sandeau, was holidaying at a neighbour's. A law student in Paris, he combined with his rather delicate physical charms some awareness of the literary world of Paris. Aurore met him, was captivated by him, and in a short time was carrying on an affair with him in a summerhouse on her estate. Casimir said nothing but one day Aurore came upon a letter in his desk marked *Not to be Opened until my Death*. Aurore opened it and learned precisely what Casimir thought of her. In high dudgeon she informed Casimir that henceforth she was spending six months of the year in Paris. She would leave the children in the care of a good tutor at Nohant and she was to be supplied with money. From now on, Aurore's overpowering and almost masculine personality began to operate. Casimir seems to have been completely dominated, for he gave in. He even wept when she said good-bye.

In Paris, Aurore, thanks to some introductions, met a few key literary men and soon became part of a circle of young intellectuals. She began to write for magazines and, although the novel she brought with her did not sell, she worked on another with some help from Jules Sandeau, her acknowledged lover. Her haughty mother-in-law, the baroness, had remarked that if she intended to publish a book, 'I sincerely hope you will not set the name I bear on the title page.' She therefore put a compromise name derived from her lover's, J. Sand, on the book. *Rose et Blanche* was a success and sold rather well. She was gaining some reputation but unfortunately her love life was once more unhappy.

Jules was now suffering from tuberculosis. A number of Aurore's lovers were semi-invalid or became so before she was through with them. Her hearty rural upbringing had given her the robust body of a country squire and she was a demon of nervous energy. She tended to choose delicate souls for her lovers towards whom she was, in a sense, maternal (de Musset was 'the urchin') and, in a sense, masculine. She often wore men's clothes in Paris, and indeed the long-nosed, strong face was not particularly feminine. Yet her temperament was feminine and passionate. She worried about Jules. 'And how I tremble at the thought that I have done him more harm by my devotion than by my resistance. I am killing him and the pleasure I give him is bought at the cost of his life. I am his scrap of Wild Ass's Skin.' Curiously enough she accepted the sexually destructive role which had been outlined in Balzac's novel.

She wrote her next book, *Indiana*, while she was back in Nohant. Since Sandeau had had no part in it, there was some discussion about the signature, which was finally changed to George Sand, the name by which she is known to us.

Indiana made her a celebrity. The preface expresses her programme as far as she ever had a programme. Indiana, she wrote, 'stands for *Woman*, a weak creature charged by the author with expressing those passions which have been compressed, or, if you will, *suppressed* by human laws. She is Choice at odds with Necessity;

she is Love blindly butting its head against all the obstacles set in its path by civilization. . . .' In other words, Sand insisted that woman had a right to her sexuality, and a right to change her partner if she could not find love. She also rebelled against the laws which made a woman the chattel of her husband. Unfortunately poor Sand herself, although she changed her partners frequently, so frequently that she almost became a kind of female Don Juan, never achieved satisfaction, either physical or emotional. Both de Musset and Chopin were frail and delicate and in the end she overpowered them. On the physical side something had gone wrong from the beginning. She wrote in one of her novels (which were always auto-biographical as far as the emotions were concerned), 'When he was fulfilled, satisfied, sated, I lay there motionless beside him. It seemed to me that I could feel the agitation of physical passion, a momentary imperative of bodily desire. . . . I fought against these lying urgencies of my suffering, knowing full well that it was not in his power to calm them.' On the one hand she complained of the animality of her men, and on the other she yearned for some demon lover into whose body she would dig her nails, at the same time 'feeling the fierce sharpness of his teeth'. We suspect that, although she was passionate, she never achieved an orgasm.

Her biographer, André Maurois, sums up her protest against the double standard as follows: 'In the name of what justice, human or divine, could a woman be bound by a code of loyalty which a man refused in his own case to regard as other than empty and ridiculous.'

Thanks to the frankness of continental tradition, the physical element in Sand's rebellion is clear. Marian Evans, who was to become George Eliot, in accordance with her Victorian background, was first and foremost the moralist. A child of middle-class parents (her father managed an estate) she had a country upbringing in the Midlands. Being somewhat isolated she formed a very strong attach-ment for her brother, Isaac. All during the formative period of her life she looked for someone to lean on. When her brother became engaged and went out of her life, she suffered a crisis. What formed her was a chance contact with intellectual neighbours, Charles and Caroline Bray, when she was living with her father at Coventry, her mother having died when she was rather young. Bray had written a philosophical work with freethinking tendencies. Marian read it and lost her evangelical orthodoxy. The Brays deduced her intellectuality from her large head and great phrenological development. In fact they could hardly wait to have her bumps read by an expert. At their house she met radical intellectuals.

Her intellectual development was not, however, applauded by her father. When she gave up going to church, he sent her off to her brother's house. Here she was wept over and reasoned with. She had been reading Wordsworth and Spinoza, however, and confounded clergymen by clear thinking and agile debate. She had decided that theology did not matter, what was important was morality and good works. The Brays became her mentors and closest friends. Through them she undertook to replace the daughter of a middle-aged German scholar, Dr Brabant, as a helpmeet. Brabant seems to have been a rather foolish character, for he and Marian became inseparable although he was sixty-two and she twenty-five. They took walks together; she basked in the sun of his intellect and wrote to the Brays that she had found a soulmate. Brabant's wife took a dim view of the matter and Marian was sent home.

Eventually she was commissioned to translate an important German work, D. F. Strauss's *Life of Jesus*. In order to match up to the author's erudition, she taught herself Greek, Latin, French, and Italian. By this time she decided she was in favour of divorce but she still had found no one to give her what she needed. As she plodded through the 1,500 pages of Strauss and looked after her now ailing father, poor horse-faced, emotional Marian Evans seemed in a fair way to become an erudite old maid. She was an admirer of George Sand's delineation of human passion and when she met Emerson in 1848 she surprised and pleased him by telling him that the book which had impressed her most was Rousseau's *Confessions*. Young girls became Marian's disciples, lost their religion, and had to be snatched away. She was thirty when her father died. For ten years Marian had done her duty tending an invalid with whom she was not compatible and who considered her a lost soul. Now she was free. She went on a European holiday with the Brays and stayed behind in Switzerland to try to collect herself. All during her years of dutiful martyrization she had suffered from sick headaches, evidently with a strong psychological component, which remained with her all of her life.

She soon wearied of *pensions* and ephemeral personal contacts and returned to England to pursue a literary career. John Chapman, a publisher whom she had met a few years before, was in need of an assistant. He was planning to buy *The Westminster Review* and realized that Marian's extensive knowledge of European literature would be valuable. Chapman was a curious character on the fringe of the radical movement of his time. He was handsome in a Byronic style and affected the Byronic open collar. He liked to be a part of the intellectual vanguard; he was a Darwinist, and opposed monogamy. Actually, in a Victorian way, he was an exploiter of women. Susanna, his not very attractive wife, had brought him enough money to buy him a publishing company and had given him three children. By 1851, after ten years of marriage, she was a prey to various elderly diseases, sciatica, headaches, etc. Chapman's custom was to invite young women with talent who might be useful to him to come and stay in his house; Eliza Lynn, a woman novelist, had been the first of these. He made love to her, it is not known with what success, for she later spoke of him with scorn.

When Marian was invited to join his ménage it also included Elizabeth Tilley, the young and pretty governess of his children who was functioning as his mistress. Into this harem entered Marian Evans full of intellectual good intentions and evidently fascinated by Chapman. Eliza Lynn, who met her at this time, said she was badly dressed, unkempt-looking, and held her arms like a kangaroo. Marian immediately became useful to Chapman as an editor but Elizabeth, who was not endowed by nature to give intellectual companionship, became violently jealous. She prodded the wife, with whom she seemed to have a working arrangement, into hostility towards Marian. The quarrels which followed were all happily recorded in Chapman's diary. Chapman would come up to Marian's room to give her German lessons and hear her play Mozart. The wife insisted that Mozart-playing take place in the parlour.

Apparently some hand-holding went on between Marian and Chapman but he was frank enough in his diary to state that of the three women Elizabeth was the only one he cared to sleep with. He enjoyed being fought over, however. The comedy was increased by Eliza Lynn, who wrote a novel which Chapman considered to be too highly spiced. He allowed all the other three women to read the love scenes. They were for once agreed in their disapproval. Chapman and Marian went on a mission to make Eliza revise. Eliza refused. Chapman wrote in his diary, 'As I am a publisher of works notable for their intellectual freedom, it behooves me to be exceedingly careful of the *moral* tendency of all I issue.' After this the other two members of the Chapman harem united their forces and drove Marian out.

As Chapman said good-bye, she asked him what his feelings were for her. He explained that for her and the other two women he had different sorts of affection. She was in tears as the train carried her back to Coventry. It is difficult to understand what Marian Evans thought she was doing, although perhaps it was all rationalized on a spiritual level just as George Sand's relationship with Lucien and her husband was supposed to be resolved as a Platonic triangle.

When Chapman actually bought *The Westminster Review* he needed Marian desperately. After many letters, and much negotiation with her rivals, he and Marian took 'a solemn and holy vow', fairly easy for Chapman since the lady editor was plain, but doubtless productive of more headaches in poor Marian. Back in Chapman's house, she took over the foreign book reviews for the magazine and also wrote articles. Altercations continued until Marian met Herbert Spencer, who was one of Chapman's authors. The philosopher-sociologist, tall, whiskered and neurotic, was charmed by her intelligence. They began to be seen everywhere and friends wondered whether they were engaged. Spencer, who does not seem to have been particularly masculine, did not consider himself the marrying type. They agreed they were not in love or, at least, Marian was persuaded to agree. Thanks to Spencer, things eased up in the Chapman household. Chapman himself was unperturbed; he wished to keep Spencer on his list of authors.

Philosophical hand-holding with Spencer went on for a couple of years as Marian became the power behind the throne in *The*

Westminster Review and saw to it that it became a distinguished magazine of letters. Her headaches continued.

Spencer had a habit of bringing George Henry Lewes with him when he visited Marian, who now had her own establishment. Lewes, a clever, homely journalist who was an editor of *The Leader*, was full of vivacity and broad humour. He came of a theatrical family and had been an actor and an unsuccessful playwright. He wrote the best drama criticism of his time. Lewes, although accepted in male literary circles, was anathema to the conventional because of his scandalous private life. He and his wife and four other married couples had participated in a free-love experiment based on the ideas of Godwin, Shelley and Fourier. The group included his co-editor Thornton Hunt and Hunt's two unmarried sisters-in-law. The result of this tangle was that Lewes' wife had two children by Thornton Hunt. Although Lewes continued to work amicably with Hunt he was estranged from his wife and had achieved a reputation of being on the town. He was frail physically and, like Marian, suffered from headaches. One night in 1853 when Spencer got up to go, Lewes remained behind. He poured all his troubles into Marian's willing ear. At last she had found someone who needed her and someone on whom she could lean.

At this time Marian was translating Ludwig Feuerbach's *The Essence of Christianity*, a book which convinced her that marriage without love was immoral. Lewes' marriage was clearly immoral but, because of his own affairs, he could not obtain a divorce and his wife had no intention of divorcing him. Since Lewes was overworked and ill, Marian nursed him, wrote his editorials for him, and tried to make her friends recognize his virtues. Finally, with the philosophy of Auguste Comte added to that of Feuerbach, she was ready for the decisive step. She and Lewes left for Germany in 1854. She was thirty-five, he thirty-six, and each was able to give what the other needed. Lewes grew stronger and was able to work. Marian wrote, 'I am really strong and well and have recovered the power of learning in spite of age and grey hairs.'

Most of their friends were estranged by the shocking step they had taken. Marian's conventional brother cast her off for ever; even the Brays did not write. The sinful couple, though isolated in continental lodgings, were happy after their fashion. During the long evenings they read to each other and Lewes sang arias from Mozart's *Figaro*. Lewes finished his *Life of Goethe*, which became a commercial success. They came back to England and resumed relations with Spencer, Charles Bray and, surprisingly, Eliza Lynn who reported that Marian looked unusually well. Caroline Bray, however, wrote letters but did not feel she could receive the unmarried pair. Marian, who took a high tone, wrote to her, 'If we differ on the subject of marriage laws, I at least can believe of you that you cleave to what you believe to be good, and I don't know of anything in the nature of your views that should prevent you from believing the same of me.' There is a parallel with George Sand who was right in what she did because her God sanctioned it. Marian knew herself to be Moral and fully justified.

Lewes, who adored her with an unselfishness without precedent in the Victorian male, felt Marian had redeemed him but that he had not done enough for her. He had begun to suspect that she had a talent for fiction. Spurred by his encouragement and helpful criticism, Marian wrote *Scenes from Clerical Life*, stories which first appeared in *Blackwood's Magazine* in 1858. Partially because her reputation might affect the reception of her work and partly because she, like Sand, competed with the dominant male, she contrived the pseudonym George Eliot, partly borrowed from her lover. The book was a success and there was great speculation as to who the author might be. An obscure and untalented clergyman was often named. Later on, when the secret was out, a partisan group still championed the clergyman and even complained that he had received no royalties.

Marian and Lewes had to work extremely hard, for he had a wife and two sets of children, one his own, to support. Once more the headaches returned. Somehow they managed to alternate their illnesses.

George Eliot was at work on *Adam Bede*. She read it chapter by chapter to Lewes, who wept at the pathetic scenes and rushed to kiss her when she had completed some particularly striking passage. Poor Lewes, who was always considered 'coarse' by the ultra refined because of his sense of humour, deserves great credit for his loyalty and understanding. Always ready to support and encourage George Eliot, he appears never to have felt the slightest jealousy at her fame, rapidly achieved by the best-selling *Adam Bede*. He continued to work at journalism and to respect and delight in a talent which he did not himself possess. Though neither a Chaucer nor a Shakespeare, in his relationship to the woman he loved he certainly achieved an insight transcending the traditional hostilities.

George Eliot became finally, according to Eliza Lynn, a sort of solemn goddess of Morality. During twenty-three years of unwedded union she produced book after book in which the leading characters firmly upheld her ethical standards. She earned the friendship of Dickens, Trollope and Wilkie Collins. Lewes took to calling her Madonna. Her wise sayings were collected in an anthology and she was even received by Queen Victoria's daughter, Princess Louise. But Victorian England did not quite forgive her. Once, when she was invited to Cambridge, the Mistress of Girton College would not receive her.

Thus, in keeping with their national backgrounds these two exceptional women, George Sand and George Eliot, registered their protest against male discrimination and proved their point by their creative achievements. The American, Victoria Claflin Woodhull born in 1838, is a fantastic contrast. Brought up in a half-educated frontier family in Humer, Ohio, her early life is obscure. Her mother was given to twirling madly in revivalist meetings and her father seems to have been a sort of confidence man. In the forties, Calvinism in the United States was breaking up in a flurry of wild sects, radical social theory, and freewheeling experiment. Spiritualism, revivalism and mesmerism often overlapped free love.

Victoria's father was run out of town when she was quite young, and the rest of the Claflin family was left high and dry. A public subscription speeded them on their way. For years they wandered about from state to state making a dubious living by table tipping and quack medical practice. Victoria later said she began having visions at the age of three. Her sister, Tennessee, was pretty and appetizing. Victoria herself, with her Dresden-china complexion and chiselled profile, was really beautiful. It seems probable that both had an early history of rough frontier sex. Victoria's protest began, not with religion or philosophy but by 'doing what comes naturally'. There were two other sisters who married and led conventional lives. Victoria at fifteen married Dr Canning Woodhull. She was later to describe him as a brutal monster who drank. Actually he seems to have been a mild man who was provided with sufficient reason for drinking. Victoria had a child by him and ran through various activities. At one time she tried her hand at acting, again in Indianapolis she practised as a medium.

After eleven years she divorced her husband and, curiously enough, went to live with her husband's family in Rochester. She soon left, to reappear united with the whole Claflin family in Chicago in 1866, where they practised spiritualism, quack doctoring by laying on of hands, and fortune-telling. Once, after having done a stint on the road, they returned to Chicago with outriders and a brass band. Eventually the medical practice which always caused trouble (Tennessee had been almost prosecuted for manslaughter when she ran a nursing home for cancer patients) caused them to be ejected from Chicago. On the road once more, Victoria encountered handsome, side-whiskered Colonel Blood. He was just what she needed. An anarchist and a mystic, he knew something of radical social theory and was enthusiastically in favour of free love and currency reform. He rapidly filled in any gaps in Victoria's knowledge of eros. Oddly, the divorced husband, Woodhull, was now back with the Claflin circus, a tolerant and loyal father figure. Colonel Blood divorced his wife, he and Victoria took out a marriage licence – and there is no record of any marriage taking place.

At any rate, thanks to Blood, Victoria was learning that what she had been doing was sanctified by Saint-Simon, Fourier and the advanced minds of the age. Actually her self-justification was simpler than that of homely George Eliot and George Sand. She was beautiful and irresistible to most men. Whatever she did was right because she did it. In addition, there appeared to her, in her séances, a Greek spirit in a tunic who prophesied a great future.

By 1870 the mountebank ménage, including Claflins, père and mère, Tennessee and Victoria, a no-account brother, Colonel Blood and Woodhull, was established in New York. At this time, the old pirate Commodore Vanderbilt, suffering from age and rheumatism, could be easily persuaded to try any sort of miraculous doctoring. The hearty Tennessee succeeded in meeting him, laid on her hands, slapped him on the back, told him jokes, and so enchanted him that he even thought of marrying her. He thought better of it but nevertheless New York was agreeably shocked and astonished by the appearance of the Claflin sisters on the stock exchange at the head of the first female brokerage firm, Woodhull, Claflin and Co. They achieved reams of publicity, dressed sensationally and, thanks to the old Commodore's tips, made a good deal of money.

At this time Victoria added a new member to her male harem which was gradually turning into a sort of brain trust. Stephen Pearl Andrews, who was living on Long Island in the anarchistic colony Modern Times (now Brentwood), was a social philosopher of some distinction, a friend of Horace Greeley's and author of 'The Basic Outline of Universology'. He had worked out a scheme of world government which he called the 'Pantarchy'. He succumbed to Victoria's beauty, vitality and charm. Somehow she had absorbed enough education along the line to be able to talk fluently and magnetically. She was delighted with Andrews, a figure of greater intellectual brilliance than Blood, for now she adored learning. With the aid of Blood and Andrews she founded *Woodhull and Claflin's Weekly*, a handsomely printed periodical which contained articles on social subjects, sponsored reform, unmasked corruption, exposed the evils of prostitution, attacked Madame Restell's abortion mill, and sponsored free love. The bluestockings had approached this subject from the point of view of marriage laws with abstract generalities but Victoria knew all about it from personal experiment.

There was more to come. Victoria's Greek spirit had told her that she would be the ruler of a great country. With the aid of her brain trust she concocted and published a manifesto. 'While others argued the equality of women with men, I proved it by successfully engaging in business; while others sought to show that there was no valid reason why women should be treated socially and historically as being inferior to man, I boldly entered the arena. . . . I therefore claim the right to speak for the unenfranchised women of the country and believing as I do that the prejudices which still exist in the popular mind against women in public life will soon disappear, I now announce myself as a candidate for the presidency. . . . I have deliberately and of my own accord placed myself before the people as a candidate for the presidency of the United States and, having the means, courage, energy and strength necessary for the race, intend to contest it to the close.'

Andrews, over her signature, wrote some of his best and most vivid political journalism for the *New York Herald* showing how, when Victoria became President, the United States would naturally become the centre of the Pantarchic world government. Victoria was outspoken on the free love issue on eugenic grounds. Woman 'will consider superior offspring a necessity and be apt to procreate only with superior men. Her intercourse with others will be limited and the proper means will be taken to render it unprolific. . . .'

In private she wore a quaint outfit which she apparently planned to reveal when she became President. It consisted of blue knee breeches and light blue stockings, a knee-length jacket, collar, cuffs and a shirtfront.

She had already been elected president of the spiritualist movement; she now set out to capture the suffragette organization. Although its more conservative members were shocked at her lurid past, Elizabeth Cady Stanton said, 'Her face, manner, and conversation all indicate the triumph of the moral intellect and the spiritual.' Mrs Stanton went on to say that she was an able speaker and writer and anyway her antecedents were as good as most congressmen's.

Unfortunately more scandals were to come. Her mother periodically hailed the rest of the ménage into court, insisting that she had been badly treated by Colonel Blood, and talking loosely about free love. Efforts to pension her off did not succeed. Everything the Claflins did got into the newspapers. The respectable suffragettes deplored the free-love publicity.

Victoria had learned of the Beecher scandal. Henry Ward Beecher, the most dramatic and well-publicized preacher of his day, had been having an affair with the wife of Theodore Tilton, a handsome poet, who was nobly trying to understand. Victoria helped Tilton to understand by taking him up on the roof of the building in which she lived, on warm summer nights. Sometimes they went on picnics and bathed together. She had planned a great lecture on Social Freedom and wanted Beecher to introduce her. Although she applied a bit of blackmailing pressure, he balked and Tilton, who had been added to her brain trust, finally stepped forward and introduced her. The division in the meeting between Victoria's admirers and enemies was intensified by the appearance of one of her respectable sisters who began to heckle her. Victoria challenged her to come up on the platform. Amid boos, hisses and cheers the atmosphere was one of such wild excitement that Victoria outdid herself. When someone screamed, 'Are you a free lover?' she shouted 'Yes! . . . The law cannot compel two to love. . . . Two people are sexually united, married by nature, united by God!' She went on to cry that the laws of marriage were the remnants of a barbaric age. 'All that is good and commendable now existing would continue to exist if all marriage laws were repealed tomorrow. . . . I have an inalienable constitutional, and natural right to love whom I may, to love as long or as short a period as I can, to change that love every day if I please!'

This scandalous affair took place in Victorian United States on 20 November 1871. It was too much for the suffragettes. When Victoria tried to capture the convention and to persuade the meeting to nominate her as its presidential candidate, Susan Anthony fought her tooth and nail and finally had the gaslights turned out, leaving Victoria talking in the dark. Victoria bolted the party with her supporters and formed the Equal Rights Party which nominated her for the office of President and named as her running mate the Negro reformer, Frederick Douglass.

She was, of course, not allowed to run and when, later, she tried to vote on the basis that she was a female man, she was firmly turned away from the polls. Victoria subsequently went from scandal to scandal, even spending some time in gaol for libel, but in the end married an English landed squire and lived until 1927, an aged gracious lady of the manor. Outrageous publicity seeker that she was, although she depended on a male brain trust, she had nevertheless enormous magnetism and a wild impudence which made the subject of female emancipation a nine days' wonder. Her Barnummountebank style was, in its way, authentically nineteenth-century American.

All three of the figures just sketched, although they espoused various advanced causes, were fundamentally driven by the desire to vindicate women sexually and to challenge male rejection, suppression and legal enslavement of their femininity. They were pioneers and precursors, but once the gap was made in male defences they were to be followed by more and more rebels who would achieve greater successes for their sex as a whole. This was naturally a new danger to the already burdened male ego. By refusing to act the role outlined for them, women now added the challenge of competition and formulated the need for something called 'fulfilment'. As a result male writers, at the turn of the century, expressed still more extreme forms of misogyny.

CHAPTER TWENTY-FOUR

The Menace of Fulfilment

The theatre in the last years of the nineteenth century and the early decades of the twentieth provides us with new versions of the *femme fatale*, who is now not only seductive but, as the result of the Western revolt of women, endowed with a new sense of independence and a ruthlessness not encountered before. The Swedish novelist and dramatist, August Strindberg (1849–1912), whose work ran the gamut from naturalism to fantasy, came to feel himself the conscious enemy of the Women's Movement; the German, Frank Wedekind, a writer half *fin-de-siècle* and half a precursor of the expressionists, created the monstrous Lulu who shocked (as she was meant to) even the most advanced. Eugene O'Neill, an admitted disciple of Strindberg, required the nine acts of the novelistic play *Strange Interlude* to record the anthropophagous crimes of Nina.

To what was evidently a not very stable disposition in Strindberg was added the catalyst of family relationships. His mother who had been his father's mistress, worked as a waitress and bore two illegitimate children before the father, who had certain pretensions, married her. An elder brother left no room for August in his mother's affections so that early in life he felt rejected. The father played the conventional role of nineteenth-century patriarch and disciplinarian. Crowded into the small space of three rooms were two adults, five children and, incredibly, two servants. It seems quite possible that in such close quarters the primal scene may have played some part in troubling his unconscious.

Puritanical Swedish Protestantism added fears of masturbation when August came across a terrifying book and was lectured by clergymen who informed him that this childhood habit would lead to madness or tuberculosis of the spine. The playwright-to-be has recorded the fact that he suffered on this score.

His early loves fall into the usual pattern. When only fifteen he became involved with a woman of thirty to whom he wrote letters and whom he worshipped as an ideal. In Strindberg the nineteenth-century ambivalence which created the virgin and the prostitute was expressed in classic form.

After writing plays which did not succeed and living a Bohemian life as a teacher, editor and journalist, he met the wife of an army officer, Baron Wrangel. Siri von Essen was pretty, had been an actress, and had borne the Baron three children. At first Strindberg worshipped her as the virgin. He could scarcely believe that her relation with her husband had anything physical about it. 'The union appeared essentially spiritual' in spite of the three children. Siri was bored with her husband, who had two mistresses, and she also felt he had made her sacrifice her career. When she showed an interest in August, he at first retreated. Then began the familiar struggle between the 'bestiality' of sex which a pietistic religion had taught August to fear and attempts to maintain a spiritual triangle. Eventually sex won and an amiable divorce was worked out, after which all three drank together sentimentally. August and Siri were married in 1877.

Strindberg recorded all the crises of his life in curious auto-biographies which, although distorted by his fantasies, were all the more revealing. He wrote that Siri fondled and kissed him like a little child and he asked himself, 'Are my feelings perverted because I want to possess my mother? Is that unconscious incest of the heart?' A dozen years later Freud would have been prepared to answer his question. When Siri returned to the stage and had a success, August's inner problems were accentuated (he himself had failed as an actor). With unerring masochism, in all of his marriages he chose women who were either actresses or journalists, fields in which competition with him resulted in emotional disaster.

Actually, even before his marriage, he had written that the Women's Movement was a mistake, saying that every man withdrawn from industry by the employment of emancipated women would mean one less marriage. Now, with his wife employed, his fanatical jealousy began. He accused her of betraying him with both men and women. In addition he distrusted his own potency, fearing that she would go back to the baron whom he imagined as more virile than he. In fact she once told him he was unsatisfactory as a lover, a charge he brooded over for years. Siri was soon demoted from virgin to prostitute and the marriage became a perfect hell. He recorded this in a significant image. 'I forgot my sex in the arms of the mother who was no longer female, but sexless. Sometimes she regarded me with the eyes of a conqueror, sometimes she looked at me kindly, seized with the tenderness which a hangman is said to feel for her victim. She was like the female spider which devours her mate immediately after the hymeneal embrace.'

Siri, who seems to have been a sloppy Bohemian but certainly not guilty of most of August's charges (after their divorce she was awarded the children) was treated to unbearable scenes. Strindberg alternately left her and returned to be reconciled in moods when Siri was allowed to regain her status as virgin. It is not surprising that when he read her mail he discovered a friend had suggested that he be committed. Thereafter he was sure that Siri was telling everyone he was mad. Along with his unbalanced attitude towards Siri went an increasing antagonism towards the Women's Movement. He had at first admired Ibsen; now, interpreting *The Wild Duck* in paranoid fashion, he decided that he was a character in the play. He came to hate Ibsen as a defender of the New Woman and he broke with Björnson over the same issue. He wrote a group of stories against women in one of which he said since women were inferior to men, 'Consequently the aping of the masculine, the equality of the sexes, means retrogression and is utter folly.' The Women's Movement in his mind became such a menace that he was convinced it was unsafe to write against it. When his stories were suppressed in Sweden for 'blasphemy' it was of course the Women's Movement working against him. After a trial in which the book was cleared, he had a success with a new play, but success or failure did not seem to change his marital relations. His suspicions of his wife reached such a point of frenzy that he attacked her and beat her about the face. Finally he decided that Siri was trying to poison him and, according to his autobiography, he took her down to the river to drown her like a kitten but thought of the children and changed his mind.

He divorced her and in 1893 married the Austrian writer Frieda Uhl, only to become a prey to delusions again. When this marriage broke up he became obsessed with the idea that he could manufacture gold. In a Paris garret he conducted chemical experiments, noting that the chemical symbols were the same as his former wife's initials. Scientists who did not find gold in his samples were in league against him. He was even convinced that he was being persecuted by an electrical machine which influenced him from a distance. His magical thinking assumed such proportions that he was sure he could kill whoever he wished. With the aid of some therapy and a conversion to Swedenborgianism he achieved better mental health only to marry Harriet Bosse, an actress, a step which brought on more delusions and a third divorce.

A glance at *The Father*, which came out of the turmoil of his first marriage, will show the image of the *femme fatale* as Strindberg envisaged it. The Captain, hero of the play with whom he identifies, has been quarrelling with his wife, Laura, over the education of their daughter. The Captain is convinced that all the women of the household are plotting against him. The familiar feline image crops up. 'It's like going into a cage of tigers. And if I didn't hold a red-hot poker under their noses, they would soon pounce on me and tear me to pieces.' The wife is shown shedding false tears and lying brazenly to convince a new doctor that her husband is insane. She finally tells the Captain that he may not be the father of his daughter, a statement which eventually also turns out to be a lie but which has a weakening influence on the Captain's intellect. Laura tells him, 'Yes, it's curious . . . but I have never been able to look at a man without feeling myself his superior.' By the second act we learn that Laura has cancelled the Captain's orders for books, a device which is supposed to have destroyed his success in mineralogy. 'You were opposed to my doing anything that might bring me recognition! It would have exposed your own inferiority!' he cries. Then he tells her he has been opening her letters and has discovered that she is telling everyone he is crazy. The terrible Laura answers, 'What has all this struggle for life and death been, if not for power?' Then follows a scene which dramatizes Strindberg's oedipal guilt in a curious fashion.

> LAURA: . . . Do you remember it was as your second mother I first came into your life. Do you? You were big of body and strong but you were lacking in stamina. . . .
>
> CAPTAIN: . . . Yes – I am afraid you are right. My father and mother did not want a child; and so I was born without a will of my own . . . I . . . listened to you as if I were your foolish little boy.
>
> LAURA: . . . Yes, that's the way it was, and that is why I loved you, as if you were my child. But I don't think you could have helped noticing that each time you approached me as lover, with feelings of another nature, I felt ashamed. . . . And the joy of being in your embrace turned into a sense of guilt – as if the shame had crept into my very blood. The mother turned mistress! Ugh!

Laura goes on to tell him that the mother was his friend, but the woman was his enemy and 'love between the sexes produces strife'.

Thus Strindberg projects his own oedipal guilt onto the woman and endows her with the fear of sex which he himself feels. That this is wholly irrational is clear enough. There is no reason why his character, Laura, should have such feelings and no indication that Siri ever did. There is also no reasonable connection between feelings of sexual guilt and Laura's determination to destroy the Captain. She is a completely unconvincing melodramatic villainess, a creature of Strindberg's tortured fantasy.

The play ends by the Captain's being goaded into throwing a lamp at his wife; he is eased into a straitjacket by his old nurse and, after a long raving scene in which he alternately curses and yearns for his wife, he has a stroke.

Strindberg's misogyny is, of course, schizophrenic yet it arises from the familiar sources, tensions concerning sex, feelings of sexual inferiority exacerbated by a curiously conscious oedipal conflict which ended by his endowing woman with every possible criminal tendency and imagining himself being destroyed as if by a female spider. A further intensifying factor was his hatred of and fear of competition with the career woman. By combining the virgin and the prostitute in the same person he created a conflict which almost tore him to pieces. Although he was frankly pathological, his pathology is a caricature of the most prevalent nineteenth-century male attitude.

Frank Wedekind, originally christened Benjamin Franklin in memory of his father's eight-year residence in the United States, is a curiously neglected dramatist whose life span runs from 1864 to 1918. He is more sophisticated, more complex intellectually and more gifted poetically than either Strindberg or O'Neill; indeed, as a dramatic innovator he stands somewhere between Georg Büchner and Bertolt Brecht. Although his meanings and attitudes are sometimes difficult to unravel, the image of the destructive woman emerges in his work as a type conditioned by the Women's Movement.

Wedekind's father was a left-wing rebel who went to America after the failure of the 1848 revolution in Germany. While in the United States he married a singer of German parentage. She was half his age and he masterfully made her give up her career. He seems, in spite of his political liberalism, to have been the usual nineteenth-century patriarch, and there was eventually conflict between him and his wife. She maintained that he ruled her, and gave her no freedom. Wedekind wrote at one time, 'Is it not surprising that when a person comes from a hair-raisingly inhuman family life he does not exactly fit into everyday normality?' There were six children of whom Frank was the second. As with Strindberg, it is possible that he did not feel himself his mother's favourite, for there is evidence of a platonic interchange with a much older woman when he was about nineteen. At about the same time there was a violent conflict with his father, who beat him. Frank broke with him, gave up studying law, and took a job in the advertising business. He had been given a good education in liberal Switzerland and had grown up in a sophisticated sceptical home. As a result there are traces of Schopenhauer, Nietzsche and Karl von Hartmann in his thinking. He became an atheist early in life and, subscribing to scientifically materialist attitudes of his time, combined with them a critical attitude towards bourgeois society. In some ways he seems to have identified with his father and repeated a similar rebellious pattern.

After travelling with a circus, entering Bohemian literary society, working as a journalist and writing plays, which the public of his time would not at first accept, he, like his father, married a career woman half his age, the actress Tilly Neves. He did not interfere with her career; they played the leads in his dramas. He was jealous of her as an artist, however; they clashed often, and she accused him of wishing to make a servant of her. She stuck to her guns as an actress and told him that she felt the need to stand on her own feet. Although the relationship was full of conflict, the marriage lasted. It had been preceded, in his Bohemian period, by many affairs with demimondaines. The general outlines of Wedekind's personal life, therefore, are not unlike those of earlier nineteenth-century writers.

The two plays which are most significant for our theme are *Earth Spirit* and *Pandora's Box* in which the career of the *femme fatale*, Lulu, is traced from adolescence to her tragic death. It is certainly significant that the two titles carry us back both to the earth mother and to the Pandora legend, establishing from the very beginning the dangerous nature of female sexuality. Lulu herself is a girl of mysterious origin whom the cynical, sophisticated tycoon, Dr Schön, picked up when he encountered her as a flower girl at the age of twelve. He subsequently educated her and trained her as a dancer. We meet her at the opening of the first play as the wife of old Dr Goll, a connoisseur of the arts. In the course of the action we are led to believe that Schön seduced her when she was young but then, sensing the menace in her character, married her off to Goll. At one point she confesses that she poisoned Schön's wife because she hoped to supplant her. Apparently Schön is unaware of this but is nevertheless determined to free himself, for he is engaged to a young woman with a good position in bourgeois society. Meanwhile Lulu is having her portrait painted by the sentimental idealist, Schwartz. The painter makes love to her in a scene in which she shows no soft emotions but allows him to kiss her. Goll breaks the door down, rushes in, wildly jealous, and dies of a stroke.

Lulu is unemotional about the death of her husband and, by the next scene, provided with a dowry by Schön, has married Schwartz, who idealizes her and bores her. She has continued to visit Schön who is still trying to free himself but has not yet married his fiancée. She complains to Schön that she cannot bear Schwartz's innocence. She wants the doctor either to make a sophisticate out of the painter or at least to make him take a realistic view of her. Schön obliges by opening Schwartz's eyes to her chequered past. He cynically tells him to remember 'You married half a million.' Schwartz goes into the next room and cuts his throat with a razor. The scene ends with Schön wiping Schwartz's blood from his hands after he has taken the artist's keys to look at his papers.

SCHÖN: It's your husband's blood.
LULU: It doesn't leave any stain.
SCHÖN: You monster.
LULU: You'll marry me in the end.

Schön does not marry her immediately. Instead he pushes her into the theatre where she dances in a pantomime composed by Alwa, Dr Schön's son, also destined to become one of her victims. When Schön brings his fiancée to see her dance the skirt dance, an act which she considers an affront, she pretends to faint. Schön comes into her dressing room where the final struggle takes place between them. Lulu wins, forcing Schön to write a letter breaking off with his fiancée.

Once married to Schön, she takes on a motley crew of lovers – the coachman, an acrobat, Rodrigo, a schoolboy, Hugenberg, Alwa, the Doctor's son – and is also courted by the lesbian Baroness Geschwitz. In a Grand Guignol music-hall scene in which lovers are hiding all over the room, Schön from a balcony sees her dining with Alwa. He enters with a pistol, drives out her admirers and orders her to shoot herself. One of her lines is revealing, 'You may have sacrificed the evening of your life to me, but you have had my whole youth in exchange,' a statement which indicates that, even though she more than once insists he is the only man she ever loved, she also hates him for seducing her in the first place.

When Schön turns, distracted by the schoolboy who is hiding under the table, she shoots him in the back. As Schön dies he says to his son, 'Don't let her escape, you are the next one.'

The second play, *Pandora's Box*, opens with Lulu's escape from prison, engineered by Baroness Geschwitz. Lulu is still surrounded by the gross acrobat, Rodrigo, the schoolboy, Hugenberg, and the old man from her past, Schigoltz, who is sometimes thought to be her father but who is not her father, and Alwa who, although he called the police, testified in her favour at the trial. She has her first really sensual love scene with Alwa who says, '. . . Yet if it were not for your big brown childlike eyes, I should be forced to regard you as the most designing bitch that ever brought a man to ruin.' To which she replies, 'I only wish I were.'

The scene shifts to Paris, where, now called the Countess Adelaide, Lulu is surrounded by demimondaines in a gambling establishment. Rodrigo is still with her, as is Alwa, but she has also been the mistress of the white slave trader and police spy, Casti-Piani. All her followers, except the Baroness, are now trying to exploit her. Casti-Piani wants to sell her to a brothel in Cairo. Here she makes it clear that she is not the prototype of a conventional whore because she only wants men she desires. Casti-Piani threatens her with the police. So does Rodrigo, who wants to squeeze money from her. She persuades the unhappy Baroness to pacify Rodrigo by sleeping with him, promising the lesbian her reward, a debt which Lulu does not intend to pay, for she has no interest in the other woman. Lulu escapes with Alwa in disguise just as the police officers break in.

The last scene in a miserable garret shows Lulu moving further and further into the darkness. Degraded and poverty-stricken, she lives with Alwa and old Schigoltz, both of whom she is supporting by prostituting herself. Alwa, looking at her youthful portrait painted by Schwartz, says, '. . . Let him, who can, feel safe in his role in bourgeois society when faced by these full red lips, these great innocent child's eyes, this exuberant pink and white body, let him be the one to cast the first stone.' Again, he says, 'A woman blossoms for us precisely at the right moment to plunge a man into everlasting ruin; such is her natural destiny.' Lulu brings home four grotesque clients; one, an African Prince, kills Alwa. The faithful Baroness is still attempting to save Lulu but, rejected once more, contemplates suicide. In a touching speech to Lulu's portrait she says, 'I wonder if there have ever been people who were happy in love.' Lulu's last client is Jack-the-Ripper, who kills the Baroness and finally murders Lulu.

All critics agree that Lulu is a symbol of pure sexual drive. As Paul Fechter wrote enthusiastically, 'She is the age-old woman, beautiful as the world on the day of creation, with a smile on her lips and nothing in her heart.' She is, however, a good deal more than this and the play must be understood on several levels. In the first place Wedekind is the conscious product of a cynical, complex European tradition. He had come to believe that the only motivation of human action was naked self-interest, *Trieb*, or 'urge'. He repeatedly tells us that human beings are animals. It is an almost Freudian point of view. He cannot, however, make up his mind how he feels about it. Among his attitudes are romantic disillusionment, horror, cynical laughter, and, at least in the case of Baroness Geschwitz, pity. Interestingly enough, in these shifting viewpoints tragedy and comedy become interchangeable (the contemporary playwright Ionesco also consciously confounds the two). In the Wedekind play there is no romantic moralizing or confused mysticism as in Strindberg or O'Neill; in some ways he is more modern than they.

Having decided that egoism is the key to all human behaviour, he then attacks bourgeois society for being hypocritical and covering up with lying moral platitudes. From this comes deliberate use of violent shocking episodes which force the audience to see itself in a sort of Coney Island mirror. Like Brecht, Wedekind creates a feeling of alienation but unlike Brecht he is not a conscious revolutionary. Disgusted by bourgeois society, he still clings to it with nostalgia very much as does Genet in his contemporary poems of decay.

This, then, is the most intellectual level of Wedekind's drama and accounts for many of the minor characters and subsidiary meanings. Lulu, however, is not only in herself a symbol of egoism writ large which, carried to extremes, destroys all bourgeois pretensions, but also a half-conscious and unconscious symbol of Wedekind's own deepest reactions to the other sex. Let us remember that while Alwa, who is sometimes Wedekind's spokesman, says that no one can contemplate Lulu's appetizing body and remain safe in his bourgeois role, he also says, 'A woman blossoms for us precisely at the right moment to plunge a man into everlasting ruin; such is her natural destiny.' This is, of course, Wedekind's most profound feeling. As an embodiment of female sexuality Lulu is amoral and all of her victims perish because sex drives them into her net. But there is another level of meaning here, for it is made clear that Lulu is not a prostitute, a merchant of sex; she is fulfilling herself, or trying to. Fulfilment, of course, has reference to the Women's Movement. The menace of female sexuality has thus gone into a new phase from bad mana to sin, to fulfilment. Wedekind uses the image of a wild animal in connection with Lulu; in the Prologue she is a snake and she is called Eve by Schwartz. Elsewhere she says Schön has 'chained her' when he marries her to another man. In the play *Death and the Devil*, Wedekind refers to woman as the 'tigress triumphant'; and so the age-old unconscious symbols of fear, applied to woman in Western culture, return again. There is a faintly suggested notion in *Earth Spirit* that Lulu's abstract sexual power needs to be 'mastered'. In other words, the fear and hostility aroused by female sexuality is to be expressed by beating down the wild animal (drawing the teeth from the menacing vagina). Both Wedekind and his father in their own lives tried to 'master' their women unsuccessfully.

Lulu, therefore, is a supreme example of the dangerous sex, and sex, in general, plays a destructive role in the two plays. In this connection Lion Feuchtwanger writes, 'The only man who can live a natural life is he who puts himself beyond the range of this society and its laws and who robs and betrays it with every means that comes to hand. According to which the true hero of this society is the unscrupulous thief and swindler, the industrial brigand in the grand style. His female counterpart is the whore born for pleasure.' But this is not the whole of Wedekind's thought. Schön is the industrialist thief but he is destroyed in the end; Lulu is killed by Jack-the-Ripper. All of Lulu's victims, including the abnormal Baroness for whom Wedekind wrote the most pitying lines, are destroyed by their sexual urges.

When we return to the short play *Death and the Devil*, Wedekind's attitude towards sex is further developed. Casti-Piani reappears in conflict with a feminist, Elfriede, who has come to demand the release of one of his victims. Casti-Piani defends himself as an

idealist and a rebel against bourgeois society while Elfriede insists
that his victims have been deceived by him for profit. 'Sensual
enjoyment is the one unqualified delight,' Casti-Piani insists. A
whore and her customer are brought on who, speaking in verse,
reveal the reality of sex. The prostitute speaks –

> LISISKA: . . . Desire, the monstrous beast,
>   Still rages unassuaged within this breast.
>   Do you think a devil's child like me
>   Had ever come into this house
>   If happiness could have freed me
>   From the beating horror of my heart?
>   Joy evaporates, a water drop
>   Upon a stone!
>   And lust, left unappeased,
>   Is ravening despair
>   Which plunges downward, seeking death
>   In bottomless abyss!

Each time the customer tries to speak of spiritual values Lisiska
repeats:

> And there was always this demonic urge
> In which there was not any place for joy.

Taken together, both the Lulu plays and the statements in *Death
and the Devil* indicate that Wedekind felt sex was painful, destructive and tragic. Atheist that he was, his fundamental male apprehensions were embodied in plays which depicted woman as a demon and
the implied moral was exactly the same as that so loudly repeated by
the medieval homilist. The death of Lulu has further implications.
The sex murderer, Jack-the-Ripper, punishes her for being female,
just as Cresseid was punished by Robert Henryson with leprosy.
In addition, death by ripping up the offending organs of the woman's
body is the ultimate 'mastery', a mastery also achieved in the
monstrous fantasies of the Marquis de Sade.

When we come to Eugene O'Neill we are dealing with a playwright who had some acquaintance with the techniques and attitudes
of Strindberg and Wedekind but who was at bottom a rather naïve
writer. Eugene O'Neill's play *Strange Interlude* sums up all his

attitudes towards the other sex. The plot of this novel-on-the-stage is contrived and unconvincing, for it is controlled by O'Neill's symbolical ideas, behind which his compulsions can be read. Nina, the daughter of a professor, has lost her fiancé, who is shot down in World War I. Her possessive father has prevented the consummation of their union. Nina is therefore so filled with guilt at not having slept with Gordon that she becomes a nurse in a veterans' hospital and gives herself indiscriminately in order to punish herself. (O'Neill had just undergone analysis before the play was written, with the result that various half-digested bits of psychology are used as motivation.)

We are told that Nina is disturbed and she remains so, with variations, during the entire action which goes on for years. Charles Marsden, who is too strongly attached to his elderly mother, has been Nina's Platonic admirer all along. When she returns from the hospital with Dr Edmund Darrel, under whom she has worked, Marsden realizes what has been going on and in one of his asides expresses his fear of sex in terms which appear again and again throughout the play. '. . . Our impotent pose of today to beat the loud drum on fornication . . . boasters . . . eunuchs parading with the phallus!' He goes on to his own traumatic experience: '. . . that house of cheap vice . . . one dollar! . . . why did I go? Jack, the dead game sport . . . how I admired him! . . . afraid of his taunts . . . he pointed to the Italian girl . . . "take her!" . . . daring me . . . I went . . . miserably frightened . . . what a pig she was . . . pretty vicious face under caked powder and rouge . . .' And his final reaction is: '. . . back at the hotel, I waited till they were asleep . . . then sobbed . . . thinking of Mother . . . feeling I had defiled her . . . and myself . . . forever . . .' Marsden, thus, repeatedly sees Nina as the prostitute.

O'Neill, who used many bits of biographical experience, returns to the episode of disgust at a first experience with a prostitute in the late play *A Moon for the Misbegotten* whose leading character is partly modelled on his older brother, James. We know that the older brother, who felt rejected and attempted to destroy Eugene under the guise of seeing to his worldly education, carefully introduced O'Neill to houses of prostitution. James considered all women to have the souls of whores. He undoubtedly played the same role as Jack in Marsden's soliloquy. Eugene may have had the experience himself, or lived it imaginatively as he identified himself with James to whom he felt attached as a sort of *alter ego*, or both; but in any case the image of the prostitute is one which stirred a deep ambivalence in him.

As the play continues we learn that Darrel takes an interest in Nina's case, feels she is ruining herself, and recommends (in defiance of any sensible therapy) that she marry her other admirer, the fatuous eternal-college-boy, Sam Evans. In this therapeutic union she is supposed to 'mother' him and also to produce children, which will take care of her emotions. Marsden is enlisted to help convince Nina that she must marry Sam. She first confesses her affairs to him, which produce his usual reaction. 'She's hard! . . . like a whore! . . . tearing your heart with dirty fingernails! . . . my Nina! . . . cruel bitch! . . . some day I won't bear it! . . . I'll scream out the truth about every woman! no kinder than a dollar tart!'

During a thoroughly bogus scene Nina is lulled into identifying Marsden with her dead father and taking his advice. In the course of one of her speeches another image of woman is painted. 'We should have imagined life as created in the birth-pain of God, the Mother. Then we would understand. Then we would understand why we, Her children, have inherited pain, for we would know that our life's rhythm beats from Her great heart, torn with the agony of love and birth. And we would feel that death meant reunion with Her, a passing back into Her substance, the blood of Her blood again, peace of Her peace!' This is the other aspect of woman as mother goddess and virgin which has been appearing all along in Western tradition. O'Neill is more confusedly ambivalent than the Victorians who so clearly separated women into virgin and prostitute because he had read Sir James Frazer, and therefore knew something about fertility goddesses, and he was also reared as a Catholic. In Irish Catholic tradition there is a split between good and bad women plus a continual harping upon all sex as sin which harks back to the Middle Ages. O'Neill's female characters were thus moulded by his inner compulsions as a man and ৭ Catholic (in childhood) plus his antagonism towards his own mother, whom he never forgave for her withdrawal from him into narcotic addiction, plus his conscious playing about with symbols.

In his play *The Great God Brown* he split the female image into two characters whom he described in a defence of the play, when the critics were confused by the masks and the cloudy symbolism. 'Cybele is an incarnation of the Earth Mother,' he wrote, and went on to explain that she was a whore and a solace to man. ' "Margaret" is my image of the modern descendant of "Marguerite" of Faust – the eternal girl woman with the virtuous simplicity of instinct.' But Margaret, he also wrote, was only concerned with perpetuating the race. Again in *Welded*, a play of tortured and ambivalent marriage relationships, which George Jean Nathan told him was third-rate Strindberg, he introduced the prostitute to whom the husband turned after his troubles with his wife. She was described as 'the solacing earth-mother whore'.

Obviously Nina is all of these people, and a few more, in one. O'Neill's attitudes are therefore complex, although the virgin-whore dichotomy is at the bottom of them. When he speaks of the whore as solace, he clearly does *not* mean as a sexual solace. Nina's speech is significant when she talks of death 'as reunion with Her, passing back into Her substance, peace of Her peace . . .' 'Solace' therefore means creeping into the desexualized womb, the same panacea advocated by Ruskin. The rejecting mother combines both qualities, she is the pace-giving womb which the son never succeeds in finding; she is also the girl-virgin Margaret, but when hostility is excited she is also the revolting whore who lures the shrinking boy. One of O'Neill's friends wrote, 'O'Neill was nearly always the seduced instead of the seducer, sometimes he resented it. . . .' Clearly the story of his first marriage dramatizes a violent reaction to the sexually ensnaring female for, after marrying Kathleen Jenkyns and making her pregnant, he set off for Honduras and never saw her again. She could not have been the solacing earth mother but rather the virgin Margaret, solely concerned with perpetuating the species. But O'Neill never wanted children and rejected them when they came. There are indications that his own lack of virility created the usual feeling of inferiority when he was faced with the sexually demanding woman. His biographers write, concerning his second marriage to

Agnes Boulton, that he sought for emotional excitement in the relationship 'as a substitute for the violent physical passion he did not seem to be capable of achieving'. So he drank, made scenes, and sometimes resorted to physical violence. An admirer of Strindberg, he already found in that writer's life and work a pattern of ambivalence towards women which was evidently close to his own.

When we return to the story of Nina we see how all of these attitudes shape the character, so much so that she never achieves any reality as a person.

Once safely married to Sam, she becomes pregnant, but on a visit to his parents she learns the melodramatic fact that most of his relatives have gone insane and have been committed. O'Neill uses the unscientific notion of inherited insanity and creates the problem of what to do about the baby. Nina gets rid of it by an abortion. Sam, who is prone to the convenient psychology that without a child he loses all will power and belief in his virility and himself, and in fact loses his job, must now be saved. Nina therefore traps the doctor, Darrel, into giving her a child, for Sam's sake. Nina is, of course, the sexually ensnaring female in this role. Darrel falls in love with her but is kept to his bargain of secrecy, which is all the more necessary because Sam, bolstered by his spurious virility, immediately becomes a noisy success in the advertising business.

Through all of this, Marsden lingers on the outskirts, waiting to become Nina's father. Eventually, for theatrical reasons, there are points where Sam is almost told the truth about his son's paternity but Nina always checks Darrel. Darrel, as a result of his love for Nina, loses his direction, never achieves anything as a scientist, and has to make up for it by helping another biologist with money he has gained from investments with Sam. By the end of the play, Nina has returned, we are told, to her neurotic behaviour of the beginning of the play and is busy trying to pry her son, Gordon, away from his fiancée, once more playing the role of the sexually devouring female. When she fails and Sam dies, she creeps into Marsden's lap as 'good old Charlie' happily accepts the role of father image.

At one point Nina expresses her insatiable need for men in a soliloquy. 'My three men! . . . I feel their desires converge in me . . . to form one complete beautiful male desire which I absorb and am whole . . . they dissolve in me, their life is my life . . . I am pregnant with the three! . . . husband! . . . lover . . . father . . . and the fourth man! . . . little man! . . . little Gordon! . . . he is mine, too! . . . that makes it perfect . . .'

This is a concept of the cannibalistic womb which includes a two-way incest. In a sense Nina castrates most of her men. Marsden is, of course, already castrated by his own mother but Nina helps to preserve his eunuchoid condition. Darrel has been castrated creatively. Although he is supposed to have been truly her lover, he speaks of having been her slave and goes on: '. . . does she think she can still own me . . . touch of her flesh . . . it's dangerous . . .' Sam achieves a spurious success in the advertising business which O'Neill makes clear is worthless but Sam is also cheated of his own child. Perhaps he does enjoy some 'solace' since he is 'mothered', hence able to relax in the desexed womb of the earth mother. Only young Gordon escapes when Nina is beaten by another female, who may well turn out to be as destructive as she.

It might be pointed out that O'Neill married two career women; Agnes Boulton was a journalist and Carlotta Monterey an actress. As we move into the twentieth century, the dangerous sex is still condemned to the split personality of the virgin and the prostitute but more and more her role as competitor and liberated woman becomes an issue in the relationship between the sexes. Nina is not the melodramatic creature of evil found in Strindberg's plays. Something nearer to Wedekind's idea of fulfilment lingers in the background of *Strange Interlude*, something halfway between psychology and mysticism, like so many of O'Neill's concepts. Most of the women he knew in his Greenwich Village days were attempting to make careers for themselves as artists and were also seeking freedom in their sexual lives. It was a period of free unions without marriage in which the old religious concepts were rejected. Now that the rebellion had taken place against the inherited stereotypes, the second sex was groping for new roles. Artists such as O'Neill were aware of this, but their compulsions as males prevented them from accepting the aspirations of women wholeheartedly. They continued to feel deeply threatened. Nina's fulfilment is at the expense of her men.

Finally, as the twentieth century moved into the middle decades, a public awareness of some aspects of depth psychology reinforced the idea of the female as a castrator, in particular in the United States.

CHAPTER TWENTY-FIVE

The Diminished Male

One of the opening guns in the contemporary campaign against women was fired by Philip Wylie two decades ago with his *Genera-tion of Vipers*. A popular novelist, Hollywood writer, journalist and advertising man, Wylie in deliberately exaggerated and provocative terms insisted that the United States had become a matriarchy and created the concept of 'momism'. His official target was not the new woman but the non-working wife and mother. Although the senti-mentalities which he attacked are no longer so prevalent, the basic charge that women have somehow got the upper hand and are ruining their men is still current. As Wylie put it, '. . . Momworship has got completely out of hand. Our land subjectively mapped, would have more silver cords and apron strings crisscrossing it than railroad and telephone wires. Mom is everywhere and everything and damned near everybody. And from her depends all the rest of the U.S. Disguised as good old mom, dear old mom, sweet old mom, your loving mom, and so on, she is the bride at every funeral and the corpse at every wedding.'

What Wylie is saying is that the survival of the Victorian cult of the virgin was grafted on to the frontier situation in America in which men were popularly supposed to be so concerned with taming the continent and building industry that ethical and cultural values were left to the woman. As a result she retained a kind of moral superiority. Satan having 'taught the gals to teach their men that dowry went the other way, that it was a weekly contribution and that any male worthy of a Cinderella would have to work like a piston after getting one so as to be worthy, also, of all the other moms in the world . . . the pretty girl then blindfolded the man so he would not see that she was turning from a butterfly into a caterpillar. . . .

268

Finally leaving him sightless and whirling, she snatched his check-book. Man was a party to the deception because he wanted to be fooled about Cinderella. . . . Mom had already shaken him out of that notion of being a surveyor in the Andes which had bloomed in him when he was nine years old, so there was nothing left to do anyway, but to take a stockroom job in the hairpin factory and try to work up to vice president. Thus the woman of America raped the man not sexually but morally since neuters come hard by morals.'

It is clear from the word 'neuter' in this passage that the concept of 'mom' is spread to all women and Wylie's charge is really one of spiritual and creative castration. The shade of O'Neill's Nina is really being evoked. Wylie also resents the role of women in politics. 'Although politics never interested her (unless she was exceptionally naïve, a hairy foghorn, or a size forty scorpion), the damage she forthwith did to society was so enormous and so rapid that even the best men lost track of things.' Since there is no objective indication that the nature of American politics changed after women were allowed to vote, this type of complaint is merely male resentment at female competition. The undertone of sex apprehension, however, rises to the surface in the following: 'If she gets to Hollywood and encounters the flesh and blood article known as the male star, she and her sister moms will run forward in a mob, wearing a joint expression which must make God rue his invention of bisexuality, and tear the man's clothes from his body, yes, verily, down to his B.V.D.'s.' Wylie goes on to assert that moms have taken over the male function and 'donned the breeches of Uncle Sam', finally winding up: 'I give you the harpies, the witches and the fates. I give you the woman in pants, and the new religion; she popery. I give you Pandora. I give you Proserpine, the queen of Hell. The five-and ten-cent store Lilith, the mother of Cain, the black widow who is poisonous and eats her mate, and I designate at the bottom of your programme the grand finale of all soap operas: the mother of Cinderella.'

Wylie's windup, enumerating so many of the stereotypes which we have been discussing all along, is testimony to the strength of the misogynist tradition. Also the fact that mom makes the man 'work like a piston' seems to emerge from the writer's unconscious. The image of the spider eating her mate puts him in a class with Strind-berg. Although Wylie's social criticism is freewheeling, popular writer that he is, we can assume he is voicing certain notions that are in the air.

The fact that his book was published in 1942 suggests that the increased participation of women in all productive activities during World War II has touched off the new offensive. Actually Wylie's attack was followed by other semipsychological articles in popular magazines which helped to solidify the stereotype of 'momism'. The most telling bit of evidence was, of course, the holiday Mother's Day, an institution which commercially sentimentalizes the parent-child relationship but which owes its existence more to American merchandizing than to a profound infantilism in the male.

Geoffrey Gorer, however, picked up the obsession with the female breast which undeniably runs through American advertising, car-toons, men's magazines, cinema titillations, girlie shows, and folklore and culminates in the pin-up girl so well endowed that she looks as if she had been inflated at a gas station. Ben Hecht writing in *Esquire* called it the 'canonization of the female breast' and pointed out that the nipple must never be shown. 'The American male likes his mammary fetish a bit under cover. (His mother was no exhibi-tionist.) Unlike the Frenchman his libido shies away from a line of fifty unbraziered beauties.' Gorer tried to equate this breast cult with rejection of the past and the immigrant's rebellion against the patriarchal authority of his father as he attached himself to his new country. Gorer also charged that the American male was reared by women and that women stood for ethical and cultural standards, the only bulwark against the rapid competition in capitalist society. This is, however, only another version of the Ruskinian attitude that woman must refine man's baser instincts. Ruskin chose the image of the tranquil all-encompassing womb as man's retreat; the modern American apparently chooses the pacifying nipple.

The charge of infantilism is repeated by another Briton, Eric Dingwall, who assembles a mass of material drawn from sociologists, novelists, movies, fashions and letters to Dorothy Dix. He accepts without question the dominance of women. 'Now one feature of life in the United States that no informed person can deny is the exaggerated devotion to the Mother . . . which carried to the extent that it is in the United States, cannot fail to influence the unconscious, as well as the conscious minds of American men.' He complains that men are reduced to the status of household servants, that the father, 'Poor old Pop', is a national figure of fun and that American women entertain castration fancies and from this 'there arises a desire for revenge followed by a symbolic castration of the opposite sex'. In addition the woman is restless and filled with romantic ideas of the ideal lover but the American male is too passive and too unskilful to supply her need. 'In the United States female tranquillity is an impossibility. The failure to find the mate she needs is finally accepted, and the domination which was partly the cause of the failure becomes a kind of compensatory device whereby her own self-respect may be maintained. The American mother becomes Mom, and takes her place in the curious matriarchal set-up of American society.' Dingwall's thesis (a bland assumption) is that woman needs to be dominated and because of the infantilism of American men she has gotten out of hand and made them and herself unhappy. This sounds suspiciously like Wedekind with his notion that the dangerous beast must be 'mastered'. At any rate he winds up with a quote from a popular magazine in which John Fisher states, 'Never in history has any country contained such a proportion of cowed and eunuchoid males.'

It is illuminating to set against this a curiously passionate little book written by the sociologist Pitirim Sorokin, who is quite sure that there is too much sex in the United States. 'Increasing divorce and desertion and the growth of prenuptial and extra-marital sex relations are signs of sex addiction somewhat similar to drug addiction.' The unreasoned, emotional and wholly unscholarly tone of Sorokin's book is testimony to the distress of another harassed male. Although he does not attack women directly, his fear of heterosexual activity which automatically involves the female is therefore allied to fear of women in general. Sorokin blasts Freud who wrote 'degrading' fairy tales and even attacks anthropologists who have written of sexual freedom in primitive groups. Such freedom, according to Sorokin, is the chief reason why they have not progressed! The less sex, the more civilization, he maintains, and suggests that in order to control their sinful addiction, Americans should give up liquor, avoid reading novels, plays, eschew television and the movies and cease to patronize dances and night clubs. The medieval tone is familiar and indeed Sorokin enlists everyone from Saint Augustine to Beethoven against sex.

Thanks to continual and never very well-founded assertions in popular media, the notion of the American matriarchy has become a current catchword. Eve Merriam, writing in a rebuttal (*The Nation*, 1958) maintained that there was a general reaction in the wake of Wylie. She quoted Russell Lynes, who wrote that the father has been reduced to 'part man, part time mother and part time maid. He is the chief cook and bottle washer; the chauffeur, the gardener, the houseboy, the maid, laundress and charwoman.' Lynes is echoing Shakespeare's *Antony and Cleopatra* in which the Egyptian queen dressed Antony in her own garments while she wore his sword. Amaury de Riencourt also states, 'Man has become a member of an oppressed minority. Preconditioned to female dominance by his mother, he is a volunteer for slavery.'

The case is pretty much summed up by a book put out by the editors of *Look* magazine, complete with cartoons by Osborne. 'From the moment he is born, the American boy is ruled by women. First the hospital nurses, then his mother, dictate his every move. When he goes to school his teachers take over and today most of them are women. He becomes accustomed to female domination.' Margaret Mead's thesis of 'conditional love' is then tossed into the hopper. If the poor afflicted boy does not behave he will not be loved, he is told by the blackmailing female. To this is added an incautious statement by Davis Riesman that the boy after being filled with conflict because of his mother is then afraid to fail before girls and thus his masculinity is overburdened.

The sexual indictments of the *Look* editors are the most revealing. 'More and more wives identify economic achievement with masculinity. Occupational success is now an important part of sex appeal, and men are unsexed by failure.' But that is only the beginning. In the first place girls are now being taught sexual know-how. Gone are the happy days of Victorian oblivion. The dominating woman now decides when sex shall take place and how much. Then, too, the wife will now make her husband realize how important it is that she be satisfied. But women have a greater sexual potential than men. The male being faced with these responsibilities, Sorokin is brought in to point out: 'A man who forces himself into constant overwork may be evading the sexual demands of his marriage.' Since success is a symbol of potency, the poor male therefore has to work day and night to satisfy his wife economically and to avoid satisfying her in bed. An Italian film, *The Conjugal Bed*, oddly enough, dramatizes precisely this situation. When the husband is persecuted by his demanding wife, he goes to the office at night and pretends he has work to do. The implacable queen bee, however, turns up at the office, pulls up her skirts to display her stockings and, wallowing on the couch lasciviously, finally gets what she wants. The result of this situation is that 'Today's American male, if the experts are right, has even lost much of his sexual initiative; some authorities believe his capacity is being lowered.'

We come back, therefore, to the old charges that the modern American woman is on the one hand the 'wooing lady' of the Middle Ages, and on the other pretty close to Wedekind's rapacious Lulu. In spite of the fact that statistics show she is always paid less than and obliged to defer to men when she makes a social contribution, she can't win.

Still one more bit of evidence is the tragi-comedy *Oh Dad, Poor Dad, Mamma's Hung You in the Closet and I'm Feelin' So Sad*. Arthur Kopit's avant-garde farce depicts a woman who has not only destroyed her husband but stuffed him and carries him about with her as a trophy. She is sexually prurient; she spends her evenings wandering about the beach at a resort throwing sand at amorous couples. Her son has been so overwhelmed by his mother, who cherishes Venus's-flytraps and a carnivorous piranha fish, that he is almost afraid to look at a girl. When one does succeed in making a pass at him, she is a patent combination of the virgin and the prostitute. The actress who played the part succeeded in combining a frilly, demure, childlike quality and a subtle insinuating lechery to an amazing degree. Kopit's unfortunate little hero, tied to his mother and effectively castrated, has no recourse but to murder the girl.

Kopit's humorous cartoon, whether tongue-in-cheek or not, is a genuine reflection of the contemporary complaints. Although women have come to stay in the American scene, men are still fighting a rear-guard action which consists mainly of verbal lamentation. There is, however, a serious side to the situation. As in the past, when men can no longer bear the company of women they run away from them.

CHAPTER TWENTY-SIX

The Flight from the Female

In earlier chapters we have touched on institutional homosexuality insomuch as it reflected a withdrawal from women. Today, although homosexuality is not institutionalized, some authorities believe that it has been increasing. Abram Kardiner cites the fact that arrests in England have risen 400 to 500 per cent since the end of World War I. He suggests that perhaps 25 per cent of the male population is removed from meaningful relations with women.

Granted that such estimates are only conjectural, Robert Lindner, basing his calculations on the Kinsey report, feels that about 5 or 6 per cent of the male population of the United States is exclusively homosexual.

Actually homosexuality is a complex phenomenon. It varies from casual sexual experience with the same sex to a permanent behaviour pattern excluding relations with the female. Males (or females), deprived of contacts with the other sex in prisons, schools, and similar restrictive situations, turn to their own sex as a substitute for physical and emotional gratifications. Again, as we have already pointed out, the male warrior group may practise it as a part of its social exclusion of women and yet retain the marriage relation and produce children. Albert Reiss has pointed out how young delinquents sell their services to older men but remain emotionally uninvolved and as long as they do not do it for pleasure consider themselves to be heterosexual. Apparently anyone may obtain erotic release from the same sex under certain circumstances.

It cannot be denied that there are many active male homosexuals whose inversion is related to their neurotic compulsions, in other words a symptom of personality difficulties. Freud believed that the libido in childhood could be directed towards either parent, the

275

infant being pansexual. The process of growing up resulted in the repression of homosexuality and other perverse expressions of sex. When this character development did not take place, infantile forms of sex expression persisted. Failure to develop normally could result from pathological family relationships.

Freudian revisionists have pointed out that the exclusively homosexual personality cannot be traced to one specific type of childhood experience. The knowledge that the parents wanted a girl, a strong attachment to the father, and a feeling of rejection by the mother, gentle unaggressive qualities which cause others to label the boy a cissy, all may play a part in turning a young male towards his own sex; but then, again, they may be successfully surmounted. Clara Thompson writes, 'In short, homosexuality is not a clinical entity, but a symptom with different meanings in different personality set-ups.'

We are here concerned, however, with homosexuality from the sociological point of view. If, as we have been suggesting, there has always been an undercurrent of anxiety in males in their relation to the opposite sex, which is expressed in various forms of extreme attitudes towards women, when the tensions burdening the male in his society particularly trouble him, what is the meaning of homosexuality today? In our crisis world it is related to the old problem of the relationship between the sexes.

Abram Kardiner, who believes homosexuality is increasing, writes, 'It seems more like a wholesale flight from the female – a flight from masculinity.' Accepting the point of view that homosexuality is a symptom of distorted personality development, in other words that it may germinate at the level of early childhood experience, he points out that full participation of the adult in his society, his way of earning a livelihood, his conception of himself as husband and father and his reactions to what others expect of him are also part of his development. All these factors are imaginatively becoming a part of his psyche by puberty when the choice of his sexual role can be actively made.

In our society the norm of masculinity is probably more confused and poorly defined than in any other period. Although, as Margaret Mead has demonstrated, male norms differ in different cultures, in earlier periods the image of the warrior and hunter was clear-cut.

Today the male is supposed to be a 'success', but increasingly women are also out to obtain success. Similarly in family relationships, more formalized cultures set up a network of privileges and responsibilities. In general, throughout Western history up until the feminist movement, women were supposed to obey. Writes Hendrik Ruitenbeek, 'The typical "manly" or masculine vocations are rapidly disappearing, at least from the list of honourable activities. As occupations, blacksmith and hunter have now disappeared; farmer, miner, lumberjack, and fisherman now work as much with machines as with male brawn. Even the professional soldier, insofar as he holds a position of command, sits behind a desk or perhaps at a computer. The day of military leader on horseback is over. The most masculine figure of modern warfare drops bombs on women and children, or, at best, on airplane carriers.'

Now we have the image created by mass media of the woman who controls her ineffectual husband. Kardiner calls this stereotype of the henpecked male Mr Bumstead. 'He is the submissive breadwinner, while Mrs Bumstead is the real power in the family. She rescues her child husband from difficulties of his own making and he pays for assistance by loss of dignity. Although Mr Bumstead is a caricature, his situation represents the tyranny of the nonworking wife out to achieve status by driving her husband to higher and higher standards of living. If he fails the penalty is degradation and occasionally the withdrawal of sexual contacts.

'What kind of a masculine ideal is furnished to the children by a father like this? The boys of the Bumstead family stand a good chance of developing into homosexuals. In this case homosexuality can result from fear of the female based on the idea that "if Mother can do this to Father, another woman can do it to me".'

The important point, however, is that while we have no way of knowing whether Bumsteads are overrunning American society or not, the mass media are predominantly in the hands of men. Men write the scripts, men produce the shows at the beck of Madison Avenue agencies and sponsors, also predominantly male. This sort of comedy, therefore, is a symptom of something going on in the male psyche. It either indicates an unconscious fear of the modern female or a desire to placate her by representing her as all-powerful.

Kardiner goes on to point out that curtailment of opportunities for male expression is more of a disaster for the male than the female. So far society has not expected so much of her. 'The male is compelled to interpret curtailment as castration or demasculinization. The female doesn't always interpret it as defeminization. The female always has a retreat; the male doesn't.'

In Kardiner's view homosexuality can thus become a retreat from too great demands upon masculinity. 'Evidently there is a voluntary element operating here. . . .' The contemporary man who feels uncertain of himself, who cherishes hostility towards society for the high demands it makes upon him, who is afraid to face the challenge of competition, looks for a way out, or some means of reassurance. It might be added that in recent years a divided world which lives under the threat of annihilation is not the most encouraging place in which to grow up. The nineteenth-century male, for all his intellectual and emotional problems, nearly always had faith in the future. He felt that society was progressing towards worthwhile goals. The disillusionment of fascism, the hardening of socialist idealism into competitive nationalism, have contributed to a mood of fear and doubt.

In addition, the alienation of the individual resulting from the monolithic centralized political structures of modern times helps to make him feel impotent. Despite the mechanisms of the vote and the father images built up by mass media, the average man's sense of being controlled by large impersonal forces, of being a cog in a mechanized world without truly human goals, is disheartening and no doubt fairly unbearable for weaker individuals.

As Kardiner puts it, 'If the male fears demasculinization by the female or society, he receives constant reassurance from his male partner that his masculinity is still there. Under these conditions the strength that he cannot get from the female, because she depletes him still more, he gets from the male who has the desired symbol of power. By pairing with a male he now obtains the assurance that his masculinity is appreciated by the one who, like himself, is threatened.'

In other words, two penises are better than one and all the more so when the threatening vagina can be avoided. Kardiner goes on to point out that this consolation and substitution is rarely satisfactory because it involves a sense of guilt on both sides, and generally undercurrents of exploitation. He adds that most homosexual relationships are temporary, unstable, often being mere pickups based on fantasy with no possibility of development. At best, when male unions are maintained in an equivalent of marriage, there is always a sense of alienation from society and the awareness of the disapprobation of most of the world.

This results in a cult attitude towards inversion, the formation of a subculture, a kind of secret society which displays a good deal of hostility towards the heterosexual world. This type of male group is very different from that which we have described among primitives where the male clubhouse is a recognized institution integrated into the culture as a whole.

If the modern homosexual flight from women be regarded as a retreat from the challenge of masculinity, in view of some of the attitudes we have been describing in past eras, it appears that males have been troubled about their maleness all along. Juvenal's descriptions of Roman homosexuality show it to be clearly of the cultic, hostile type. On the other hand the hit-and-run sex expression of the eighteenth-century gallant is a kind of reverse of cultic homosexual withdrawal. The gallant, by protesting his maleness too much reveals his own insecurity.

As the depth psychologists have told us again and again, the burdens of civilization are very difficult to bear; it appears that the proliferation of industrial society has made them heavier and heavier. Hendrik Ruitenbeek writes, 'Man stands alone now; class, rank, family, even the fundamental sex role no longer props him up. He must choose the very basis of his existence. Life as a homosexual is one of the turnings he can take. It is a road an increasing number of men are following.'

It would seem therefore, for social health, men more than ever need to improve their relationships to women. One prerequisite is certainly a dispassionate understanding of the chimera of the dangerous sex. Though, as we have attempted to show, it is deep-seated and compulsive, like most irrational fears, if faced intelligently it should lose its menace.

CHAPTER TWENTY-SEVEN

Now and Tomorrow

We have been endeavouring to show by the facts assembled in this study that male attitudes towards women and the images of women created by men are strongly influenced by deep anxieties, which are probably universal and basic as the young male grows up in the family relationship, and also shaped by the pressures in the various cultures which man has created. In other words, since men have a tendency to be afraid of women they also create situations which rationalize these fears and perpetuate them. In addition, since no human being can easily face his own compulsions, the male tends to project his fears and antagonisms in terms of derogatory attributes by insisting that women are evil, inferior and valueless (because different) and hence should be made to obey, be kept in their place, or fulfil some unreal role which neutralizes them and removes them from the sphere of competition. From all of this, traditions and stereotypes are born which can always be called upon to justify the inherent tendencies in male behaviour.

We have shown that in preliterate cultures there is a world-wide fear of women's sexual functions which is institutionalized in sanctions and restrictions which are not without survivals in contemporary times. We have analysed some of the basic myths of both primitive and early urban cultures to reveal the ethical and pietistic rationalizations of the underlying compulsive hostility towards women. We have traced the violent and primitive reaction which took place in the Middle Ages, a period in which women were rejected even more drastically than in earlier times, and the ensuing witchcraft fantasy in which the old castration fears assumed new forms. We have also indicated the curious exaggerated social form of the men's club in which phallicism led to passive or active homosexuality, another symptomatic rejection of women. We have sketched the misogynist tradition in Western literature through which the writer, as shaman, has expressed the same age-old fears and hostilities, creating the image of the *femme fatale* and the split figure of the virgin and prostitute. We have also dealt with the contemporary scene in which the charges against women derive from the same primitive unconscious apprehensions. While there is no denying that there is always a certain economic factor in man's treatment of woman; as a dehumanized sexual possession and as a status symbol she is used to bolster his ego and exploited out of self-interest, we are here concerned with emphasizing the psychological factors which, as outlined in this study, still play an important role in distorting the relationship between the sexes today.

Assuming there is truth in this thesis, let us see, for instance, how it affects the problem of the working woman. It is a bitter irony that, thanks to the manpower shortage caused by two major wars, women have been admitted into industry and white-collar work in large numbers. In fact in Western civilization today Alva Myrdal estimates that about a third of the working force is composed of women. Nevertheless, in spite of the *fait accompli* the controversy still goes on as to whether the working mother can be a successful housewife, whether her children suffer from this situation, whether her abilities are inferior to those of men, in short men are simply not happy about her economic freedom. We have also seen how the Nazi movement attempted to drive her back into the kitchen. Now that we are faced with technological unemployment will something similar happen if the working force begins to be reduced on a large scale?

Myrdal feels (and so does Amram Scheinfeld), on the basis of various statistical studies, that 'Experience has settled the long controversy about feminine abilities and has proved that women are fit for a much wider range of activities than those compatible with the commonly accepted idea of the "weaker" sex.' Indeed, as Myrdal has pointed out, in agricultural societies women have worked alongside men and in the early nineteenth century men were happy to exploit women in industry and pay them less than a living wage. With the rise in industrial wages, women tended to leave the factory in order to imitate the non-working status of their bourgeois sisters. Then in the twentieth century women fought their way back (aided by war) into most fields already occupied by men. On the other hand, as we have seen, in many primitive groups men's and women's work is rigidly separated on the basis of sexual taboos.

Everything tends to show that men's attitudes towards working women are involved with ideas about their masculinity. All the material we have been discussing indicates that men have always been fragile in their sex life. Women can fulfil their sexual role in society without effort, by mere acceptance; their need for orgasmic experience has varied with the culture's expectations. Men, however, must be capable of erection and discharge or they are not performing their duty in carrying on the race. At the same time loss of semen and erection in the sex act seems also to have troubled them. Thus men have worried about their potency from the beginning of history. The primitive sometimes sees the woman as a direct castration threat and full of bad mana. The man in a highly developed society equates his work and his achievement with his potency. When women compete with him, his ego suffers; all his ambivalent reactions to the sexual act reinforce his distress. Women not only make frightening physical demands upon him (especially now that more and more women feel that if their mates do not give them orgasmic satisfaction they are cheated) but castrate him creatively by possibly doing his work better. Just as the die-hard southern segregationist, now that Negroes are actively demanding first-class citizenship, begins to wail that they are out to deprive him of political supremacy and to disenfranchise him, so the insecure male announces that women have made the United States into a matriarchy. At worst he retreats into homosexuality.

Interestingly enough, women still feel that they must play down their abilities or they will ruin their matrimonial chances. Forty per cent of a group of college girls interviewed in 1943 believed that they must play dumb or they would frighten men off. Twenty years have not changed the situation greatly. As recently as 1958 an investigator was told by a woman department store executive, 'A woman should not try to get ahead of the men at any time. They'll only buck her and give her trouble, but if you will work with them and sort of take the attitude that he who is humble shall be exalted and so forth, you'll make out much better.' Thus men's attitude still 'vacillates between a wish to have a girl friend who is an intelligent companion and a good sport, and a desire for a combination mother-image and Venus de Milo; a woman for whom they are the sole aim in life and with whom they are proud to be seen'.

One result of this confusion is the so-called Hollywood love goddess, the final betrayal of both femininity and sex. Balzac made of the *grande courtisane* a heartless *femme fatale*, the Victorians made of her a brutalized outcast; it has remained for Americans to make of her an abstract commodity. No more dehumanized victim could be found than a Marilyn Monroe or an Elizabeth Taylor. As women and human beings such stars are not allowed to exist. In Monroe's case, the bitter conflict between herself as an industry and a frustrated, undeveloped, and wholly unrealized female destroyed her. Hers was a feminine American Tragedy. In a merchandising civilization everything is marketable. By marketing legs, breasts and haunches, a male-dominated society panders to the same type of fantasy that created the 'wooing lady' of the Middle Ages, but it goes further by patenting and mass-producing a pseudo image upon which a nationwide audience may vent its hostile and degrading eroticism. In the long run Marilyn Monroe was treated no better than the poor drab of the London pavements whom we encountered in 1850. Let us set against this metaphorical gang rape the image of Eleanor Roosevelt with her sense of purpose, her active support of progressive public policies, her contributions to statesmanship and social betterment.

In spite of the relative emancipation of some women, a reaction seems to be taking place. Betty Friedan devotes a whole book, *The Feminine Mystique*, to the thesis that in the last decade or so a counter revolution has been in progress in the United States designed to sell the image of the woman as housewife. She finds that in women's colleges the emphasis has shifted from career training to an orientation towards marriage. In addition American merchandising has concentrated on woman as the consumer and has unloosed a barrage of propaganda designed to sell homemaking as fulfilment and housework as creative achievement. College girls, she maintains, are no longer interested in careers; they are accepting the old happy housewife stereotype. Friedan seems to think that this arises from a kind of feminine 'failure of nerve', a reluctance to face the problem of creating a new identity. We have already mentioned the spectre of technological unemployment. It may be already affecting our society. We suspect, however, that male anguish is basically to blame, for, as we have repeatedly stated, it is still a man's world. Some of Friedan's own research bears this out. In discussing the type of story now published in women's magazines which glorifies the domestic ideal, she reveals that most of the new writers who exalt the happy housewife are men. The women writers who created the career girl image have dropped out of the field. An editor told her, 'The new writers were all men, back from the war, who had been dreaming about home and a cosy domestic life.'

The novelist Brigid Brophy, in an article in the *Saturday Evening Post*, November 1963, repeats the complaint that although the bars are down, women are still imprisoned in a zoo without bars. 'All the zoo architect needs to do is run a zone of hot or cold air, whichever the animal concerned cannot tolerate, round the cage where the bars used to be.' This barrier is social pressure – the fear of not being considered a real man or a real woman. Attacking the myth that the man naturally wants to leave the house while the woman prefers to stay in it, in her view some men might be good housekeepers and enjoy it. 'Many masculine neuroses would be avoided and many children would enjoy the benefit of being brought up by a father with a talent for child rearing instead of a mother with no talent for it but a sense of guilt about the lack. . . .' Women, hampered by the same social myth, are ashamed of being logical thinkers for fear of being called masculine. Brophy is therefore repeating the same idea expressed by the college girls of twenty years ago, that a woman 'is inclined to think that an intelligence would be as unbecoming to her as a moustache; and pathetically many women have tried in furtive privacy to disembarrass themselves of intellect as though it were false hair'. Brophy boldly suggests that the sex stereotypes should simply be dropped. 'If modern civilization has invented methods of education which make it possible for women to think logically and for men to feed babies, we are betraying civilization if we do not set both sexes free to make a choice.'

They can never be free, however, as long as reasons for the clichés are not recognized and the cowardly compulsions are not brought out into the open. It is certainly too much to expect a woman to become an ideal mother into whose desexualized and innocuous womb a man may creep. It is also too much to expect a woman to become an appendage to masculinity, a disembodied paean of approval and encouragement.

It may be objected that women have been submissive so long that the modern revolt is only a temporary phenomenon. Actually the rebellion of women as a conscious group has merely followed in the wake of other and more easily formulated social changes and is intimately connected with the rise to power of the bourgeoisie. The fact that women, as a group, cut across social classes and that they were intimately and personally related to men made it far more difficult to clarify their aims. It was not until widespread educational opportunities had been approved by bourgeois society that the female sex began to produce educated leaders and individual males became their allies. Their changed socio-economic and legal status is therefore a part of social evolution and not likely to be reversible.

Viewed dispassionately, the women of history seem to have put up with a good deal from their nervous and easily disturbed mates. Studies show that women are physically tougher; they break down less often and are less prone to suicide. They have needed to be. Often treated as property, abused and scolded, blamed for every disaster when the going got tough, they have nevertheless come up smiling, lipstick in hand. They have been loyal to the lord and master, admired him and bowed to the inevitable when their sons also turned out to be poseurs and bullies.

It seems essential that the contemporary male reconceive his notion of masculinity. Studies tend to show that men excel in activities requiring strength, women in those which require dexterity. Men seem to excel in mechanics and in abstract areas such as mathematics, women are better in languages. The male who worries about his ego should take a good look at the uncharacteristic Victorian, Mr George Lewes, who with perfect good nature was able to live with a wife considered more talented than he, and moreover did not feel frustrated but delighted in her success. On the other hand he was no handmaid or parasite, for he worked serenely at his trade of journalism; indeed only recently a collection of his essays on nineteenth-century actors has been published in a paperback, showing that he possessed a critical ability which has now become a contribution to theatre history. With a little insight and courage it should not be too much for American men to learn to respect the abilities of each sex and to overcome the terrors of competition.

Myrdal points out that the continually increasing life expectation of the Western world, the increase in domestic conveniences, the decreasing infant mortality and smaller family mean that less time must be spent on raising children; women simply cannot occupy their lives exclusively with household tasks. He estimates that the average married woman is only employed full time at such occupations for a third to a quarter of her life. If she is to be a healthy human being she must be allowed to make a social contribution during these other productive years. 'Modern mothers who make no plans outside the family for their future will not only play havoc with their own lives but will make nervous wrecks of their over-protected children and of their husbands,' writes Myrdal, and it is hard to disprove him.

The question of women's creativity is connected with that of image and role. Men have always been concerned with their image, whether they put enormous bone ornaments in their noses to make themselves look fierce, like the Asmats, or developed touchy concepts of honour and ritual dances, including the duel. Women, up to the present, have not had to worry – they have been firmly told what was ladylike and unladylike. Great actresses in the past, they have played roles written for them by the male author. Whether they have done this out of love for him or because they preferred to be interpretative artists is a question. Sometimes the feminine role has been hammed to the point of caricature. The platonic love queen, inspiring the warrior in the metal suit, the Victorian Mrs Ellis, silent when her husband speaks – we wonder, was it almost tongue-in-cheek?

When the question of female traits is realistically viewed by Viola

Klein in *The Feminine Character*, after reviewing the finding of various social scientists, she admits, 'An attempt to draw up a table of feminine traits, and to list all the respective authors' agreements or disagreements on each point must fail because there is hardly any common basis to the different views. The difficulty is not on specific characteristics and their origin, but that the emphasis is laid on absolutely different attributes.'

It is true that only a few important women artists have made contributions and, so far, mostly in literature. They have been hampered by the fact that, since male standards prevail, as rebels they have been forced to mould themselves by these patterns. Since they have different capabilities, their task is to explore their own image of themselves. They have centuries of accumulated domination to unravel, a tremendous job of critical evaluation to perform before they can discover what they are and what they really want to be.

Naturally in their present condition women are unsure of themselves and, dissatisfied with the role of imitation males, may out of confusion and neurosis become the hostile or actively castrating harpies which Lundberg describes in *The Lost Sex*. But when this author insists that motherhood must be 'rehabilitated' he is merely repeating the dated clichés.

Morton Hunt's inquiry into the contemporary status of women in America tends to picture them caught in a dilemma. Raising children and working makes for a hectic life but if the woman stops working and devotes herself to her children, once they are out of the nest she finds herself, with her skills dated, out of the labour market and may never succeed in getting back. As a result she has a bleak prospect with half her life left over. Myrdal's suggestion that working conditions should be adjusted so that the working mother can fulfil tasks inside and outside the home is a realistic approach to the problem. Women's major problems still remain unsolved, however. In a conference on the Potential of Women held at the University of California in the autumn of 1963, a psychologist, Dr Eleanor Maccoby, pointed out that women who succeed in making intellectual contributions are generally tomboys in their childhood and rebel against authority. When the girl goes to school, however, she faces a social pressure to conform to the domestic ideal. She may fight this pressure, 'and she may do this successfully in many ways, but I suggest that it is a rare intellectual woman who will not have paid a price for it. And I hazard the guess that it is this anxiety which helps account for the lack of productivity of women who make intellectual careers.' And so, like Brigid Brophy, Maccoby also feels that the stereotypes should be revised so that a woman may be dominantly active and still not lose her sexual attractions. Marya Mannes, a married woman and a writer, at the same conference summed up with some bitterness, 'If she has children, she must pay for this indulgence with a long burden of guilt for her life will be split three ways between them, her husband and her work. What she gives to one she must take from the other, and there will be no time when the one or the other is not harmed.'

In the area of sex relations, the heritage of tradition and the basic anxieties still confuse the issue. The result is a series of equivocations and hypocrisies which make life very difficult for the mating young of the species. The shadow of the double standard looms darkly although there is a general agreement not to mention it any more.

In actual practice the double standard means that sexual experimentation before marriage and rejection of ironclad monogamy is permitted to the male while the female is allowed the same privileges only secretly and if she is not stigmatized by unlegalized pregnancy. If she is, she may encounter serious social sanctions.

Since official Western legal and religious codes set up monogamy and premarital chastity as the rule for both sexes, the double standard is obviously a folk invention, one of those mores that defy articulate intellectual rules. We know from cross-cultural studies that it is by no means universal or inevitable. Primitive groups range from puritanical attitudes as severe as those of early New Englanders to an acceptance of sex as a harmless amusement. Margaret Mead and Bronislaw Malinowski's studies of Samoa and the Trobriand Islands have publicized the relaxed promiscuity of the young before marriage in these particular areas and have probably exerted some influence on actual contemporary behaviour.

We have already suggested that the male's insistence on a monopoly of his wife's sexual services and the requirement that she be
intact at marriage is involved with his feelings about private property. In the Middle Ages, as we noted, marriage was combined
with the acquisition of property and continued to be in later periods.
This, however, is not enough to account for the long history of
jealousy and the emotional 'never darken my door again' Victorian
attitude of the father (infuriated when the daughter upon whom his
unacknowledged incestuous desires were fixed betrayed him with a
lover). It seems likely that the stubbornly persisting double standard
is really largely dependent upon male anxiety. Even as property, a
woman's person is an extension of the male ego. When we add to
this the fact, of which the man is keenly aware, that a woman's
ability to perform sexually is limitless compared to his own, there
is always the fear and suspicion that he has not fully satisfied her and
that she will turn to a more potent male. Schopenhauer and Strindberg were good examples of this apprehension. As a result, a fanatical
desire to control her sex activity arises. Thus the faithless woman,
Cressida, was made into a stereotype and punished by male writers.
Don Juan, on the other hand, despite occasional punishment in
another world, is a hero and always regarded by the male writer with
a certain admiration. Perhaps there will come a time when feminine
artists will give Theseus the treatment he deserves for deserting
Ariadne so callously and Jason's story will be told from an angle
which will throw a different light on Medea.

The problem of the double standard is also tied up with the denial
of women's need for sexual fulfilment. Men have always assumed
that they are the active element, women the passive. Mechanically
men, of course, are active, since they must become aroused and
carry out the act of penetration. Women, although they play the
role of acceptance, can always say yes or no. As long as they exercise
this prerogative they are not passive. Despite cultures in which
marriages are arranged by an older generation, women have always
attempted to pick and choose, to encourage the men they preferred.
A woman of the Lesu culture when she wants a man, quite simply
stimulates him by exposing her sex.

Victorianism made an intolerable attempt to deprive women of any sexual rights. As the histories of the pioneer feminists Sand, Eliot and Woodhull show, one of the first and most intense aims of the rebels was freedom of sexual expression. This immediately re-aroused the fears of the predatory female; male writers resorted to the feline image which is probably unconsciously related to the toothed vagina; fulfilment was a cannibal act committed upon the male.

The question as to whether the woman's sexual needs are to be recognized without alarm and treated with as much respect as those of the male's thus also relates to the double standard. There has been much discussion whether an actual orgasm is essential to female satisfaction. Margaret Mead writes that perhaps 'the capacity to learn a total orgasmic response is present differentially in all women and that the differentials are perhaps very slight'. Whether such a response is 'learned' or not, it can evidently be repressed. Havelock Ellis reports that no complaints of frigidity in women are on record in the eighteenth century. Indeed *Fanny Hill*, though written by a man, is indicative of the cultural attitude of the time towards female pleasure. It took the nineteenth-century prude to impose frigidity.

Although the female orgasm is not so clearly defined as that of the male, there is no doubt that something pleasurable goes on which most women do not want to miss. An interesting bit of evidence from primitive life can be drawn from Edwin Grant Burrows' report on the poetry of the Ifaluk Islanders, a Melanesian group which lives near Yap. Uncorrupted by any missionary teaching, these people live a fairly free and cheerful sex life. Here women have orgasmal experience. There is no puberty ceremony for men and when the anthropologists described circumcision they were shocked by the idea. The Ifaluk natives do observe menstrual taboos and during the fishing season men live in the canoe house and abstain from women. There are records of wars in Ifaluk poetry but headhunting is unknown. Discreet love affairs are accepted among young people before marriage but the boys are not supposed to engage in such practices until they are about sixteen. If the girl becomes pregnant the pair normally marries. The Ifaluk people do not discuss sex in mixed company and affairs are always carried out in the strictest privacy. The islanders, on the whole, do not seem to have developed an exaggeratedly phallic culture like that in some other areas of the Pacific. Most significant is the fact that they possess a large body of love poetry exclusively composed by women. Such poems are sung, accompanied by dancing somewhat similar to the hula. The erotic poetry is not supposed to be mentioned in mixed company but women sing the songs among themselves and sing them to their lovers in amorous situations. Men, among themselves, will also reminiscently sing the songs. An example will show the frank and hedonistic character of Ifaluk female love poetry.

LOVE AND PARTING

Flower of the Sevang tree,
Ango that blooms in the taro swamp,
My lover comes to me,
Stays close to me;
Our feelings are the same.
I understand what he says.
He told me, 'I'll never leave you.'
I asked 'Truly?' and he said 'I wouldn't lie to you.'
He is like a vein in my body;
Grips me like the breadfruit roots underground.
He love me too much to leave me.
Wherever he goes the thought of me is with him.
My love is meat and drink to him.
I am like a garland on his head,
Like a feathered tropic bird
His head is adorned with plumes.
He makes a fine showing in the canoe house
Or as he goes into the meeting house Katelu.
He cannot bear to stay away from me;
He comes around by the back way,
Comes through the woods to find me.
We go into the woods together,
Find a pleasant clearing;
There we lie down side by side
Where the gabwi grows low about us.
I take off my skirt, spread my legs,
Show him my sex,
He admires my thighs,
Caresses my sex with his hand,

Strokes the hair with his hand.
I adore his caresses . . .
If he leaves me I will be in despair. . . .
Though he is far away, I will not forget.
He has left his perfume behind;
Left it on my skirt,
Left it on my body;
For a long time it stays.
He has gone far away
To the island of Lamotrek.
As he lies down to sleep
In the canoe house there
He dreams of his lover,
Dreams I am sleeping beside him . . .
There, he is holding me like a child,
There, we are in the woods again
In our favourite clearing,
Always he holds me tight.
Flower in my ear,
Fragrant ango flower,
It is well.

Ruskin's horror at such poetry can be imagined but the South Sea island Sappho would not be out of place among the beats.

Since the primitive generally institutionalized his fears of women, he often narrowed her activities, but the evidence just cited from Ifaluk shows that he is at times able to accept her on the basis of equality as a lover. Ovid, though he was somewhat guilty of Don Juanism, also respected feminine eroticism. The courtly love movement exalted woman as an erotic partner even though it had to compromise and equivocate because of clerical sanctions. In our time nineteenth-century rationalizations and evasions still shape official attitudes. We are all aware, from Mr Kinsey's studies, that actual practice is at variance with public ideas. It is because of these contradictions that dating becomes such a social no-man's-land. A situation in which the boy tries to get all he can when he goes out with a girl, regardless of the emotional and social consequences to her, while the girl is traditionally made to feel she should give as little as possible, yet is torn by the fear that if she does not give enough she will not be popular is certainly the result of confused male attitudes. On the one hand, there is enough of the Don Juan impulse in the boy to require conquests to bolster his ego, on the other hand he is not prepared to publicly grant the girl the same freedom he assumes himself. The resulting guilts, conflicts and tensions are a poor preparation for choosing a mate.

To quote Max Lerner, 'Given the gap between actual behavior and formal codes, Kinsey estimates that 85 per cent of the younger male Americans could be convicted as sex offenders. In the gap and conflict between these two forces he finds a source of much of the American sense of guilt and anxiety which form the heavy psychic toll that Americans pay. . . . Despite the fluid nature of American society, there is a tenacity in the codes that is hard to break through, and their hold is all the greater because the loose sprawling character of the society frightens most Americans and makes them cling all the harder to the challenged codes.' Nevertheless when prohibition became 100 per cent hypocrisy, we gave it up. Some groups have faced the sex issue. The Swedes, with a basically Protestant culture, have radically altered their legal and social attitudes towards sex. Although there is no reason why their system should suit the United States, a study of how the change came about should be instructive.

In some primitive cultures premarital liaisons are an accepted social form. As such, there is no conflict and tension. We moderns, in what is still predominantly a man's world, are still hedging and avoiding the issue. Back in the twenties Judge Ben Lindsay suggested a concrete institution, companionate marriage, in which young people would live together and practise birth control. He was not heeded and since his time there has been nothing but viewing with alarm and vague circular discussion. Sex relationship as a pleasure and a part of emotional fulfilment is always accepted in practice in the Western world. Unrealistic attitudes towards abortion penalize the second sex. Human society has always tended to regulate sex relations in some way and rightly, for human beings require order and pattern to life and promiscuity results in demoralization. What is needed, however, are social forms which realistically approximate the needs and desires of members of a specific culture. If something like Lindsay's suggestion were accepted as a respectable social form by which young people could lead normal lives at the time when their urge is strongest, the result could be revolutionary as far as encouraging honesty, respect and real friendship between young people. For this to happen, however, the contemporary male, and this includes the older pillar of society and upholder of law and custom, as well as his mating son, would have to deal with the bogeys that harrow his psyche; he would have to take a long and painful look at his culturally inherited and inherent fears.

In a sense the present book has been an attempt to put men on the couch, to make them aware of the shameful burden of fantasy and rationalization which they have been trailing down the ages. The male has accused woman of bewitching him with sex, of destroying him with her organ and her appetite, or of betraying him with a real or imaginary stallion-like rival. Or he turns upon her and calls her carrion and identifies her with sin or describes her as a tiger or a cannibalistic spider. By using this symbolic magic he has either imprisoned her, made her an outcast, or treated her as a scapegoat.

The facts speak for themselves. We have apparently reached a crisis in relations between the sexes. After a major shift in the social balance in which women have partially freed themselves and begun to assert their need to participate in contemporary culture on a new basis, at present there seems to be a stalemate. Whether women (as spokesmen for the old clichés) or men have brought it about, the conclusions of this study suggest that the dominant male attitude is fundamentally to blame.

If we are to go forward, therefore, it is time the male abandoned his magical approach to the second sex. It is time he learned to accept his existentialist anguish; it is time he realized the menace of the female lies within himself. And when he is ready to accept her as a partner in work and love, he may even begin to find out what she is like.

Note

D. O. Hebb in his book, *The Organization of Behavior* (New York, 1949), attempts a synthesis of physiology and experimental psychology and makes some suggestive points concerning the development of emotional patterns. He accepts, in the first place, an innate potential ambivalence of reaction, pleasure-love and rage-fear, which is the same as that formulated by depth psychology. He points out that experiments with chimpanzees raised in darkness indicate that some new visual experiences aroused a general sort of excitement; it was not until the apes were older (and hence their experience was more varied and more organized) that they showed fear of strangers and also fear of a model of a decapitated head (which would come under the category of the strange or unusual). Experience, therefore, caused tension (or excitement) and was eventually fitted into the categories of acceptance-rejection. Hebb also makes the point that organized behaviour tends to reduce emotional reaction. Thus, by analogy, when life's most disturbing experiences are fitted into the ambivalent philosophy of mana and rituals are built about them, distressing tension is contained and man copes with his world.

Bibliography

CHAPTER ONE

BEAUVOIR, SIMONE DE, *The Second Sex*. London, 1953.
BOK, EDWIN, Interview, *The New York Times*, April 18, 1909.
BROWN, HENRY BILLINGS, *Woman Suffrage: Paper read before the Ladies' Congressional Club of Washington, D.C.* Washington, 1910.
FOWLER, HENRY, *Phrenology and Physiology Applied to the Selection of a Suitable Companion for Life*. Philadelphia, 1841.
HAWES, JOEL, '*A Looking Glass for Ladies*', or, *The Formation and Excellence of the Female Character*. Address delivered at the eighth anniversary of the Mount Holyoke Female Seminary, South Hadley, Mass., 1845. Boston, 1845.
LA BARRE, WESTON, *The Human Animal*. Chicago, 1954.
MASON, OTIS T., *The Origin of Invention*. New York, 1902.
—, *Woman's Share in Primitive Culture*. New York, 1899.
MOEBIUS, P. J., *Über den physiologischen Schwachsinn des Weibes*. Halle, 1907.
MONTAGU, ASHLEY, *The Natural Superiority of Women*. London, 1954.
—, 'The Origin of Subincision in Australia'. *Oceania*. Melbourne, 1937.
PARKMAN, FRANCIS, *Some of the Reasons Against Woman Suffrage*. Pamphlet written for the Massachusetts Association Opposed to the Further Extension of Suffrage to Women. Boston, 1910.
PARSONS, ELSIE CLEWS, *The Old-Fashioned Woman: Primitive Fancies About the Sex*. New York, 1913.
REIK, THEODOR, *Ritual*, tr. Douglas Bryan. London, 1958.
The Trial of Isaac Preston. London, 1786.
WEININGER, OTTO, *Geschlecht und Charakter*. Leipzig, 1920.

CHAPTER TWO

CAZENEUVE, JEAN, *Les rites et la condition humaine*. Paris, 1958.
FREUD, SIGMUND, *Anxiety*, Standard Edition of the Complete

Psychological Works, Vol. XX. London, from 1953. *Beyond the Pleasure Principle*, Vol. XVIII. *The Ego and the Id*, Vol. XIX. *Group Psychology and the Analysis of the Ego*, Vol. XVIII. *Totem and Taboo*, Vol. XIII.

HAYS, H. R., *In the Beginnings*. New York, 1963.

RADIN, PAUL, *Primitive Religion*. New York, 1936. London, 1957.

RÓHEIM, GÉZA, 'Psychoanalysis of Primitive Cultural Types'. *International Journal of Psychoanalysis*, Vol. XIII. London, 1932.

—, *The Riddle of the Sphinx*. London, 1934.

THOMPSON, CLARA, and MULLAHY, PATRICK, *Psychoanalysis: Evolution and Development*. London, 1952.

CHAPTER THREE

CAZENEUVE, JEAN, *Les rites et la condition humaine*. Paris, 1958.

CRAWLEY, ERNEST, *The Mystic Rose*. London, 1961.

WEBSTER, HUTTON, *Magic*. Stanford, 1948.

—, *Taboo*. Stanford, 1942.

CHAPTER FOUR

CAZENEUVE, JEAN, *Les rites et la condition humaine*. Paris, 1958.

CRAWLEY, ERNEST, *The Mystic Rose*. London, 1961.

ELLIS, HAVELOCK, *Studies in the Psychology of Sex*, Vol. I. Philadelphia, 1901–28.

HAYS, H. R., *In the Beginnings*. New York, 1963.

PLOSS, HERMANN, and BARTELS, M. C. A. and P. R. A., *Woman: an Historical, Gynaecological and Anthropological Compendium*, 3 Vols. London, 1935.

CHAPTER FIVE

BROMBERG, WALTER, 'Psychological Considerations in Alcoholic Hallucination, Castration and Dismemberment Motif', *International Journal of Psychoanalysis*, Vol. XV. London, 1934.

CRAWLEY, ERNEST, *The Mystic Rose*. London, 1961.

DALY, C. F., 'Hindumythologie und Kastrationskomplex'. *Imago*, Vol. XIII. Vienna, 1927.

FENICHEL, OTTO, *The Psychoanalytical Theory of Neurosis*. New York, 1945.

FREUD, SIGMUND, *The Taboo of Virginity*. Standard Edition, Vol. XI.

GESSAIN, ROBERT, *Le motif vagina dentata*. 32nd International Congress of Americanists, Copenhagen, 1958.

HAYS, H. R., *In the Beginnings*. New York, 1963.

HOGBIN, HERBERT IAN, 'The Native Culture of Wogeo'. *Oceania*, Vol. 5. Melbourne, 1934–5.

HORNEY, KAREN, 'The Dread of Women'. *International Journal of Psychoanalysis*, Vol. XIII. London, 1932.

MEAD, MARGARET, *The Mountain Arapesh*, Part 2. American Museum of Natural History Anthropological Papers. Vol. XXXVII. New York, 1940.

MELVILLE, HERMAN, *Selected Tales and Poems*. New York, 1939.

PLOSS, HERMANN, and BARTELS, M. C. A. and P. R. A., *Woman: an Historical, Gynaecological and Anthropological Compendium*, 3 Vols. London, 1935.

RÓHEIM, GÉZA, 'The Evolution of Culture'. *International Journal of Psychoanalysis*, Vol. XV. London, 1935.

—, *The Riddle of the Sphinx*. London, 1934.

SARTRE, JEAN-PAUL, *Existential Psychoanalysis*. London, 1953.

CHAPTER SIX

BATESON, GREGORY, *Naven*. Cambridge, 1936. London, 1958.

BRIDGES, E. LUCAS, *The Uttermost Part of the Earth*. London, 1948.

HANDY, E. S. CRAIGHILL, *Polynesian Religion*. Bernice P. Bishop, Museum Bulletin, No. 34. Honolulu, 1927.

HAYS, H. R., *In the Beginnings*, New York, 1963.

HIRSCHFELD, MAGNUS, *Handbuch der gesamten Sexualwissenschaft*, Bund III, *Die Homosexualitat*. Berlin, 1914.

HIRSCHFELD, MAGNUS, and GASPAR, ANDREAS, eds., *Sexual History of the World War*. New York, 1934.

JONES, ERNEST, 'The Phallic Phase'. *International Journal of Psychoanalysis*, Vol. XIV. London, 1933.

KRUSE, ALBERT, 'Mundurucú Moieties'. *Primitive Man*, Vol. VII. New York, 1934.

LAYARD, JOHN W., *Stone Men of Malekula*. London, 1942.

LOTHROP, SAMUEL K., *The Indians of Tierra del Fuego*. Anthropological Contributions of the Museum of the American Indian, Heye Foundation, Vol. 10. New York, 1908.

MALINOWSKI, BRONISLAW, *The Sexual Life of Savages*. London, 1929.

OVESEY, LIONEL, 'The Homosexual Conflict'. *Psychiatry*, Vol. 17. New York, 1954.

PLOSS, HERMANN, and BARTELS, M. C. A. and P. R. A., *Woman: an Historical, Gynaecological and Anthropological Compendium*, 3 Vols. London, 1935.

QUAIN, BUELL HALVOR, *Fijian Village*. Chicago, 1948.

RADIN, PAUL, *The Indians of South America*. New York, 1942.

RÓHEIM, GÉZA, 'Psychoanalysis of Primitive Cultural Types'. *International Journal of Psychoanalysis*, Vol. XIII. London, 1932.
SAULNIER, TONY, *Headhunters of Papua*. New York, 1963.
SCHURTZ, HEINRICH, *Altersklassen und Männerbunde*. Berlin, 1902.
WARNER, WILLIAM LLOYD, *A Black Civilization*. London, 1958.
WEBSTER, HUTTON, *Primitive Secret Societies*. New York, 1908.
WILLIAMS, FRANCIS EDGAR, *Papuans of the Trans-Fly*. Oxford, 1936.
WILLIAMS, THOMAS, *Fiji and the Fijians*. London, 1868.

CHAPTER SEVEN

FINK, GERHARD, *Pandora und Epimetheus*. Furth Bayern, 1958.
FRITZ, KURT VON, 'Pandora, Prometheus and the Myth of the Ages'. *The Review of Religion*, Vol. XI. New York, 1947.
HARRISON, JANE, *Prolegomena to the Study of the Greek Religion*. Cambridge, 1922.
HESIOD, *Collected Works* (Carmina, recensuit, Aloisius Rzach). Stuttgart, 1958.
JAMES, EDWIN OLIVER, *The Ancient Gods*. London, 1960.
KRAMER, SAMUEL NOAH, *Sumerian Mythology*. London, 1962.
PANOFSKY, DORA and ERWIN, *Pandora's Box*. London, 1956.
SOLMSEN, FRIEDRICH, *Hesiod and Aeschylus*. Ithaca, 1949.
TURCK, H., *Pandora und Eva*. Weimar, 1931.

CHAPTER EIGHT

FRAZER, JAMES, *Folklore in the Old Testament*. New York, 1925.
GORDIS, ROBERT, 'The Significance of the Paradise Myth'. *The American Journal of Semitic Languages and Literatures*, Vol. LII. New York, 1936.
LEVY, LUDWIG, 'Sexualsymbolik in der Biblischen Paradies-geschicht'. *Imago*, Vol. V. Vienna, 1917.
POSNINSKY, S. H., 'The Death of Maui'. *Journal of the American Psychoanalytical Association*, Vol. V. New York, 1957.
POWDERMAKER, HORTENSE, *Life in Lesu*. New York, 1933.
REIK, THEODOR, *Myth and Guilt*. London, 1958.
RÓHEIM, GÉZA, 'Eden'. *The Psychoanalytical Review*. Vol. XXVII. New York, 1940.
TYLER, E. B., *Primitive Culture*. Oxford, 1936.
WILLIAMS, FRANCIS EDGAR, *Papuans of the Trans-Fly*. Oxford, 1936.

CHAPTER NINE

JUVENAL, *Satires*, tr. Rolfe Humphries. Bloomington, 1958.
OVID, *Art of Love*, tr. Rolfe Humphries. Bloomington, 1957.

CHAPTER TEN

AUGUSTINE, SAINT, *A Select Library of the Nicene and Post-Nicene Fathers of the Christian Church*, ed. Philip Schaff, Vols. I–VIII. New York, 1886–90.

CATULLUS, *Poems*, ed. Elmer Truesdell Merrill. Cambridge, 1951.

DODD, E. R., *The Greeks and the Irrational*. Berkeley, 1951.

ENGLE, BERNICE ATTIS, 'A Study of Castration'. *The Psychoanalytical Review*, Vol. XXIII. New York, 1936.

GRAILLOT, HENRI, *Le Culte de Cybèle, mère des dieux, à Rome et dans l'empire romain*. Paris, 1912.

JEROME, SAINT, *A Select Library of the Nicene and Post-Nicene Fathers of the Christian Church*, 2nd series, ed. Philip Schaff and Henry Wace, Vol. VI. New York, 1893.

KLIGERMAN, CHARLES, 'A Psychoanalytic Study of the *Confessions* of St Augustine'. *Journal of the American Psychoanalytical Association*, Vol. III. New York, 1957.

LEA, HENRY CHARLES, *The History of Sacerdotal Celibacy in the Christian Church*. New York, 1957.

MEAD, MARGARET, *New Lives for Old*. London, 1956.

TARACHOW, SIDNEY, 'St Paul and Early Christianity', *Psychoanalysis and the Social Sciences*, Vol. IV. New York, 1955.

TAYLOR, G. RATTRAY, *Sex in History*. London, 1953.

TERTULLIAN, *The Ante-Nicene Fathers*, ed. Alexander Roberts and James Donaldson, Vol. IV. New York, 1925.

WESTERMARCK, EDWARD, *Christianity and Morals*. London, 1939.

CHAPTER ELEVEN

Amis and Amiloun, ed. MacEdward Leach. Early English Text Society, Original Series, No. 203. London, 1937.

PAINTER, SIDNEY, *French Chivalry*. Baltimore, 1940.

WRIGHT, THOMAS, *Womankind in Western Europe from the Earliest Times to the Seventeenth Century*. London, 1869.

WULFF, AUGUST, *Die Frauenfeindlichen Dichtungen in den Romanischen Literaturen des Mittelalters bis zum Ende des XIII Jahrhunderts*. Halle, 1914.

CHAPTER TWELVE

Chaucer, Geoffrey, Students' edition, ed. Walter W. Skeat. Oxford, 1894.

GORDON, ROBERT KAY, *The Story of Troilus as told by Benoît de*

Sainte-Maure, Giovanni Boccaccio, Geoffrey Chaucer and Robert Henryson. London, 1934.

KIRBY, THOMAS A., Chaucer's Troilus: A Study in Courtly Love. New Orleans, 1940.

LEWIS, CLIVE STAPLES, 'What Chaucer really did to il Filostrato'. Essays and Studies by Members of the English Association, Vol. XVII. Oxford, 1932.

ROLLINS, HYDER E., 'The Troilus and Cressida Story from Chaucer to Shakespeare'. Publications of the Modern Language Association of America, Vol. 32, 1917.

SHAKESPEARE, WILLIAM, Troilus and Cressida, Collected Works, ed. William Aldis Wright. Garden City, 1936.

CHAPTER THIRTEEN

CAMPBELL, GEORGE A., The Knights Templars: Their Rise and Fall. London, 1937.

SIMON, EDITH, The Piebald Standard: A Biography of the Knights Templars. London, 1959.

CHAPTER FOURTEEN

CHRISTIAN, PAUL, The History and Practice of Magic, 2 Vols. London, 1952.

KEATS, JOHN, Poetical Works, ed. H. W. Garrod. Oxford, 1956.

KITTEN, A. M., 'La légende de Lilith', Revue de la Littérature Comparée, Vol. II. Paris, 1932.

LAVATER, LUDWIG, Of Ghostes and Spirites Walking by Nyght, 1572, ed. J. Dover Wilson. Oxford, 1929.

MALINOWSKI, BRONISLAW, Sexual Life of Savages in North-Western Melanesia. London, 1929.

SUMMERS, MONTAGUE, The Vampire, His Kith and Kin. New York, 1929.

—, The Vampire in Europe. New York, 1929.

THOMPSON, REGINALD CAMPBELL, The Devils and Evil Spirits of Babylonia, Being Babylonian and Assyrian Incantations, 2 Vols. London, 1903-4.

CHAPTER FIFTEEN

GUAZZO, FRANCESCO MARIA, Compendium Maleficarum, tr. E. A. Ashwin, ed. Montague Summers. London, 1929.

JONES, ERNEST, On the Nightmare. London, 1949.

MURRAY, MARGARET A., The Witch-Cult in Western Europe. Oxford, 1962.

RUNEBERG, ARNE, *Witches, Demons and Fertility Magic*. Helsingfors, 1947.
SPRENGER, JACOB, and KRÄMER, HEINRICH, *Malleus Maleficarum*, tr. Montague Summers. London, 1928.
SUMMERS, MONTAGUE, *The History of Witchcraft and Demonology*. New York, 1926. London, 1946.
WRIGHT, THOMAS, *Narratives of Sorcery and Magic*. London, 1851.
ZILBOORG, GREGORY, *The Medical Man and the Witch during the Renaissance*. Baltimore, 1935.

CHAPTER SIXTEEN

DRYDEN, JOHN, *All for Love, Twelve Famous Plays of the Restoration and Eighteenth Century*. New York, 1933.
SHAKESPEARE, WILLIAM, *Antony and Cleopatra, Collected Works*, ed. William Aldis Wright. Garden City, 1936.

CHAPTER SEVENTEEN

BELLOC, HILAIRE, *Milton*. London, 1935.
HANFORD, JAMES HOLLY, *John Milton, Englishman*. New York, 1949.
MILTON, JOHN, *Complete Prose Works*, 3 Vols., ed. Don M. Wolfe, Ernest Sirluck, Merritt Y. Hughes. New Haven, 1953-62.
—, *Paradise Lost and Other Poems*. New York, 1961.

CHAPTER EIGHTEEN

ALLPORT, GORDON, *The Nature of Prejudice*. London, 1954.
CASANOVA DE SEINGALT, *My Life and Adventures*, tr. Arthur Machen. New York, 1932.
GORER, GEOFFREY, *The Life and Ideas of the Marquis de Sade*. London, 1964.
KESTEN, HERMANN, *Casanova*. New York, 1955.
LÉLY, GILBERT, *Vie du Marquis de Sade*, 2 Vols. Paris, 1952-7.
RICHARDSON, SAMUEL, *Pamela*. London.
ROCHESTER, JOHN WILMOT, EARL OF, *Poems*, ed. Vivian de Sola Pinto. Cambridge, 1953.
SADE, DONATIEN, MARQUIS DE, *Oeuvres Complètes*, Vol. III, *Justine*. Paris, 1963. tr. Walton, London, 1964.
WOOD, ANTHONY À, *Athenae Oxonienses*, 2 Vols. London, 1691-2.
Works of Wycherly, Congreve, Vanbrugh and Farquhar, ed. Leigh Hunt, London, 1860.

CHAPTER NINETEEN

BAUDELAIRE, CHARLES, *L'Oeuvre Poétique*, ed. Guillaume Apollinaire. Paris, 1917.

BRAGMAN, LOUIS J., 'The case of Algernon Charles Swinburne'. *The Psychoanalytical Review*, Vol. XXI. New York, 1934.

CHEW, SAMUEL, *Swinburne*. Boston, 1929.

FEUILLERAT, ALBERT, 'Baudelaire et la légende de Don Juan'. *Renaissance*, 2–3. New York, 1944–5.

Laus Veneris. Antioch Press, Yellow Springs, Ohio, 1942.

POE, EDGAR ALLAN, *Complete Tales and Poems*. Intro. by Hervey Allen. New York, 1938.

STARKIE, ENID MARY, *Baudelaire*. London, 1933.

SWINBURNE, ALGERNON CHARLES, *Letters of Algernon C. Swinburne*, ed. Cecil Y. Lang, 6 Vols. New Haven, 1959.

WAGENKNECHT, EDWARD C., *Edgar Allan Poe: the Man Behind the Legend*. New York, 1963.

WERTHAM, FREDERIC, *Dark Legend*. New York, 1941.

CHAPTER TWENTY

COPLESTON, FREDERICK, *Arthur Schopenhauer, Philosopher of Pessimism*. London, 1946.

MCGILL, V. J., *Schopenhauer: Pessimist and Pagan*. New York, 1931.

SCHOPENHAUER, ARTHUR, *Parerga und Paralipomena*. Berlin, 1862.

—, *Studies in Pessimism*. New York, 1925.

CHAPTER TWENTY-ONE

BALDICK, ROBERT, *The Life of J.-K. Huysmans*. Oxford, 1955.

BALZAC, HONORÉ DE, *La peau de chagrin. Oeuvres Complètes*, Vol. II. Paris, 1896.

HUYSMANS, J.-K., *À Rebours. Oeuvres Complètes*, Vol. 7. Paris, 1928–1934.

—, *Against the Grain*, Intro. by Havelock Ellis. New York, 1931.

—, *Certains*. Paris, 1908.

—, *Là-Bas. Oeuvres Complètes*, Vol. 12. Paris, 1929–34.

LAVER, JAMES, *The First Decadent: Being the Strange Life of J.-K. Huysmans*. London, 1954.

ZWEIG, STEFAN, *Balzac*, tr. Will and Dorothy Rose. London, 1947.

CHAPTER TWENTY-TWO

ACTON, WILLIAM, *Prostitution*. London, 1870.

CRUSE, AMY, *The Victorians and Their Reading*. London, 1935.

MARE, MARGARET and ALICIA C., *Victorian Best-Seller: The World of Charlotte Yonge*. London, 1947.
'Prostitution', unsigned article, *Westminster Review*, Vol. 53, 1851.
RUSKIN, JOHN, *Works*, Vol. 18. London, 1905.
SACHS, EMANIE LOUISE, *'The Terrible Siren'*, Victoria Woodhull *(1838-1927)*. New York, 1928.
TENNYSON, ALFRED, LORD, *Poetic and Dramatic Works*. Cambridge, 1898.
THOMSON, PATRICIA, *The Victorian Heroine: A Changing Ideal, 1837-1873* London, 1956.

CHAPTER TWENTY-THREE

HAIGHT, GORDON S., *George Eliot and John Chapman*. Oxford, 1940.
HANSON, LAWRENCE and ELISABETH, *Marian Evans and George Eliot*. London, 1952.
MAUROIS, ANDRÉ, *Lélia*, tr. Gerard Hopkins. London, 1953.
SACHS, EMANIE LOUISE, *'The Terrible Siren'*, Victoria Woodhull *(1838-1927)*. New York, 1928.

CHAPTER TWENTY-FOUR

COLEMAN, STANLEY, 'Strindberg, the Autobiographies'. *The Psychoanalytical Review*, Vol. XXIII, 1936.
FECHTER, PAUL, *Frank Wedekind, der Mensch und das Werk*. Jena, 1920.
GELB, ARTHUR and BARBARA, *O'Neill*. New York, 1962.
HAGEMANN, FRITZ, *Wedekinds 'Erdgeist' und 'Die Buchse der Pandora'*. Neustrelitz, 1926.
KUTSCHER, ARTUR, *Frank Wedekind, Sein Leben und seine Werke*, 3 Vols. Munich, 1922-31.
MCGILL, V. J., *August Strindberg*. New York, 1930.
STRINDBERG, AUGUST, *Seven Plays*, tr. Arvid Paulson. (Bantam). New York, 1960.
WEDEKIND, FRANK, *Five Tragedies of Sex*, tr. Frances Fawcett and Stephen Spender. New York, 1952.
—, *Gesammelte Werken*, ed. G. Muller. Munich, 1912-24.

CHAPTER TWENTY-FIVE

DINGWALL, ERIC JOHN, *The American Woman: A Historical Study*. London, 1956.

GORER, GEOFFREY, *The American People: A Study in National Character.* New York, 1948.

HECHT, BEN, 'Bosoms Away', *Esquire*, July 1957.

Look Magazine, Editors, *The Decline of the American Male.* New York, 1958.

MERRIAM, EVE, 'The Matriarchal Myth'. *The Nation*, November, 1958.

SOROKIN, PITIRIM, *The American Sex Revolution.* Boston, 1957.

WYLIE, PHILIP, *A Generation of Vipers.* New York, 1942.

CHAPTER TWENTY-SIX

CORY, DONALD WEBSTER, *The Homosexual in America.* New York, 1951.

KARDINER, ABRAM, *Sex and Morality.* New York, 1954.

RUITENBEEK, HENDRICK M., ed., *The Problem of Homosexuality in Modern Society.* (Dutton) New York, 1963.

CHAPTER TWENTY-SEVEN

BROPHY, BRIGID, 'Speaking Out: Woman is a Prisoner of her Sex', *Saturday Evening Post*, November 1963.

BURROWS, EDWIN GRANT, *An Atoll Culture: Ethnography of Ifaluk in the Central Carolines.* New Haven, 1953.

FRIEDAN, BETTY, *The Feminine Mystique.* (Dell) New York, 1964.

HUNT, MORTON M., *Her Infinite Variety.* New York, 1962.

KINSEY, ALFRED, *Sexual Behaviour in the Human Female.* London, 1953.

—, *Sexual Behaviour in the Human Male.* London, 1948.

KLEIN, VIOLA, *The Feminine Character: History of an Ideology.* London, 1946.

LERNER, MAX, *America as a Civilization: Life and Thought in the U.S. Today.* London, 1958.

LUNDBERG, FERDINAND, and FARNHAM, MARYNIA, *Modern Woman – The Lost Sex.* London, 1947.

MARINE, GENE, 'New Look at the Oldest Differences'. *The Nation*, March 1963.

MEAD, MARGARET, *Male and Female.* (Mentor) New York, 1955.

MYRDAL, FRU ALVA, and KLEIN, VIOLA, *Women's Two Roles: Home and Work.* London, 1956.

SCHEINFELD, AMRAM, *Women and Men.* New York, 1944.

Index